INDIANA WINE

INDIANA UNIVERSITY PRESS
Bloomington and Indianapolis

INDIANA WINE

A HISTORY

James L. Butler & John J. Butler

This book is a publication of

Indiana University Press
601 North Morton Street
Bloomington, IN 47404-3797 USA

http://iupress.indiana.edu

Telephone orders 800-842-6796
Fax orders 812-855-7931
Orders by e-mail iuporder@indiana.edu

The paper used in this publication meets the
minimum requirements of American
National Standard for Information
Sciences—Permanence of Paper for Printed
Library Materials, ANSI Z39.48-1984.

Manufactured in the United States of
America

**Library of Congress Cataloging-in
Publication Data**

Butler, James L., date
  Indiana wine : a history / James L. Butler
and John J. Butler.
       p.   cm.
Includes bibliographical references and index.
  ISBN 0-253-34036-5 (cloth : alk. paper)
  1. Wine and wine making—Indiana—
History.   I. Butler, John J., date.   II. Title.
TP559.I6 B87 2001
641.2'2'09772—dc21
                                    2001002123

1 2 3 4 5 06 05 04 03 02 01

C O N T E N T S

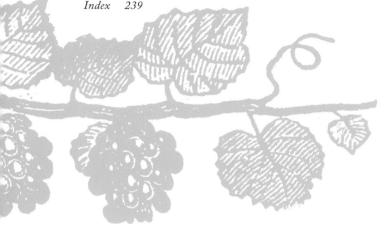

Foreword

IN THE YEAR 1000, Norseman explorer Leif Eriksson discovered such an abundance of grapevines thriving along the north Atlantic coastline that he named the New World "Vineland." Centuries later, that land became the colonies and territories that became a unification of states—virtually all of which now lay claim to some measure of American wine-growing history.

Early American wines were, however, a bitter disappointment. Sixteenth-century Huguenots arriving in Florida found wild muscadine vines bearing thick-skinned fruit which made wine unlike anything back in France. Unfortunately, this experience heralded many more colonial wines which provided relief from the pains of the times but gained little epicurean fanfare. Captain John Smith expressed his frustration over Virginia vines that grew to the tops of trees and produced bountiful fruit but displeasing wine. European wines were expensive to transport and most colonists were poor. John Mason offered to trade most of what is now the state of New Hampshire in return for 300 tons of good French wine. To the great frustration of all concerned, Old World vines planted in New World soils repeatedly died young—phylloxera, a microscopic root louse yet to be identified, was the culprit. It was a grim situation for pioneers accustomed to good wine as a staple of their diets.

As a consequence, colonists commenced to lose interest in wine-growing, turning instead to brewing beer and other manners of fermented potions. Governmental countermeasures included New York's promotion of seventeenth-century wine-growing with tax incentives and Virginia's law requiring farmers to cultivate vines. Another century passed with little success. The likes of William Penn, Benjamin Franklin, and Henry Clay encouraged development of an American wine industry without success. Following his term as ambassador to France, Thomas Jefferson returned with a fresh enthusiasm for wine-growing and hired European experts to grow Old World vines at Monticello. His dream was also doomed as the silent, invisible phylloxera worked its devastation.

It is unlikely that many people, even enophiles, would figure Indiana to have a leadership role in the development of American wine-growing during this time, but this did happen. Jean Jacques (John James) Dufour arrived from his native Switzerland in the latter 1700s to pursue his dream of fine wine-growing in the New World. His relentless pursuit to succeed where others had failed with greater resources and obstacles is a story of monumental determination. Decades before wine-growing flourished in New York's Finger Lakes district or California's Napa Valley, the Dufour legacy was the "Little Rhineland"—a narrow strip of terraced hillside vineyards along the Indiana side of the Ohio River in what is now Switzerland County. The region grew to embrace hundreds of acres of vines producing wines of a quality which attracted the attention of many American wine enthusiasts, including Henry Clay and Thomas Jefferson.

We are now approaching the 200th anniversary of Jean Jacques Dufour's initial land purchase in Indiana. If he could be here, he would surely be proud of this fascinating account of his great struggle, which is so eloquently portrayed by authors James and John Butler. Dufour would doubtlessly be equally proud of the Butler family, which carries on his dream of producing wine in Indiana as they operate the award-winning Butler Winery and Vineyards in Bloomington. James, an Indiana University alumnus, and son John, currently an Indiana University graduate student in history, are eminently qualified to accurately and thoroughly write the Dufour story. Both have spent years gathering a plethora of primary source material, much of which was very difficult to trace and then confirm, in order to fully chronicle Dufour's remarkable quest to bring America its first wine-growing region. For wine and history lovers alike, this is (quite literally) vintage Americana—a delightful book which is difficult to put down.

RICHARD P. VINE, PH.D.
Professor of Enology
Purdue University

Acknowledgments

WE WOULD LIKE TO THANK the following organizations and people for their cooperation and assistance with this work. The Lilly Library in Bloomington, Indiana; the Indiana Historical Society in Indianapolis; and the Indiana State Library in Indianapolis were wonderful sources of books, letters, and documents. The records and files in the Switzerland County Historical Society and the Vevay Public Library were also of great value.

For the chapters on the modern era we would like to thank Sally Linton and the Indiana Wine Grape Council for the maps for each of the wineries and the wonderful people of the Indiana wine industry for providing labels and information. Thanks also to Professor William Oliver, Ben Sparks, Mark Easley, and Dr. Donald MacDaniel for providing documents and taking time to talk with us about the early days of the modern industry.

Special thanks go to Tom and Mary Jane Demaree and Tom and Donna Weaver of Vevay for arranging access to the great relics of the early Vevay, Indiana, wine industry. Drs. Richard Vine and Bruce Bordelon of Purdue University offered helpful comments and suggestions. We're also indebted to numerous other people who gave us help and encouragement along the way.

Lastly we would like to thank Indiana University Press for their patience and willingness to take on the project, our editor Kate Babbitt for holding us to a high standard, and Amy Butler for her diligent organization of the index.

Introduction

IN RECENT YEARS, the Indiana wine industry has gained recognition both at home and beyond the borders of the state. As the number of wineries has increased, many people have wondered, "Why Indiana?" The industry appears to have come out of nowhere. But this is not true. Today's modern Indiana wine industry is a rebirth of a grape-growing and wine-making tradition that began two hundred years ago. Indiana played a significant role in the development of the American wine industry. In fact, the first commercial wine production took place in Indiana. This achievement is more easily understood when placed in the larger context of the story of American wine. This is the story of the land, the people, and the laws that have made Indiana wine what it is today.

INDIANA WINE

1. In the Beginning

MANY OF THE EARLIEST European explorers of North America noted the amazing abundance of grapevines in the New World. They returned to Europe with glowing reports that gave their backers and financiers hope that wine could be successfully grown in the Americas, and within a short time, the possibilities of producing wine in the New World took on mythic proportions. Like Noah after the flood, the early colonists set about planting vineyards as soon as they landed. One of the earliest recorded attempts to cultivate vines in North America can be credited to the Spanish. They planted a vineyard on what is now Paris Island, South Carolina, in 1568, but there is no record that a successful crop was ever taken from the vineyard. Yet this attempt illustrates how quickly the settlers tried the cultivation of European grapes in the New World.

Of all the European nations engaged in colonizing the New World, the English were probably the most persistent in planting the vine. The reason lay in the northern latitude that England occupies. The cool, wet weather made grape-growing difficult on their island homeland. To satisfy their wine needs, the English imported wine primarily from France and Portugal, nations that were blessed with a more Mediterranean climate. Thus, it is not surprising that the English hoped North America could be turned into an English Mediterranean. When one looks at the latitude occupied by North America, it is easy to understand why they reasoned that the vast lands they held in the New World could supply the British Empire with wine, silk, and olive oil. The French and Spanish, who were quite capable of producing these commodities on their own soil, had no great need for a "Mediterranean" across the Atlantic and therefore did not actively encourage the planting of grapes in North America to the degree that their English rivals did.

The first English attempt at viticulture was at Jamestown, Virginia, in 1607. There colonists made wine from the abundant wild grapes but were not satisfied with the results. Many of the native wild grape varieties had flavors that seemed odd to the Europeans, and the wines were often too tart and astringent. Also, although the wild varieties grew quite copiously, they often yielded less fruit than the vineyards of Europe. It soon became obvious it would be difficult to base a successful wine industry on the wild American vines.

The next logical step was to attempt to improve the native vines. At this time, 250 years before Gregor Mendel's experiments with pea plants and Darwin's theory of natural selection, it was still believed that the mere act of caring for wild grapevines by planting them in a vineyard would tame the vines within a few years. Unfortunately for the early vine-growers, this was simply not true. The native grapevines might have grown more luxuriously if watered and fertilized, but their basic characteristics, such as flavor, sugar content, and acidity, would not have changed.

During the early 1600s, the Virginia Company made several attempts to encourage grape-growing at Jamestown. In 1619, a law was enacted that required every household in the colony to plant ten vines. European grapes were supplied to the colonist, and instruction was provided by the importation of French vinedressers (a vinedresser is one who takes care of a vineyard), since it was assumed that part of the colony's problem was a lack of expertise. Ultimately, the European vines and the French advisors were no more successful than the English had been with the native vines. The English colonists accused the French vinedressers of purposely failing, of concealing their true knowledge and not making an honest effort.

Added to these difficulties was the fact that a new vineyard does not come into full production for several years; the vines take time to grow and mature. What the settlers really wanted was a quick and reliable cash crop. Tobacco showed great promise from the start and soon filled that important niche. Interest in wine production fell as interest in tobacco increased, and soon all the wealthiest colonists had fields filled with tobacco. Throughout the 1700s, any decline in the tobacco markets sparked renewed efforts to promote the vine. But as soon as the tobacco industry rebounded, the vineyard schemes were abandoned. The colonists obviously preferred the tangible profit that could be made by planting tobacco to the theoretical profits to be had from making wine. The English colonists were never able to overcome the failure of their European vines or the basic undesirability of the native wild grapes.

The Virginia experience was repeated, under slightly different circumstances, by the English at Massachusetts Bay Colony, the Dutch in the New Netherlands, William Penn in Pennsylvania, Lord Baltimore in Maryland,

James Ogelthorpe in Georgia, and many others too numerous to mention. For 200 years, European settlers attempted to establish their imported grapes on the eastern shores of North America with no success. The prospect of American wine was dim, and the hope of bountiful grape harvests remained unfulfilled.

The reasons for their failures were not immediately apparent to these pioneering viticulturists. North America had more species of native wild grapes than any other continent. Because of all of these wild grapes, it seemed that the New World would be a paradise for the European vine. Colonists hoped that all one needed to do was plant the reliable European varieties and await the harvest. However, they did not understand that a land teeming with wild grapevines was also a land infested with grapevine diseases, pests, and insects. The native North American grape varieties had evolved with these native enemies and had long ago established a measure of resistance to molds, mildews, and pests. The diseases and pests endemic to North America were unknown in Europe, and the European vines had relatively little natural resistance to the pests encountered in the New World. During the first season of growth, the European vines would flourish, often growing faster and more luxuriantly than they had in Europe. But soon the promising vines would succumb to black rot, mildews, and phylloxera. The colonists were at a loss to describe the sudden shriveling of the fruit due to black rot, the loss of leaves caused by mildew, or the stunted growth and decline of the vines from phylloxera. There were no methods to combat the diseases or even to sort out the symptoms of one disease from another. Indeed, many of the organisms that caused these diseases would not be identified until they made their way to Europe in the mid- to late 1800s and wiped out large portions of the European wine industry.

The climate was another factor in the failure of European grapevines in the New World. The Europeans simply looked at a world map and decided that 40 degrees north latitude in North America would have the same climate as 40 degrees north latitude in Europe. Much to the colonists' chagrin, the winters in eastern North America were colder than the winters at comparable latitudes in Europe. This difference is due to the Atlantic Gulf Stream that carries warm water toward northern Europe, thus moderating its climate. The native American grapes had evolved a significant degree of hardiness to cold, but it was soon obvious that the European grapes could not tolerate the extreme cold temperatures sometimes encountered in eastern North America.

A significant renewal of interest in wine production and grape-growing occurred just before the American Revolution. Several of the nation's founding fathers were involved. George Washington planted grapes at Mount Vernon as early as 1768. In the mid-1770s, he attempted a major vineyard planting of 2,000 native vines. Despite years of work and some expense, his attempts came to naught. Thomas Jefferson, a celebrated Francophile, was one of the most noted American wine connoisseurs of his day, so it is not surprising that he too was interested in establishing an American wine industry. In 1775, he became involved in a vineyard scheme with an Italian gentleman by the name of Philip Mazzei. Jefferson offered him 2,000 acres near Monticello and enlisted shareholders, at 50 British pounds each, to pay for the enterprise. Because of the start of the American Revolution, the plan was abandoned before the success of it could be determined, but Jefferson's relationship to wine and grape-growing lasted throughout his long life. When he was ambassador to France, he toured the French vineyards; as president, he encouraged the vinedressers and winemakers with whom he corresponded; and in retirement, he continued to extol the benefits to be gained from a domestic wine industry.

Jefferson often lamented the fact that the wines imported into the United States were regularly fortified with distilled spirits. He believed that wine was the beverage of moderation and wished that Americans had the opportunity to drink unadulterated wines at reasonable prices. Jefferson wanted the import duty on wine lowered so that it would be more affordable. His often-quoted statement that "no nation is drunk where wine is cheap; and none sober, where the dearness of wine substitutes ardent spirits as the common beverage" reflects this philosophy. Unfortunately, until the Americas had a domestic wine industry, they would not have access to inexpensive quality wine.

The European wines that were available in America fell into several different categories of style and quality. The best wines were those from the better French vineyards that shipped their product either bottled or in barrels. These wines were expensive and thus available only to the wealthiest members of society. Much of the imported wine was of the sherry or Madeira style, which, due to the addition of brandy, had a higher alcohol content than standard table wine. This helped the wine withstand the prolonged crossing of the Atlantic, and it also made the wine more popular with many of the colonists. The cheapest wines in the colonies were wines that had been shipped in bulk from the Netherlands and England, where they had been doctored with a long list of odious ingredients, ostensibly to improve them but more likely to stretch them and increase the profits of the shippers.

The failure to successfully cultivate European wine grapes and the expense and poor quality of imported wine had profound effects on the drinking habits of the colonists. One substitute was hard cider, and almost every farm on the eastern seaboard had an apple orchard from which farmers made their own cider. Another alternative was West Indian rum, which was processed cheaply from the abundant sugar cane fields. Its high alcohol content made it a popular American import. Finally, whiskey production became very popular when a great number of farmers took up the cultivation of corn and began to use their excess crop to make alcohol.

In the closing decades of the colonial period, grape-growing had already been attempted in what would later become Indiana. The French are said to have planted most of the larger and smaller fruits (which certainly would have included grapes) at their outposts on the Wabash River as early as 1735. The trading town of St. Vincent (present-day Vincennes) was one of the major outposts. There, the French settlers used wine for various events and social gatherings; one of the most well known was the "King of the Ball," or "Le Roi du Ball." A young unmarried man was selected as king of the ball and was welcomed by singing. One of the verses went:

> Rights superb have you my Lord,
> King of the ball, our king and bard.
> The sheaves of harvest you'll have prime,
> When comes the day of reaping time.
> Into your gifts you'll enter here,
> With pomp the honor wine we bear,
> The vat for you with grace will ring,
> For this is a good right of kings.

But if wine was the right of kings, it certainly wasn't the daily beverage for the common man in St. Vincent in the mid-1700s.

In 1763, the French and British signed the treaty of Paris to end the Seven Years' War (the North American portion of this war was called the French and Indian War), at which time the British took over the administration of the Northwest Territory. A lieutenant in the British Army named Fraser traveled through the territory shortly after it was acquired from the French. In his report he wrote about "St. Vincent on the Oaubash River." He reported that the French had tried to grow the European vines but had given up on the attempt. He felt that this was mainly due to a lack of skill, but he also felt that a fear of competition might have been the motive, since he had heard of "the Monarch's Injunctions prohibiting the raising [of] any thing which might interfere with the staple commodities of the Northern Country." Fraser also noted they made a wine from wild grapes, which in his opinion was, "a very bad wine. . . . This Wine tho' seemingly very unhealthy is sold at a most exorbitant price, when they have none else to drink." This disparaging comment is most likely the earliest recorded critique of an Indiana wine.

As in all opinions of taste and art, it is helpful to get an alternate viewpoint to balance the record. About fifteen years after Fraser's trip through this area, Thomas Hutchins, the first U.S. national geographer, traveled through the Wabash River Valley. He also described the French settlement at Vincennes and the efforts of the settlers there at wine-making. He reported that the grapes had a thin black skin and grew in abundance along the banks of the river. He stated that the inhabitants made a "well tasted red wine" for their own consumption.

A Dr. Saugrain visited Vincennes in 1788. His notebook recorded the following observation: "They go into the woods to gather the grapes which are found on vines encircling the trees, and an indifferent sort of wine is made." In 1789, a pamphlet appeared in France to promote the settling of land owned by the Scioto Company in the Ohio Country. This lengthy advertisement stated, "One finds both on the hills and on the plain a great quantity of grapes growing wild, and of which the inhabitants make a red wine, which suffices for their own consumption. They have tried the experiment of pressing these grapes at the settlement of St. Vincent, and the result is a wine which by keeping a little while, becomes preferable to the many wines of Europe."

While the preceding reports differ on matters of taste, they give us a fairly good idea about the state of wine production in Vincennes. The European vines had apparently been tried, but they failed to survive due to diseases, not from lack of skill or fear of competition as Fraser had speculated. The French frontier winemakers relied upon the wild grapes that grew abundantly in the woods. Although Fraser does mention that the French sold their wine, it would be hard to qualify this attempt as an example of successful commercial viticulture without a cultivated vineyard.

From this example, we can see that the French experience in Indiana was very similar to the other colonial experiments with wine production.

For 200 years, most attempts to produce wine in North America had failed. No workable solution had been found to overcome the basic problems confronting New World vintners. To have a successful wine industry in America, it was necessary to either adapt European vines to the climate or improve the flavor and yield of the hardy wild vines. Ideally, a vine could be found that would combine the desirable characteristics of both flavor and hardiness. Until this happened, the American wine industry would lie dormant, waiting for someone to break the paradoxical curse laid upon North American viticulture.

2. Wandering in the Wilderness

THE UNLIKELY HERO who would eventually lead the revolution in American viticulture was John James Dufour. He arrived alone and unnoticed on the shores of North America. Had some gentleman been waiting on the docks, looking for a vinedresser who could save American viticulture, he probably would have passed over Dufour at first glance. This was because Dufour did not fit the stereotypical English view of a vinedresser. First, though he was from the French-speaking part of Switzerland, he was not French. And even though Switzerland was a wine-producing country, it was unimportant compared to France in both production and reputation. Second, Dufour was maimed in his left arm. The extent of his injury and whether it was there from birth or was the result of an accident are lost to the historical record. What is known is that because of his handicap, some people thought him unfit for his chosen profession. Yet, despite these facts which seemed to disqualify him on first inspection, Dufour had qualities of character that enabled him to be successful where so many before him had failed.

Dufour was born in 1763 in the Canton of Vaud (pronounced "Vo") near the town of Vevey, which lies on the eastern end of Lake Geneva. This western region of Switzerland, which shares a border with France, is a traditional wine-producing area. It is known for its dry white wines and for the famous Fête des Vignerons, or festival of vine-growers, that has been held in Vevey every year since 1651. Dufour was the oldest son of a family of grape-growers that had been engaged in this pursuit for at least three generations, and it was naturally expected that he would be the next to take up this noble profession. Thus, Dufour had not only the practical experience of working in his family's vineyards in his youth, he also inherited a long tradition of Swiss grape and wine production. Tenacity and perseverance were his by nature, but perhaps his greatest asset lay in his keen powers of observation. He had the presence of mind to take in what others had done and to learn from their mistakes as well as from his own.

The spirit of the New World captured Dufour at an early age. Near the end of his life, he wrote about what had influenced him to come to America and attempt grape-growing.

> When I took the resolution to come to America, to try the cultivation of the grape, I was but fourteen [1777]; and I came to this determination by reading the newspapers, which were full of the American Revolutionary War, and contained many letters from the officers of the French army aiding the Republicans, which complained of the scarcity of the wine among them, in the midst of the greatest abundance of every thing else; and by inspection of the maps, I saw that America was in the parallel of the best wine countries in the world—like Spain, South of France, Italy and Greece: I then made the culture of the grape, of it's natural history, and of all that was connected with it, my most serious study, to be the better able to succeed here.

As this quote illustrates, Dufour became interested in growing grapes in the New World early in his life. But this desire lay dormant for two decades because Dufour, at fourteen, had neither the resources nor the knowledge to set such a grandiose plan in motion. He spent the intervening twenty years working in his family's vineyards, biding his time and building his experience. According to family legend, Dufour's cause was helped by none other than Benjamin Franklin, American ambassador to France, who (if we are to believe the family story) advised Dufour's father to send his children to America, "where they could enjoy greater advantages and where with the means he could give them they could secure a good tract of land for the cultivation of vineyards." What influence this had on Dufour and his family is hard to say, but the turbulent events that swept through Europe at the end of the eighteenth century had a major influence on the economic and social order of Switzerland, which in turn had an effect on the Swiss grape-growers.

In the late 1700s, Europe was going through an incredibly tumultuous period. The American Revolution had had serious repercussions in France, where the American ideals were adopted by a populace eager for change. Unfortunately for the French, their revolution took a decidedly different turn, and rather than fighting an external enemy as had happened in America, they set about fighting among themselves. Soon the revolution dissolved into a bitter power struggle between different elements of French society, and the end result was a bloody period of class warfare. The revolution culminated in a complete upheaval of the French power structure, and thousands of public executions were carried out with the dreaded guillotine. The end of the revolution brought little relief for the French, since their new democracy was usurped by Napoleon Bonaparte, who then embroiled France in almost twenty years of constant warfare with the great European powers.

The traditional geographic and cultural ties of western Switzerland and France guaranteed that the troubles convulsing France would have an effect on the Swiss. At first the troubles were mainly economic in nature. As Dufour stated, "The revolution has allowed the wines of France and Savon into the Canton of Bern, which will inevitably lower the price of wine in the Vaud country." Later, the troubles were political and religious, as the process of overthrowing the old order spread to Switzerland. In 1792, the revolution came to Geneva. It had all the trappings of the French revolution, including violence and plundering, but on a smaller scale. In 1794, a mob gained control of the government in Geneva, taking over the town hall and turning it into a drinking parlor. It proceeded to levy death sentences against the aristocracy, of which eleven were carried out. These events did much to unsettle the lives of the Swiss vine-growers in Vevey, which lay at the opposite end of Lake Geneva. They wrote, "The convulsions and wars that are now raging in Europe [are] an effect of the too considerable population, and are destructive of the right of property and have a tendency to destroy the notions of justice that are the basis of social happiness." The only way to escape the continuing violence and economic upheaval was to leave Europe and its excessive population behind and make a new start in America.

Dufour set his American dreams in motion in March of 1796, at the age of thirty-three. Starting his journey with funds from his father as well as his own, he headed for Paris. Not only was Paris the largest French city at this time, it was also the transportation and economic hub of Europe. While Dufour was there, he purchased fifty-nine silver and gold watches, which he would use as currency for the Atlantic crossing and afterward on his arrival in America. From Paris he traveled to Le Havre, a bustling French port on the Atlantic Ocean, where he secured passage and board on the brig *Sally* for $50. He left France on June 12, 1796, bound for the New World. The crossing was apparently uneventful, and after a brief stop at the Azores for supplies, the *Sally* arrived in America two months later. On August 12, 1796, Dufour recorded in his daybook (an account book that contained brief entries on his travels and finances) that he had paid 59 pounds for the duty on his trunk in Wilmington, Delaware.

Soon after arriving, Dufour traveled through southeastern Pennsylvania and northern Maryland to inspect all the vineyards he could find and learn from their successes and failures. First, he visited the estate of Mr. Carroll in Carrolton, Maryland, where there was a small vineyard kept by a French vinedresser. Then he visited a vineyard near Middletown, Pennsylvania, on the Susquehanna River. Established by a German, the vineyard was overgrown at the time of Dufour's visit because the owner had died. He also stopped at the vineyard of Peter Legaux at Spring Mill, Pennsylvania, which was about a dozen miles outside of Philadelphia.

Legaux's plantings were the first notable post–Revolutionary War attempt to establish a vineyard. Here he mostly planted imported European vines. Because he needed money to continue his struggling vineyard, he obtained an act from the Pennsylvania legislature in March of 1793 to form the Pennsylvania Vine Company. This was to be funded by subscription of one thousand shares at $20 each. In 1794, he unsuccessfully petitioned the U.S. Senate for support of his vineyard. When Dufour visited him in 1796, Legaux had not yet sold all the shares of the vineyard.

Legaux wrote to Thomas Jefferson in 1801 in an effort to sell him vines and get him to support his company. Jefferson did not subscribe to his plan, and Legaux was unable to count the president among the members of his company. It was not until 1802 that the minimum number of shares were sold and the company was officially incorporated. Legaux was a consummate self-promoter, and his claims far surpassed his results. But even his minimal results were more than many others had achieved.

Looking back upon his early eastern vineyard tour, Dufour remarked,

> But none of the different and numerous trials which were made in several parts of the United States, that I visited after my arrival in 1796, were found [worthy of] the name of vineyards. All of them, except the vines planted in the gardens of the cities of New York and Philadelphia, and about a dozen of the plants in the vineyard of Mr. Legaux at Spring Mill, near the latter place, did not suffice to pay for one half of their attendance.

While Dufour was in Philadelphia, he heard that the Jesuit priests had at one time established a successful vineyard at Kaskaskia on the Mississippi River (in present-day southern Illinois) when the French controlled the Northwest Territory. He was also informed that the French government had ordered the Jesuits to destroy the vineyard for fear that successful grape culture would spread throughout America, thereby hurting their overseas wine trade. After hearing this, he decided that "as I had seen but discouraging plantations on that side of the Allegheny, and as the object of my journey to America, was purposely to learn what could be done in that line of business; I was desirous to see if the West would afford more encouragement."

Dufour sold several gold watches and with that money purchased items to sell or trade on his trip to Kaskaskia; these included quantities of cloth, ribbons, combs, needles, thimbles, eyeglasses, and silk stockings. On September 30th, 1796, he weighed his trunk for shipment and headed west from Philadelphia. In the 1790s, there were three different modes of travel across Pennsylvania: on foot, on horseback, or by wagon. To travel from Philadelphia to Pittsburgh (a straight-line distance of about 260 miles) took around a month on foot. The trip by wagon took approximately twenty to twenty-four days, while on horseback it could be completed in just ten days. Dufour left no record of which method of transport he chose, but we can surmise that he traveled by foot for two reasons: he did not mention purchasing a horse or paying for a ride in a wagon, and he had paid for his trunks to be forwarded to Pittsburgh. He traveled as far west as Marietta, Ohio, where he noted in his daybook that he had purchased a rifle. Leaving Marietta, Dufour went to Pittsburgh to spend the winter, arriving there on November 11th, 1796. His cost for board and other expenses during the trip amounted to 50 cents per day. During his forty-one days on the road, Dufour searched the region for examples of successful vineyards and potential sites for his enterprise.

At this time the federal government was the largest landowner in the West. The land in private hands was largely owned by land speculators who were intent on profiting from the re-sale of the land. In early 1796, the federal government passed a law that opened up the lands of the Northwest Territory for sale. This was done in an effort to raise funds for the government's nearly empty coffers and to encourage settlement in these new lands, thereby strengthening the American claim to them. Congressman Albert Gallatin of western Pennsylvania supported the law. He attempted to make the law favorable to the average farmer, who could only afford small tracts of land, but instead the law was passed with provisions that favored the larger land speculators. The end result was that little money came in to the government and few people settled in the West.

President Washington was one of the western land speculators who held considerable acreage along the Ohio River. He owned four tracts of land on the Virginia, or eastern, side of the river between Wheeling and the mouth of the Kanawha River and five tracts of land along the Kanawha itself, for a total of about 33,000 acres. Most of this land was located in the river bottoms, giving him approximately fifty-six miles of river frontage. Washington had offered large portions of this land for sale since before his presidency but was unable to attract any buyers. In 1794, he started advertising these lands for sale at the starting price of $3 per acre.

While staying in Pittsburgh, Dufour saw Washington's lands advertised in a Philadelphia newspaper. Since he had just visited the lands along the Ohio River between Pittsburgh and Marietta, Ohio, Dufour wanted to learn more about the land that Washington owned. He also wanted to discover if President Washington would support his idea of bringing Swiss immigrants to America in an effort to cultivate the vine. On December 19th, Dufour wrote to President Washington from Pittsburgh, asking if the land was still for sale and at what price. He said that he wanted to visit the lands on his return from a trip he intended to make in Kentucky. He told the president that he was seeking land suitable for a "large family of Swiss plowmen versed in the culture of the vine, orchard management, and livestock raising."

Apparently Dufour was hoping that Washington's renowned love for the area would influence the president to give Dufour a positive response. He hoped Washington would reply by post to Limestone, Kentucky (now Maysville), as Dufour would be passing that way in the near future. In an effort to further influence Washington about to his good intentions, Dufour stated, "I do not intend to swell the masses of land speculators who so terribly hinder the progress of agriculture." Dufour was apparently unaware that the president was one of the largest speculators in western lands and that this phrase might be somewhat insulting. It is unknown if Dufour ever received a reply.

In mid-February, Dufour decided that the worst of the winter had passed and that he should embark on his trip to Kaskaskia. He had great hopes of finding some remains of a productive wine culture there, saying, "I resolved therefore on a visit to see if any remains of the Jesuits' vines were still in being, and what sort of grapes they were; supposing very naturally, that if they had succeeded as well as tradition reported, some of them might possibly be found in some of the gardens there." Dufour boarded a boat to travel down the Ohio River and up the Mississippi to Kaskaskia.

Along the Ohio River at Marietta, Dufour met a Frenchman who was making several barrels of wine a year from the grapes that grew wild on the heads of the islands in the river. The locals called it the Sand grape and believed it came from European ancestry, saying that the French had thrown their vines in the river rather than have the British capture them at the fall of Fort Duquesne (modern-day Pittsburgh). The current of the river supposedly carried the vines downstream, where they lodged on the heads of the islands near Marietta and then grew wild. At first Dufour believed this story, but as evidence presented itself, he came to doubt it: "I believed it, until I found the same kind of grapes up the Kentucky, and Mississippi rivers, where it is impossible they could have been brought from the Ohio by floating on the water."

Dufour reached Cape Girardeau on the Mississippi by the 8th of May and reached St. Louis one month later. Kaskaskia lies roughly halfway between these two cites, and here Dufour found the abandoned Jesuit site: "But I found only the spot where that vineyard had been planted, in a well selected place, on the side of a hill to the north east of the town, under a cliff. No good grapes, however[,] were found either there, or in any of the gardens of the country." The fact that Dufour found only a large bed of asparagus, still growing where the Jesuits had planted it, led him to believe that perhaps the grape-growing enterprise had not been as successful as people had claimed.

After finding nothing useful in Kaskaskia, Dufour prepared for the return leg of his trip. In entrepreneurial fashion so typical of Dufour, he purchased 6 1/2 tons of lead in St. Louis in order to have something to sell to merchants along the Ohio as he headed back east. To haul his lead, he procured a boat and six oarsmen, which took him as far as Cincinnati. For sustenance on the journey, he purchased 300 pounds of bacon and 554 pounds of biscuit. He was supplied and ready to leave by the end of August, 1797. When they reached Louisville, they had to portage the boat and cargo around the falls of the Ohio. Dufour arrived in Cincinnati on October 8th.

John James Dufour's nephew Perret Dufour (who was also a family historian) wrote in 1876, "The barge sunk and he had a great deal of trouble, and a great risk of loosing [sic] the whole cargo." Dufour makes no mention of this accident in his accounts of his travels, but an entry on October the 8th in Cincinnati may refer to it. He wrote that he spent $10.25 to replace 114 pounds of damaged biscuits. These biscuits could have been a replacement for provisions that had been damaged in the sinking. But, if they were, this is the only reference to the "great deal of trouble" of which Perret Dufour spoke.

At this time, Cincinnati was a town with a population of around 1,000 people, and Ohio was still a part of the Northwest Territory. The largest city in the west was Lexington, Kentucky. Kentucky had become a state in 1792 (the first west of the mountains), and Lexington was known as the wealthiest city of the new state. It is not surprising that Dufour decided to visit this area. He sold 1,105 pounds of lead to merchants in Cincinnati and put the remainder in storage. Dufour left Cincinnati on or around October 24th and arrived in Lexington on October 29th.

A visitor in the early 1800s described Lexington:

> We turned up the main street, which is about eighty feet wide, compactly built, well paved, and having a footway, twelve feet wide on each side. Passing several very handsome brick houses of two and three stories, numerous stores well filled with merchandize [*sic*] of every description, and the market place and courthouse.

This energetic western city must have made a favorable impression on Dufour, and the citizens of the city seem to have been equally impressed with him. According to Dufour, he was "requested and encouraged" to start a vineyard when he arrived. Despite the multiple examples of failure he had witnessed in his travels, he was not dissuaded from attempting a vineyard. Peter Legaux's idea of starting a vineyard by subscription, which Dufour had witnessed on his visit to Philadelphia, would make the project possible. Financed with capital provided by Lexington's leading citizens, Dufour would be able to overcome the high initial cost of a vineyard and reduce his own monetary risk. Using their money, he could test his ideas about growing grapes in America.

On January 17, 1798, he wrote a letter to the local paper, the *Kentucky Gazette,* presenting his plan. He began the letter with a description of his twenty years of experience as a vinedresser in Switzerland. He explained how some of the mountainous areas of Germany and Switzerland were, due to grape-growing, at least as prosperous as other areas of Europe that enjoyed flatter lands and soils of greater fertility. He thought that the hilly terrain of Kentucky would be ideally suited to the cultivation of the vine, even if it was not the best land for regular farming. He stated that within four or five years of planting vines, a vineyard "never fails to produce to the industrious cultivator the same yearly increasing income." He estimated that six to twelve acres ought to be planted and that a variety of species, imported vines as well as indigenous, should be tried.

To carry out the project he suggested an investment of $10,000, to be used as follows:

One hundred acres of third rate land at two dollars	$200
Ten negroes, two must be a little acquainted with carpenters and coopers work	3700
Food and clothing, during the first year, as the produce of the farm, will supply for the next year.	300
Horses, cattle, tools, &c. for both cultivations	400
For collecting in Europe, about 40,000 plants of grapes and making the choice of the best, and importing them	400
Sum to be laid out in the beginning	5000
Wages of the chief cultivator, for five years, at the rate of $1,000 a year, to be paid in the course of them	5000
Total	10,000

Dufour estimated that by 1806 the expanded vineyard would produce 6,000 gallons of wine a year for forty years. This wine could be sold for $1 a gallon, bringing in an income of $6,000 a year. He made an impassioned plea to begin the project at once, "Now, ye citizens of Kentucky, is the time to begin to plant the vine, if you will enjoy in a few years, the riches which it produces."

In order to reap this great profit, Dufour needed subscribers to help share the financial burden. He wrote, "I with a number of well disposed citizens, and inhabitants of Kentucky, to compose a company of two hundred shares, at fifty dollars each, of which thirty dollars only to be paid immediately into the hands of its treasurer, and the balance of each share, when required by the company." Dufour offered his services to the company as chief cultivator if they would provide him with the salary he requested. He felt that $1,000 was a reasonable amount, considering the labor involved. But he also realized that in the beginning the company might have some difficulty coming up with enough cash to pay his salary, so he offered to take his first two years' payment in the form of forty shares of company stock. By all indications Dufour's proposal was met with great enthusiasm, and the Kentucky Vineyard Society was born.

Two weeks after his proposal was printed, Dufour paid for his room and board in Lexington and prepared to tour the area. He spent the next month investigating the region west and south of Lexington, looking for the best site for a vineyard. First Dufour visited Frankfort. He then proceeded to Bardstown, Rolling Fork, Greentown, and back to Rolling Fork. Next he traveled through Springfield, Harrodsburg, Danville, and finally back to Lexington. After a brief stay in Lexington, he searched the area northeast of town, where he traveled as far as Millersburg. Finally, he returned to Lexington on March 14th.

Even though the Kentucky Vineyard Society seemed to be off to a good start, Dufour still needed to earn a living and remain in contact with his relatives in Switzerland. In mid-March, Dufour left Lexington for Cincinnati. Once there, he retrieved his lead from storage and prepared to travel to Pittsburgh. Dufour used a portion of his lead to pay for the provisions he needed for the trip. At Pittsburgh he gave 1,628 pounds of lead to pay for the cost of transporting the remainder of it to that city. He arrived in Pittsburgh in early May and stayed there for approximately a month.

On June 12th, 1798, Dufour headed south from Pittsburgh to Washington, Pennsylvania, where he arrived the next day. On the 14th he traveled to old Fort Redstone (known today as Brownsville). There Dufour purchased his first horse, including saddle and bridle, for four silver watches plus $8.50. The following day he traveled another fifteen miles to New Geneva, recently founded by fellow Swiss émigré Albert Gallatin. It was Gallatin who had proposed that the Northwest Territory should be sold in small lots.

Gallatin, who loved the western frontier, had established a farm on Georges Creek, about forty-five miles south of Pittsburgh. The farm was located on a rise near where Georges Creek empties into the Monongahela River. He called his property Friendship Hill. In 1795, Gallatin and some other Swiss investors from Philadelphia had purchased, not far from Friendship Hill, a ramshackle set of buildings on the Monongahela known as Wilson's Port. The investors wanted to offer a spot of refuge for their friends and family from Geneva, Switzerland, who were suffering from the effects of the French Revolution. They transformed the rough buildings of Wilson's Port into the town of New Geneva.

The citizens of New Geneva tried their hands at a number of industries. By far the most successful industry was the town's glassworks, started in the fall of 1797, which produced both bottles and sheet glass. At the time of Dufour's visit to New Geneva, in June of 1798, Albert Gallatin was in Philadelphia attending a session of Congress. Although Dufour was unable to meet his fellow countryman on this occasion, there is evidence that they did meet eventually. Gallatin was obviously an important person with whom Dufour needed to establish an acquaintance. Gallatin supported the sale of small quantities of government lands in the West, and he produced glass bottles. Both of these would be helpful, if not essential, for the future success of his wine-making colony.

Dufour returned to Pittsburgh and arranged to have his remaining lead sold on commission. He purchased a second horse and rode to Philadelphia, arriving there on the Fourth of July. In Philadelphia, he wrote a letter to his parents and mailed it on the ship *La Liberté* bound for Bordeaux. After a stay of twelve days, during which he sold one of his horses, he took the Burlington packet (a packet was a passenger boat that carried mail and cargo on a regular schedule) to New York. Once in New York, Dufour mailed two more letters to his parents, one via Hamburg and the other via Copenhagen. Perhaps this duplication of post was necessary considering the uncertainty of the Atlantic crossing and the revolutionary events in Europe. Once he completed his business in the East, Dufour set off for the frontier. He rode back to Pittsburgh and then took a ferry to Wheeling. He crossed the wilderness in seven days by following Zane's Trace. This trail covered some 200 miles across central Ohio from Wheeling to Aberdeen, which was situated on the Ohio River opposite Limestone, Kentucky. By the end of August 1798, he was back in Lexington, Kentucky.

Shortly after Dufour's return to Lexington, a public notice was placed in the *Kentucky Gazette*. It read as follows:

Public Notice

The members of the Kentucky Association for the Establishment of a Vineyard are requested to be punctual in their attendance at Mr. Postlewhait's [a local tavern and meetinghouse] in Lexington, on Saturday the 22d inst. at three o'clock in the afternoon, as some matters of great importance are then to be laid before them.

N.B. The gentleman, in whose hands J. J. Dufour has left his subscription papers, will please send them as soon as possible to the subscriber in Lexington.

J. RUSSELL Sec. of the society
Lexington, September 10, 1798

The "matter of great importance" that prompted the placement of this ad was the purchase of land for a vineyard. Dufour, accompanied by U.S. Senator John Brown of Kentucky, inspected the land around Frankfort for a site along the Kentucky River. The next day (apparently without Senator Brown), Dufour continued his search. He traveled upstream (south) along the bank of the river. After four days and forty miles, he arrived at the mouth of Hickman Creek. Dufour described this trip as "having found nothing which pleased me, except near Frankfort, and that too high-priced." Dufour returned to Lexington on September 18th but did not stay for the meeting of the vineyard society. Instead, he left again to search for vineyard sites. This time he walked to Cleveland Landing, south of Lexington on the Kentucky River, where he acquired a boat and went down the Kentucky River, returning to the mouth of Hickman Creek. This trip was much more successful than the last, as Dufour wrote, "I reported to the Vineyard Company that I had seen 3 or 4 places which would suit me for laying out a vineyard, and they concluded to buy in the Big Bend 4 miles above the mouth [of the creek at] Hickman's, a tract of 630 acres from James Haselrig."

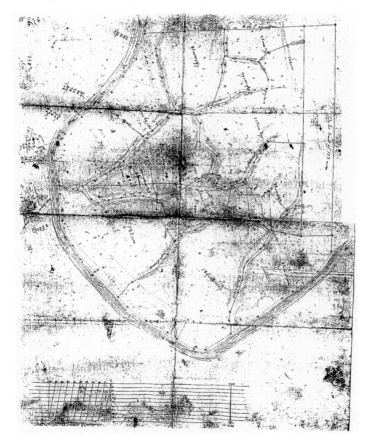

Survey map of First-vineyard, Kentucky. (Courtesy of Indiana State Library)

Dufour's dream of cultivating the vine in America was about to be realized. He had secured the backing of wealthy investors. He had located a suitable site for a vineyard, and he had obtained the land. On November 5, 1798, he recorded, "Prepared to go and begin the work on the company's land, and from that day have kept the journal for the said Company in a book which remains at Firstvineyard, name given to the place where the vineyard is being established."

A contract was drawn up between Dufour and the Kentucky Vineyard Society. Two hundred shares of stock at $50 each were to be subscribed. Once 100 shares had been subscribed to, the contract would become effective. Several portions of the contract are worth noting. First, the contract

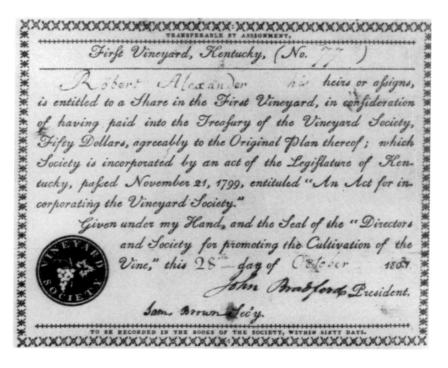

Stock certificate of the Kentucky Vineyard Society. This share, number 77, was issued to Robert Alexander on October 28, 1801.

would last for nine years. Second, Dufour was to work to discover the best method for cultivating the vine and making wine. Third, he was to teach the manner of the cultivation of the vine to the sons of the subscribers, providing that they would stay and work two years, or to the slaves and servants if they would stay for three years. Finally, Dufour was to

> furnish at his own charge so many of the plants of the vine as will set such a number of acres as the society shall find it necessary to begin with, which shall consist of a collection of all kinds of grapes as well indigenous as exotic, the greater part however, brought from Europe. . . . If Dufour should not return to Kentucky with the plants before May 20, 1801, the contract is void.

The vineyard society had given Dufour two years in which to acquire the vines, return to Kentucky, and start the vineyard. This amount of time seems reasonable when one considers the traveling that Dufour would have to do in order to procure vines from Europe. The investors were probably under the impression that events would proceed more slowly than they did in the spring of 1799.

On January 2, 1799, Dufour left Firstvineyard for Europe. Since he was no longer encumbered by his lead, Dufour was able to travel over land. He went east through the Cumberland Gap into Virginia. First he went to Charlottesville and then to Jefferson's vineyard at Monticello. Of this visit he wrote, "Monticello, [Vice] President Jefferson's place . . . had been abandoned, or left without any care for three or four years before, which proved evidently, that it had not been profitable."

From Monticello, Dufour headed farther east to Baltimore. At some point on the journey, he decided that it would be unsafe to travel to Europe to procure his vines because the United States and France were in the midst of an undeclared naval war. Also, he felt that the return trip from Europe to Kentucky would take too long to guarantee the survival of the vines.

In Baltimore, Dufour purchased a few grapevines from a gardener named Hewsler. These vines were of a variety that he called Madeira. From Baltimore, Dufour went to New York, where he purchased pruning knives and a few more cuttings of vines. From New York, he returned to Philadelphia, and while there he revisited the vineyard of Peter Legaux. Here he purchased the bulk of the grapevines that were to be planted at Firstvineyard. His March 6th entry in his daybook read: "Left Philadelphia again for Kentucky, taking with me a wagon loaded with grapevine cuttings of more than 35 different varieties having bought of one, Legau[x], 10,000 at 4 dollars and at 8 dollars a hundred, all costs being charged to the account of the Vineyard Company."

When Dufour arrived in Pittsburgh he retrieved his remaining unsold lead and put it on a boat with his vine cuttings. He headed back down the Ohio River to Limestone, Kentucky. From there, he hauled his cargo of vines and lead overland to Lexington, depositing some of his lead with various merchants along the way. The last of Dufour's lead, some 3,380 pounds of it, was sold to several of the vineyard's subscribers who happened to be merchants in Lexington.

In a matter of only four months Dufour completed a trip that had been allotted two years by the shareholders of the company. This industrious start was continued as Dufour set about planting the vines that he had brought with him from the East. His work apparently impressed the Kentucky legislature; it incorporated the vineyard society in November 1799.

By the end of the year of 1799, all of the arrangements between Dufour and the Kentucky Vineyard Society seem to have been in place. Dufour had been very busy since landing in America in August of 1796. He had traveled as far west as Kaskaskia, visited every vineyard attempt of which he had heard, and met or wrote to some of America's leading citizens. Then, in an amazingly short period of time, he had organized the Kentucky Vineyard Society, located a site for a vineyard, and procured vine cuttings. There seemed to be little that could stand in the way of Dufour's ultimate success.

3. The Swiss Colony

THE MARKED PROGRESS of Firstvineyard inspired Dufour to write to his relatives and friends in Switzerland requesting them to come join him in the New World. They responded energetically to his missive. On April 30, 1800, "relations and friends" formed a covenant that was signed by the following heads of households: Daniel Dufour, David Golay, Phillip Berney, Joseph Meylan, and J. Pierre Boralley. The covenant was a contract of thirty-one articles outlining the relationship the members of the group were to have in America. They hoped that this document would help bind them together during the years of danger and hard work to come. The group planned to leave for America in November of 1800.

The preamble of the covenant provided an explanation for their decision to leave Switzerland. They were convinced that the last ten years of European warfare had been caused by overpopulation. Furthermore, they felt that war was detrimental to the basic structure of society, causing the destruction of property and disturbing the notion of justice. The promise of liberty and justice in the U.S. Constitution was the beacon that drew them to the New World. The signers of the covenant also believed that it was necessary to settle and cultivate "the immense and fertile continent of the new world" in order "to fulfill the ends of the good providence." They wanted to bring up their children to fear God and be filled with "ideas of morality and justice." Finally, Dufour's friends and family wrote,

> those who have the wisdom and courage to quit the frivolous and dangerous resources that are now found in Switzerland shall be protected by Him and loaded with His blessings.
>
> Considering lastly, that this good providence has already signalized his powerful protection in the favor of our dear and worthy friend, J. J. Dufour who since four years his cultivating the vine with success in America and to procure our future establishment or the close alliance that we form together: that consequently we must accelerate as much as it lays in our power the execution of that enterprise by the acquisition of the land necessary for the colony.

The thirty-one governing articles of the covenant were concerned with issues ranging from economics, religion, and education to "unforseen events." Fruit trees, vine cuttings, and tools would be held in common. The head of each of the families would be responsible for the expense of their crossing, in proportion to their wealth and number. A considerable portion of the covenant dealt with the property to be acquired in America. No division of the property or production from the property was to occur in the first ten years of the colony's existence. Article seventeen stated,

> Our friend J. J. Dufour, under whose auspice the present contract should be executed, will be asked in the form of several letters that will be addressed to him to acquire the land necessary to carry out the Society's intentions, as much for the culture of the vine as for other farming which might be undertaken, this to be done beforehand, as well as to obtain the necessary dry goods until which time we can harvest the Society's own land cultivation.

This article obviously put a great deal of responsibility on the shoulders of John James Dufour. He was in charge of purchasing suitable ground, deciding what crops to plant, and providing the colony with food until the farm could support them. But Dufour would know nothing of the details of the covenant until midsummer due to the length of time it took for mail to cross the Atlantic and find its way to Lexington, Kentucky.

In the latter part of June 1800, an event in Lexington cast considerable doubt in Dufour's mind about the ultimate success of Firstvineyard and the wisdom of settling the colony there. Apparently some members of the Kentucky Vineyard Society criticized Dufour because he did not go to Europe to procure the cuttings for the vineyard. On June 23, 1800, he wrote a letter to the directors of the Kentucky Vineyard Society, which was printed in the *Kentucky Gazette*. He defended himself against the charge by saying,

> I shall only observe that when I procured the vines at New York and Philadelphia, instead of going for them to Europe, I did not so much consult my own convenience, as the advantages of the society. I had concerns in Switzerland of much more consequence to me than any thing of a private nature here; especially as my brother who had charge of my affairs in that country, had joined the army. It is fortunate however that I did not go, for had I have gone, I should not have been able to have returned: besides, experience has taught me, that to transport the Vine from Europe to Kentucky, is impractical; from New York or Philadelphia, is as far as they will bear to be transported. Had I attempted to have brought Vines from Europe to Kentucky, I should certainly have lost them; besides the 22,000 which I have planted were brought originally from Europe.

After defending his actions in regard to the society, Dufour then blamed the society for not living up to their end of the bargain. As he stated,

> Although extremely painful, yet I conceive it to be my duty to inform you, that the delay in furnishing the different portions of the expence [*sic*], has been the greatest obstacle which we have had to encounter; the vicissitudes of the season, and the rigors of the winter are nothing in comparison to it. If I have only 10,000 Vines, which have taken root, out of the 18,000, which I had right to expect out of the 22,000, which I planted, it is because by want of money, I was prevented from procuring the cuttings in due season, those which I planted the last four weeks in the season all perished.

Dufour went on to explain that the lack of funds had forced him to purchase corn and goods on credit, which was much more expensive. He also stated that the lack of money had kept the society from procuring any slaves; instead, he was forced to teach the same jobs to different workers every season. After Dufour had said his piece, he held out a measure of hope for the project by saying,

> I have now witnessed the effect of every season of the year on the Vines in Kentucky; I no longer hesitate to give you the strongest assurance of success. I can assert that during the 20 years which I spent in the cultivation of the Vine in Switzerland, I never saw it vegitate so rapidly as it has done here, and that in no instance did I ever gather fruit within 18 months after planting the Vine, as (with the blessing of providence) I shall do this autumn, and that I never planted scions taken from the stocks only eight months old, as I have done this spring.

Dufour's letter had an immediate effect on the members of the board of directors, perhaps even more than he had hoped. They wrote a reply that was published directly below Dufour's letter in the *Kentucky Gazette*. The directors demanded that the delinquent subscribers pay their shares in full and threatened lawsuits against those who did not comply.

The exchange of letters printed in the newspaper appears to have renewed interest in the vineyard enterprise. The citizens of Lexington purchased more shares until the required 100 shares of company stock had been sold. The list of shareholders reads like a who's who of early Kentucky. It included Senators John Brown and Buckner Thurston; hotel manager Cuthbert Banks; tavern owner J. Postlethwait; founder of the *Kentucky Gazette* John Bradford; and Henry Clay. The contract between Dufour and the Kentucky Vineyard Society was recorded on August 5, 1800.

Perhaps during the summer of 1800, Dufour received a copy of the covenant from his friends and relatives in Switzerland. He must have recognized the tremendous effort it would take to establish a Swiss colony in the wilderness and that the responsibility lay entirely with him. He realized that he could not entrust the colony to the whims of the Kentucky Vineyard Society, and he knew that a fairly large tract of land would be needed to support the vinedressers. The problem was twofold: Where should the colony be located? and How could he pay for the land? He had several choices about location but few options with regard to payment. He had contacts with private landowners in both Kentucky and Tennessee who offered to sell him land. But of greater interest to Dufour was the land that the federal government had just put up for sale in the Northwest Territory.

In 1799, the first legislature of the Northwest Territory met in Cincinnati and elected William Henry Harrison to represent the Northwest Territory in Congress. He understood and supported the desires of the small farmers looking for affordable land west of the mountains. Albert Gallatin shared Harrison's feelings about settling the West. Together they steered a bill through Congress that set up the system of townships and sections that became the method for laying out the boundaries in the Northwest Territory. A half section (320 acres) would be offered for sale at $2 an acre, to be paid in installments over four years at 6 percent interest. The measure passed on May 10, 1800, and was titled "An Act Providing for the Sale of the Lands of the U.S. in the Territory Northwest of the Ohio and Above the Mouth of the Kentucky River."

The federal government had secured this land for settlement in 1795 when it signed the Treaty of Greenville. Most of the land offered for sale by the act was located in the Ohio Territory. However, a portion of it was in what would become Indiana. This portion was bounded by the Ohio River to the south, by the First Principal Meridian (which forms the present Ohio-Indiana border) to the east, and by a line drawn from the mouth of the Kentucky River in a northeasterly direction to Fort Recovery in Greenville, Ohio. This triangular piece of land became known as the Gore. (The name refers to the shape of the land, which is a triangle.) The sale of these lands began on the first Monday of April 1801.

Another event that had a bearing on Dufour's land purchase problem was the election of Thomas Jefferson to the presidency. This unusual election in the fall of 1800 proved to be a stern test of the democratic ideals of the fledgling nation. Aaron Burr and Thomas Jefferson had tied in the electoral vote for president, and the matter was sent to the House of Representatives for resolution, as set out in the Constitution. Ballot after

ballot was taken, each ending in a tie vote. In the secti
voting, the South and West voted for Jefferson while N
for Burr. As the tensions grew, people worried that the co
up; perhaps there would even be a civil war. Finally, on F
after several months of political intrigue and thirty-six b
broken and the House voted for Jefferson. The hard-won ƿ
this wine lover must have pleased Dufour.

The citizens of Lexington, Kentucky, seemed to have been a little early
in their victory celebration for President Jefferson. On January 22, 1801, a
"Grand Festival" was held, to which, incredibly, the whole state of Kentucky
was invited. There were 160 ladies and 500 gentlemen in attendance, and
many toasts were raised. They toasted the memory of George Washington,
recently deceased. They toasted peace and happiness, a republican form of
government, the state of Kentucky, the new administration, and the other
states that had voted for Jefferson. One of the last toasts offered was for
Dufour: "May the virtuous and independent sons of Switzerland, who have
chosen our country as a retreat from the commotions of war, find in the juice
of the Kentucky grape, a solace for all their misfortunes."

While Dufour awaited the arrival of his family and friends, he started
planning his grand scheme for the future of the colony. It revolved around
the recently opened lands of the Northwest Territory and the Jefferson
administration. He wrote to the recently established land office in Cincinnati requesting a map to determine the boundaries of the land available for
sale, which he received on January 10, 1801. On the 1st of February, he
wrote letters to both Thomas Jefferson and Albert Gallatin.

The letter to Gallatin asked for a favor from Congress. Dufour wanted
Gallatin to help him purchase land on the Ohio River on credit. He
emphasized that he was doing this in order to establish a colony of Swiss
winemakers. No doubt Dufour was hoping that Gallatin's Swiss heritage
would make him favorable to the plan. Dufour included a map of the land
he hoped to purchase and explained that he had also wanted to include a
recommendation from the board of directors of the Kentucky Vineyard
Society. However,

> they refused, not because they cannot attest to the progress and success that
> I've had in wine making, and not because they do not wish me well, they
> would do anything to help me if the lots that are the object of my petition
> were in the borders to the state of Kentucky. Their jealousy is so obvious that
> they make it understood that I owe them this colony because they say it is the

vine I planted which attracts them and which makes them spend money. . . .
But even though I am obliged to them, I cannot repay them with the well-
being of an entire colony that owes them nothing.

Already the disparate interests of the Kentucky Vineyard Society and
the Swiss colonists had come into conflict, and Dufour had to put the well-
being of the Swiss first. He explained to Gallatin that he preferred the land
directly on the bank of the Ohio River, even though he had alternative offers
in Kentucky for cheaper land on longer terms and at a better interest rate
than the government was offering. He sent Gallatin a copy of the map that
he had received from the Cincinnati land office on which he had marked the
areas he was interested in acquiring. He calculated the total acreage to be
between 7,000 and 9,000 acres (the discrepancy was due to the scale of the
map). It lay on the north bank of the Ohio River and ran from Markland,
Indiana, to a spot about one mile below Patriot, Indiana. It consisted of a
series of bluffs that rose up behind the bottom ground. He wanted to
purchase this bottom ground first, as it was the only land that was likely to
attract conventional farmers. Then he could purchase the hillsides when
more money became available.

The letter Dufour wrote to Jefferson is very similar to the one he wrote
to Gallatin. Dufour related the trials and tribulations he had faced since his
coming to America. He told Jefferson of his travels in the West and of his
observations of grape-growing. He said the wars and revolutions in Europe
had depleted his funds and those of his family. This had made him fear that
his trip to America had been for naught until he was able to start the
vineyard in Kentucky. Having done so, he had attracted the attention of four
influential Swiss families that wanted to come to America and attempt to
cultivate the vine. Now he wished to purchase land along the Ohio River to
accomplish this goal. He continued,

> That is why I believed that Congress, whose wisdom works continually for
> the good of the country, would like, in favor of a settlement so important to
> the future wealth of the country, to make a small exception to their law
> relating to the sale of land northwest of the Ohio River and to sell me with a
> credit of 10 or 12 years the site that I have been wanting for a long time and
> which I believe to be very favorable to wine-growing.

Dufour feared his request to Congress was too late to be considered during
the ongoing session, but he hoped that it would be considered in the next
session. Dufour wanted to know if Jefferson would support his petition. If
in fact Jefferson did support it, Dufour would buy the bottom ground along

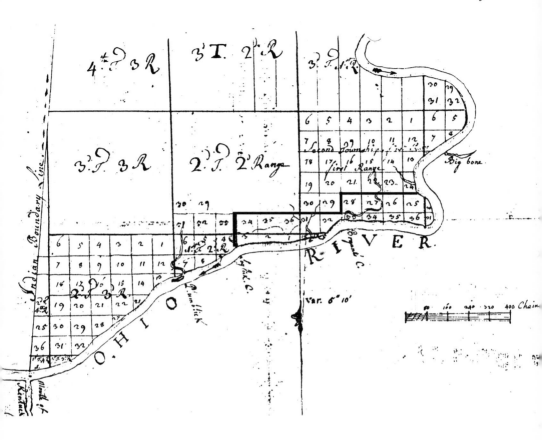

Dufour's first proposed purchase.

the river on regular government terms to keep others from buying it before Congress could approve his plan in the following session.

On the same day that Dufour wrote to Jefferson and Gallatin, he also addressed a petition to Congress. While the two previous letters were written in French and in the first person, this letter was written in English and in the third person. The introduction of himself, his travels, his Swiss friends, and their future plans was much the same as it had been in the other two letters. He also included a list of the sections of land he wished to purchase. Dufour requested they purchase the land at the stipulated price of

$2 an acre, payable in the year 1812 without interest. To demonstrate his sincerity, Dufour said the colony would forfeit the land and the improvements on it if they failed to make the payment or if the following conditions were not met:

> 1) To settle upon the land the families above mentioned as soon as possible after their arrival in the country.
> 2) To complete the plantation of ten acres of the vine before the expiration of two years after their settlement, and in every subsequent year as much more as the force of the colony would enable him to do.
> 3) To use every exertion by his example to render the Cultivation of the Vine familiar to the people of the United States.

Ten days after writing to Jefferson, Gallatin, and Congress, Dufour wrote another letter to the land office in Cincinnati. He returned the map he had received earlier with the land he wanted to purchase outlined in red. Dufour wrote that if he did not receive the terms he wanted from Congress or if he could not receive the very land marked, then he would not settle on the Ohio River, but rather in Tennessee where he had a very generous offer.

As Dufour feared, the petition to Congress arrived too late to be voted on during that session. It is unknown whether Dufour received a positive response from Jefferson or Gallatin, but he proceeded as though he had. At the sale of land in Cincinnati, Dufour purchased on regular terms two partial sections of the best river bottomland, hoping, as he had said, to tie up the larger piece. The land he bought started one mile above Markland and ran for two miles up the river. The date of record is April 10, 1801. His daybook recorded the following: "May 6th, For what I bought on account for 795.5 acres of land bought of Congress at the last public sale, at two dollars per acre, one fourth cash, besides the fees, $405.20."

Dufour's grand scheme was set in motion, and everything seemed to be going well. The Kentucky vineyard was still very young and the vines were not yet showing the symptoms of the pests and diseases that had plagued virtually every other grower in North America. The directors of the Kentucky Vineyard Society had secured more funding for the project after overcoming the recriminations between Dufour and the subscribers. The Swiss colonists had agreed to come to America and were trusting in Dufour to select the land that would eventually be the site of their settlement. The prospects for success were good, but Mother Nature and the hand of man would soon change the course of the venture.

4. The Swiss Settle in Indiana

THE COLONY did not take leave of Switzerland in the last fortnight of November 1800, as John James Dufour had been informed they would. Because of the continuing warfare in Europe the original association was broken, and a smaller group of people prepared to emigrate. Instead of the four wealthy families that had signed the covenant, the people who emigrated were "all poor people who have . . . only the means to make the trip." The group left their Swiss homeland some time after January 13, 1801.

The group included four separate families, the Dufours, Bettens, Boralleys, and Siebenthals, as well as Jean Daniel Morerod, who had yet to start a family. There were seventeen people in all, as many children as adults. The oldest Dufours were Daniel Dufour, aged 31, and his wife Frances, aged 24. All of the other Dufours (Antoinette, John Francis, Suzanne Marguerite, Jeanne Marie, and John David) were under the age of 20. The Bettens family consisted of Phillip Bettens and his wife and daughter. The Boralley family was composed of Peter Boralley, his wife, and his son and daughter. The Siebenthal family consisted of Francis Louis Siebenthal and his son John Francis. It is unlikely that the group had any concept of what life would really be like in the New World. While the adults of the group were dedicated to the establishment of vineyards in their new home, the younger members, like young people everywhere, would be more willing to explore new opportunities. A family named Golay also planned to join the colony on their voyage to America. However, they were delayed by various political events in Switzerland and did not leave for another six months. The Golays crossed the Atlantic on a later ship and settled as caretakers on a dairy farm in New York.

Daniel Dufour was a brother of John James Dufour. The other Dufour siblings were half-brothers and half-sisters to John James. Their father, John James Rudolph Dufour, put John James in charge of his brothers and sisters as a second father, asking him to look after his younger siblings in the New World. The youngest brother, Amie, who was only 7 or 8 at the time, stayed in Europe until 1812, when he crossed the Atlantic Ocean by himself. Curiously, John James Dufour's wife and his son Vincent remained in Europe.

Jean Daniel Morerod, aged 31, was not one of the original signers of the covenant. In May of 1800, prior to the great French victory at the Battle of Marengo, he helped transport Napoleon's artillery across the Alps. Morerod had apparently fallen in love with Antoinette Dufour and could not bear the thought of her leaving him behind. Knowing that she would soon be departing for America, he decided to trade a life of military adventure for a life in the unknown wilds of the New World.

The family members gathered up their most necessary belongings and bid a tearful farewell to their homeland and friends. Their aged father read the Ninetieth Psalm at their departure and asked God's blessing for them in the coming days of hardship. He recommended that particular Psalm for their future guidance and instruction and asked that it be read at the funeral service of each one of these Swiss emigrants and their descendants. Father Dufour's instructions to read the Ninetieth Psalm were followed by descendants of the colonists into the early 1900s.

John Daniel Dufour kept a diary of their Atlantic crossing. On March 20, 1801, they boarded the sloop *Useful,* which carried them and their belongings out to a "superb vessel" which lay at anchor in the roadstead of Rochelle, about three miles from shore. When they arrived on board, the captain informed them that they did not have enough supplies to complete the trip. The men returned to shore to secure more provisions. For three days they were trapped on land by high winds and bad weather. On the fourth day, even though there was still great danger, they were able to return to the ship. On the 25th of March the anchor was raised, and they departed for America.

The trip was more remarkable than the Atlantic crossing of John James Dufour. On the afternoon of their first day at sea, they were stopped and boarded by a corsair (a pirate ship) from the island of Guernsey. Fortunately, the presence nearby of a seventy-four-gun English ship prevented them from being robbed. Then on the 30th of March they spotted another ship following them. Once again it was a corsair from Guernsey. The chase was on, and both ships sailed at full speed. Throughout the day the corsair gained on their ship, and before evening the pirates had overtaken them. The passengers and crew surrendered several hundred pounds of biscuits to the pirates and some wooden baskets. For these items the pirate captain offered payment, but the captain of the immigrant's ship refused. Then the corsairs offered to trade fifty bottles of brandy for fifty bottles of wine. The immigrants, hardly in a position to refuse, delivered the wine to the pirate ship, only to watch the corsairs set sail without delivering the promised brandy.

The voyage continued despite the harassment of the pirates. On the 13th of April, as they neared the banks off Newfoundland, they encountered a terrible storm. The winds blew until the 16th, and the ship was pitched about on the crests of waves thirty feet high. Lucky to survive the storm, they forged ahead until the 29th, when they encountered a wrecked ship off the coast of Virginia. The ship was floating partly submerged without any of its masts or tackle. They immediately slowed and launched their small boat in an effort to investigate the wreck. The second mate and three sailors went over to the wreck. There they found two or three sailor's shirts, a pair of shoes, and moccasins for a child. They also discovered that the boat was loaded with wine and other merchandise. Unfortunately, since only a small portion of the deck was above water and since the seas were rough, they were unable to salvage any of the wine. They were also unable to tow the ship because the wind was from the wrong direction, and dragging the half-sunken vessel would have proved impossible.

On April 30, 1801, the voyagers dropped anchor opposite the mouth of the James River, about three hours from Norfolk, Virginia. Their long and eventful sea crossing was over. Now the Swiss immigrants had to travel hundreds of miles across the mountains and down the Ohio River to join John James Dufour in Kentucky.

The Swiss settlers traveled from Norfolk overland to Pittsburgh. The women and children who could not walk the distance to Pittsburgh were weighed as freight and rode in wagons over the mountains. The colonists were indeed a poor group. After arriving in Pittsburgh they found they were unable to afford their passage down the Ohio River. They were grateful to borrow $50 from Mr. Lewis Sanders, a Lexington shopkeeper, to fund the remainder of their journey.

John James Dufour was characteristically busy while his family was in transit. He wrote a letter to the (Nashville) *Tennessee Gazette,* which was printed on July 29, 1801. The letter outlined a proposal for a vineyard scheme that Dufour thought could be accomplished in Tennessee. The outline was very similar to the Kentucky Vineyard Society plan. He stated that he had learned several things that would be very useful to the new company but that he would be unable to oversee the proposed Tennessee venture because he already had prior commitments. However, he had brothers on the way from Europe, and they would be able to undertake the project. The letter highlights the fact that Dufour was still actively looking for alternatives to the Kentucky venture and the land on the Ohio River that he had recently purchased. He was a man of his word and would not break his contract, but he still had great ambitions for himself and his family. Obviously, the more ventures a family undertakes, the greater the chance that at least one member will succeed and that they will be well placed in a growing American industry. However, the Tennessee project was never attempted, and their efforts focused on the Ohio River site.

On June 9, Dufour received word that his family had landed in America and was on its way west. He decided to meet them en route and accompany them on the remainder of their journey. News spread surprisingly quickly on the frontier. The *Cincinnati Western Spy* ran an article in their July 29th edition that quoted the information from the *Kentucky Gazette* of July 9th that several families of vinedressers had arrived from Switzerland. It stated that three of the immigrants were brothers of John James Dufour who had come to Kentucky because of the flattering accounts given by their brother of his success with the vine. The articles made much of the fact that the Swiss settlers would be starting a colony to make wine and that they had brought several boxes of European vines with them as well as choice fruit trees and various fruit seeds. The attention in the press illustrates the novel undertaking of these immigrants.

John James traveled all the way to Marietta, Ohio, before he encountered his family descending the river. It must have been a joyous occasion for all, particularly for John James, who had not seen any members of his family for five years. They traveled together back to Lexington, where they arrived on the third of July. The next day, July 4th, the citizens of Lexington threw an Independence Day party at which they offered up their usual lengthy list of toasts. A toast was even made to the newly arrived Swiss: "Success to the vine-yard association, a hearty welcome to the cultivators of the vine, and to all peaceable foreigners who introduce their industry and arts amongst us." On July 6th, they arrived at Firstvineyard.

Tired as they must have been from their long voyage, they did not waste any time in getting organized. The day they arrived at Firstvineyard, Dufour recorded in his daybook: "My brothers and all their company, making in all 17 persons, arrived at Firstvineyard and I entered into a partnership with my brothers and sisters to work the vineyard. From this time on all has been in common. However, what was mine before the partnership is to be deducted after."

This agreement is an obvious statement that their shared work at Firstvineyard was just an interim situation until their permanent land, wherever it would be, was purchased and settled. In the meantime, the colony had to support itself. The contract that Dufour had signed with the Kentucky Vineyard Society stipulated that the colony was to obtain their support from the farm for the first few years until the vineyard began producing. There would be no help from the shareholders for the colony's support. The seeds and plants that the colonists had brought from Switzerland were set out. In addition to the staple food crops they sowed, they planted the vines they had brought from Europe among the other vines at Firstvineyard.

The arrival of the smaller and poorer colony caused Dufour to make several changes in his grand scheme. In his original plan he had requested of Congress about 7,000 acres of land. As previously mentioned, he had forged ahead and purchased 795.5 acres on standard terms while he waited for Congress to address his "little exception." Now Dufour was forced to reduce his request to fit the new circumstances of the smaller colony. Dufour wrote another letter to Thomas Jefferson dated January 15, 1802, saying,

> [The Swiss Colony desires] about three sections of land on the banks of the Ohio where they would like to settle, and it is to ask you to grant your signature to this petition that I take the liberty to write you. I already troubled you last year with a letter regarding the same concern but it was too late for Congress. Our petition is the same as last year except for the amount; I was requesting at that time a large tract because a large Colony had formed a company to come grow wine and called on me to buy them land, but because of the war this association was broken and only a small part of the colony came.

Dufour goes on to explain that he has every confidence that his vineyard scheme will be met with success if only the government will help him. He even goes farther than this: "The time is not far off when our seaports instead of receiving wines and liquors, will send some abroad," and, he added, "I foresee the time when the Ohio will compete with the Rhine or the Rhone for the quantity of vineyards, and the quality of wine." Dufour expressed only optimism about the future of the American wine industry and saw the Ohio River as the heart of this successful future.

Daniel Dufour joined his brother in beseeching powerful members of the U.S. government to help the new immigrants. On January 12, 1802, he wrote to Albert Gallatin, who at this time was the secretary of the U.S. Treasury. He began his letter by stating that even though he had not had the honor of meeting Mr. Gallatin, his brother John James "has had the honor of meeting you, and to speak with you from time to time." Daniel asked of Mr. Gallatin the same favor that his brother had requested from the president. He wrote,

> This petition is more or less the same as the one my brother took the liberty of sending you late last year with this difference; instead of 7000 acres which he asked for, we are only asking for 2 thousand, which would give each of us around 150 acres. We do not wish to extend the bounds of honesty. My brother in asking for 7000 acres was counting on the arrival of numerous colonists, but several members of the colony could not follow us because of last minute inconveniences, caused by our revolution.

The 2,000 acres were located "17 to 19 miles above the mouth of the Kentucky River." This was where Dufour had made his earlier purchase in 1801.

This time the Dufours were successful in getting their "little exception" passed through Congress. On May 1, 1802, Congress passed a measure entitled, "An act to empower John James Dufour, and his associates, to purchase certain lands." The act states,

> Be it enacted, &c., That to encourage the introduction, and to promote the culture of the vine within the territory of the United States, north-west of the river Ohio, it shall be lawful for John James Dufour, and his associates, to purchase any quantity not exceeding four sections of the lands of the United States, lying between the Great Miami river and the Indian boundary line, at the rate of two dollars per acre, payable without interest, on or before the first day of January, one thousand eight hundred and fourteen.

This congressional act opened the way for the colony to purchase the land they desired. Surprisingly, they did not select the lands that adjoined Dufour's original purchase. One can only speculate what brought about this turn of events. One clue may come from Lewis Sanders (the same Lexington merchant who had loaned the Swiss colonists money to complete their journey to Firstvineyard in 1801), who in reference to the colony at Firstvineyard wrote, "They thought the steep hillsides unfavorable to the cultivation of the grape, and preferred level lands."

Another, and perhaps more important, factor was the purchase of land by other settlers in the immediate vicinity of John James's original land purchase. In July 1801, Thomas Hopkins had purchased a partial section of river frontage immediately adjoining the western boundary of Dufour's purchase. A short distance to the east (just above where Florence, Indiana, is today), the hills come right down to the river for a distance of about two miles. Hopkins's purchase limited expansion to the west, and steep hills limited expansion to the east. If they had settled there, the colony would have been limited more or less to the river frontage of Dufour's first purchase.

The land the colony decided to buy was five or six miles downriver, where the town of Vevay is located today. They acquired approximately three miles of river frontage and a fair quantity of flat ground on the second bank above the river. The presence of this second bank, which is less prone to flooding, could be another factor that influenced the colonists to select this spot. The total acreage that they desired was greater than the four sections allotted to them by the act of Congress. The extra land was purchased by John James on the "regular terms" available to all settlers. They called their future settlement "New Switzerland."

In the summer of 1802, shortly after the land purchase, the Bettens and Morerod families moved to New Switzerland (Jean Daniel Morerod had married Antoinette Dufour on February 16, 1802, at Firstvineyard, Kentucky). They and John James Dufour went by boat down the Kentucky River to the Ohio and then up the Ohio to their new lands. According to Perret Dufour, John James stepped ashore with an axe, saying, "I will cut down the first tree on our lands." He then strode up the bank and felled a sapling. The Morerods and Bettens moved into a squatter's cabin and lived there while they cleared land for the planting of crops and vineyards. The arduous task of clearing timber and building homes in the wilderness would take a number of years.

The majority of the Swiss colony remained at Firstvineyard, and while they resided there they drew up a new covenant (dated January 20, 1803) that stipulated how their Indiana lands were to be divided. The covenant stated that the primary goal of the group was, "To plant the vine and make their principal business their cultivation." Peter Boralley, who was a signer of the original covenant and had left Switzerland with the group, did not sign the new covenant; he had died after being kicked in the head by a horse. His family took leave of their Swiss brethren and moved to Garrard County, Kentucky.

On August 10th and 11th, 1802, while work was just beginning at New Switzerland, Andre Michaux, a French botanist, visited Firstvineyard. Michaux left us one of the few eyewitness accounts of Firstvineyard. He wrote of the visit in his book about his travels through the eastern United States. He described the vineyard:

> However the success did not answer the expectation; only four or five various kinds [of grapes] survived, among which were those that he had described by the name of Burgundy and Madeira, but the former is far from being healthy. The grape generally decays before it is ripe. When I saw them the bunches were thin and poor, the berries small, and every thing announced that the vintage of 1802 would not be more abundant than that of preceding years. The Madeira vines appeared, on the contrary, to give some hopes. Out of a hundred and fifty to two hundred, there was a third loaded with very fine bunches. The whole of these vines do not occupy a space of more than six acres. They are planted and fixed with props similar to those in the environs of Paris.
>
> Such was then the situation of this establishment, in which the stock-holders concerned themselves but very little. . . . These particulars are sufficient to give, on the pretended flourishing state of the vines in Kentucky, an idea very different to that which might be formed from the pompous account of them which appeared some months since in our public papers.

Michaux seems to have visited just as the vineyard first started showing signs of disease. Of this period, John James wrote:

> Three years [1799, 1800, 1801] we were in full expectation, and worked with great courage—a great many species of vines showed fruit the third year [1801]; one vine of the sweet water was full of eminently good grapes, fully ripened by the first of September. A few bunches that I carried to Lexington, were admired beyond any thing. But alas! It was the first and last year that vine ever bore fruit, a sickness . . . took hold of all our vines except the few stocks of Cape and Madeira grapes, from each of which we made the fourth year some wine [1802], which was drank by some shareholders in Lexington in March next [1803].

The summer of 1802 was a critical time for Firstvineyard. Dufour's experience in Kentucky was mimicking all the other failed experiments to grow grapes in eastern North America. In the first year there was a flush of success as the vines flourished in the American soil. This was followed by a year or two in which the vines seemed well on their way to production. Then came the sudden and disappointing failure. But the Swiss did not take this as a sign of complete failure. Instead, they took cuttings of the surviving vines (mainly the Cape and Madeira) and used those to replant the vine-yard.

In 1805, a Frenchman named Valcourt who lived nearby visited First-vineyard on a regular basis. According to Mr. Valcourt, some of Mr. Dufour's vines were from the cooler climes of Europe, that is, the vines of the Rhine, Moselle, Burgundy, and Champagne. He also had vines from the warmer climates of Europe, such as Spain, Portugal, and Madeira. According to Valcourt, Dufour was "very much surprised to find that all the leaves of the shoots from the colder latitudes were burnt up by the sun, and crumbled into powder resembling snuff, which did not happen with the shoots of the warmer climates."

The shriveling and crumbling of the leaves of the more northern vines, which Dufour attributed to the sun, were probably symptoms of one or more of the diseases endemic to North America to which the European vines had no resistance. The survival of the vines from the warmer climate indicated that they were not true European vines but actually a cross of European Vinifera and native American vines. This made them much more resistant to the grape diseases of the New World, the major factor in the success of the Cape and Madeira grapes.

Dufour believed that his Cape grape was indeed a true European variety. He based this opinion on two things. First, when he had purchased the cuttings from Mr. Legaux, he had been told that they were from South Africa and were the famous Constantia, or Cape grape. Second, his own extensive observations of grapes had shown him that all true European grape varieties (*Vitis vinifera*) had flowers with both male and female parts, so-called perfect flowers. Dufour, however, had observed that the native North American grape varieties had flowers that were either all male or all female (imperfect flowers). The perfect flowers of the Cape grape had convinced Dufour that it was a true European Vinifera variety. At this time it was generally thought that vines were either European or American. Hybrids between the two groups had not yet been recognized. The first mention in print of hybrids between European and American grapes would occur within Dufour's circle of acquaintances. In 1806, Bernard McMahon, secretary of Legaux's vineyard company and one of the leading horticultur-ists of the day, described the Alexander and Bland's grapes as being chance crosses of two different native grapes or of Vinifera and native varieties. One can hardly criticize Dufour or anyone of this period for having a confused conception of hybrids. Dufour's observations were based on the botanical evidence of the day. The groundbreaking work of Gregor Mendel was still fifty years in the future. Had Dufour realized that hybrids between European and American vines were generally hermaphroditic, it would have saved him much argument and controversy later in his life.

Cape grape. This grape was grown commercially through the 1860s in the Cincinnati area. No known verifiable specimen exists today. (From Fleischmann, *Grapes of America*.)

Schuylkill

In December of 1804, Dufour decided to have a sample of his wine sent to President Jefferson in Washington. Unfortunately, the colonists did not have enough money to finance the trip on their own. Henry Clay, eminent Kentuckian and subscriber to the Kentucky Vineyard Society, collected a fund of $60 to help finance the journey. John Francis Dufour, then a young man of about 20, was chosen to make the trip. Julie LeClerc Knox, a Dufour descendant, wrote that John Francis "started off through the then almost trackless wilderness, [on] horseback, leading a packhorse, laden with two kegs of five gallons each." After a long overland journey of approximately 600 miles, John Francis arrived in Washington in late February. He carried the following letter from Kentucky senator John Brown:

To Thomas Jefferson

Senate Chamber 20th. Feby 1805

Sir

The Bearier [*sic*] J. F. Dufour is one of the Swiss Emigrants who have commenced the culture of the Vine in Kentucky & on the Banks of the Ohio

He requests the honor of presenting to you as a testimony of their high respect, a sample of Wines made by them last Autumn at their first Vineyard in Kentucky, & will return highly gratified should the fruits of their infant establishment be found worthy of any portion of your approbation.

I have the honor to be very respectfully Yo Mo ob Servt.

THOMAS JEFFERSON ESQR   J. BROWN

John Francis met with Jefferson two days later. Jefferson wrote a letter of reply to Senator Brown describing the meeting between himself and John Francis Dufour. Jefferson wrote that Mr. Dufour had visited him and wanted to know what he thought of the wine. Jefferson informed John Francis that it was too early to form an opinion of the wine because the wine was so young; he felt that from two to five years were necessary to age a wine. Jefferson thought about giving the wine to others so that they might taste it as well, but he decided against it because they might mistake the green-ness (youngness) of the wine for its true qualities. He therefore sampled both kinds of wine at dinner with his family. Jefferson described both wines: "They appear to possess a body capable of becoming good." Jefferson felt that the best service he could offer the Dufours was to have the wine well taken care of and tasted again in twelve months and then again in two years. After that time, he said, "We may begin to form a better judgment of it." In an interesting postscript to the letter, Jefferson asked for candid information from Mr. Dufour as to whether any spirits had been added to the wine and if so in what quantity. His concern illustrates the overdependence on the fortification of wine in the early American period.

Other Swiss settlers soon joined the colony at New Switzerland, just as Dufour had predicted they would. Some of the land that had been purchased on regular terms by Dufour was sold to the new arrivals. One of these was Louis Gex-Oboussier. He purchased 319 acres and brought his family to settle. Frederick Raymond and Frederick Deserens together purchased

Letter from President Jefferson to Senator John Brown of Kentucky concerning the visit of John Francis Dufour. (From the Alderman Library, the University of Virginia.)

150 acres, while a Mr. Stuart bought 160 acres in section 15 for $4 per acre. The Golays also arrived at New Switzerland. Their tenure on the New York dairy farm proved to be a short-lived adventure because the dairy farm was

in very poor condition and was not at all as it had been represented in Europe. After several years they sued the land agents who had lied to them about the prospects of the farm and won a settlement. In 1804, using the money they won in the suit, they joined the other Swiss vinedressers on the Ohio.

In September 1804, John James Dufour purchased sections 7 and 8 to the east of the New Switzerland purchase. This increased the total land in the New Switzerland area to about 3,700 acres. Dufour's daybook entry for October 1804 noted that the family partnership would dissolve in the near future: "The family has ceased being in partnership, Daniel wishing to go on his land and Jean Francois [John Francis], being of age, does not wish to remain any longer in partnership."

The entry for November 8, 1804, shows the further breakdown of the partnership:

> In consequence of our dissolution of partnership I have drawn up a plan of division by which each one of the children of Jean Jaques Dufour, Senior, will receive an allotment in the tract of land which Congress granted me and my associates. My son Vincent Dl. [Daniel] will also receive an allotment as an associate. I have surveyed and apportioned it on the plan as exactly as possible.

John James describes the division and concludes:

> By the above division each of my brothers and sisters will receive his portion of one-third of the products of the partnership and the Vineyard Company in Kentucky, for which I have worked alone 6 years, and all of us, 3 [years]. . . . A copy of my accounts with my father and of the above mentioned division, and also a copy of the plan of the lands above mentioned is kept at the house at Firstvineyard in the care of Jean Francois Dufour, and another copy will be given, if it so pleases God, to my father in Switzerland.

While the brothers were contemplating the breakup of the Kentucky partnership, John James Dufour, Sr., was trying to encourage the family to work together and avoid the temptations of America's religious freedom. He corresponded with his children in America and offered advice and thoughts about their lives on the frontier. On one occasion they had written to him about the religious revival movement that was sweeping through the western states. Their father warned them of trances and ecstasies and reminded them of the advice of the "Abbot of the Vinedressers of Vevey" who said, "*Ora et labora*"—pray while you work. The elder Dufour was glad that the American government did not interfere with the subject of religion, but he told his children that governments could not conduct them to eternal life. He wrote passionately that reason, abandoned to itself without faith or revelation, was liable to fall into the greatest of absurdities.

Firstvineyard did not require all of Dufour's time, nor did it exhaust his creative energy. During the slower seasons he was able to travel to various places in the Ohio Valley. In 1801, he had traveled to the Upper Blue Lick. In 1802, he went to Goose Creek. In October 1803, his journeys took him to Red Bank, Saline River, and Post Vincennes. He made one other trip to the three forks of the Kentucky River. All of these trips were made in an effort to find a salt pit in order to make salt in a new way. Whether he was ever able to do this we don't know. On January 1st, 1801, Dufour made arrangements to work with Thomas Hart and Samuel Brown. The two gentleman had formed a partnership to purchase a saltpeter cave near Madison, Kentucky. They hoped to get a contract to supply saltpeter to the government for the manufacture of gunpowder. What Dufour's role in the enterprise was we do not know. Near the end of January, he left the vineyard in the care of Jean Roux and went to the cave. Three months later he returned to the vineyard, having earned $80 for his work at the cave.

John James did not move to New Switzerland but maintained his residence in Kentucky at Firstvineyard until his return to Europe. On August 1, 1805, Dufour wrote in his daybook, "Have placed the vineyard in the care of Jean Francois for a period of 4 years, while I go to Switzerland to get my family." Four years from August 1, 1805, would be the day his contract with the Kentucky Vineyard Society would expire.

On New Year's Day 1806, Dufour settled his accounts with the vineyard company. On the 15th of January he granted his brother John Francis power of attorney over his affairs in America. He borrowed $15 from Henry Clay in Lexington in order to pay for his trip east and left for Washington. He arrived there on February 16th, and on the 18th he advertised that his horse was for sale and that he was looking for investors for a new type of steam engine that he had invented and intended to patent.

As far as we know, Dufour did not procure any investors for his steam engine, but we do know that he sold his horse for $60. With this money he repaid the $15 loan from Henry Clay by entrusting the money to Senator Thurston of Kentucky. He obtained the following letter from his friend, Senator John Brown of Kentucky:

To James Madison

Sir

The Bearer is one of the Swiss Emigrants who have commenced the culture of the Vine in Kentucky & on the Banks of the Ohio. He request to have the honor of presenting to you in testimony of their respect, a sample of wine made by them last Autumn at their Vineyard in Kentucky—

Yo Mo ob Sert
J. Brown
22d. Feby

The wine given to Madison from Firstvineyard would have been from the 1805 vintage. Little else is known about the visit. Dufour left Washington on March 8th and arrived in Philadelphia on the 12th.

In Philadelphia, Dufour was invited by Mr. McMahon, secretary of the Philadelphia Vineyard Society, to attend a meeting on March 23rd at the society's vineyard under the management of Peter Legaux. This was, of course, the vineyard where Dufour had obtained thirty-five of the grape varieties he planted at Firstvineyard. News of the success of Dufour's vineyard had reached Philadelphia and the members were curious about why their vineyard had not succeeded while Dufour's had. Of the meeting Dufour later wrote:

> I briefly answered, that all the mystery of our success consisted in nursing only the vines that were prosperous, no matter how good or how bad their fruit was; for I was fully of the opinion, that no other existing this side of the Atlantic, would ever remunerate for the trouble of attendance; that the Cape grape was the only one reared by the Swiss settlers; that it was a hardy and thrifty plant, giving regular if not large crops of grapes, . . . —making a good wine inferior but to a minority of the European wines, and that it rewarded its cultivator as well as any other American produce.

Dufour attributed his success to finding a vine that survived and sticking with it. His practical nature dictated that one must work with the plants available until more desirable plants could be found. This philosophy was the opposite of that held by the Philadelphia Vineyard Society, which kept importing European vines only to have them die. If Dufour had gone to Europe to procure his grapes as members of the Kentucky Vineyard Society had wanted him to do, his failure would have been as complete as the failures of all the other efforts in North America. It was only by happening upon the unlikely cross, which was misrepresented as the Cape grape, that he had had success.

According to Legaux's diary, a Mr. Morgan also attended the meeting. George Morgan of Washington, Pennsylvania, a person of noted standing in Philadelphia society, had started a vineyard in 1796 in Washington County, south of Pittsburgh, at his farm called Morganza. He claimed to have conducted "the first Experiment ever made West of the Allegheny Mountain by an individual . . . on the cultivation of the Grape except a few Plants in Gardens." Morgan abandoned his vineyard in 1806.

On March 24th, Dufour left Philadelphia for New York via the Burlington packet. On the 9th of April he paid for his passage to Bordeaux, France, and left for Europe aboard the brig *Edward Young*. Before he left, he posted letters for his friends and associates remaining in New Switzerland. This voyage proved to be much more exciting than his previous crossing of the Atlantic. England and France were still at war. As the *Edward Young* approached the coast of Bordeaux on May 4th, the English captured the ship. Dufour and the other passengers were taken to Plymouth, England, where they were kept in quarantine for a month. Upon his release, he made his way to London, where he visited St. Paul's Cathedral and sampled some of the British beer. From London he sailed to Rotterdam and eventually made his way to Vevey, Switzerland, where he arrived on the 14th of August, 1806. It had been ten years since he had seen his wife and son. It would be another ten years before he returned to Firstvineyard and New Switzerland.

5. Out of the Very Ground They Tread

WHEN JOHN JAMES DUFOUR went to Europe in 1806, he left behind his brothers, John David and John Francis Dufour, at Firstvineyard to fulfill his contractual obligations with the Kentucky Vineyard Society. The rest of the Swiss settlers had moved to New Switzerland in the Indiana territory. Each year they cleared land and increased the planting of vineyards and other crops. In 1805, the settlers had their first substantial wheat crop, and shortly afterward, in 1806 or 1807, they enjoyed their first grape crop. In 1808, grape production increased enough to allow the colonists to make 800 gallons of wine. In his book *The American Vine-Dresser's Guide,* John James Dufour explained that the vineyards produced approximately one ton per acre, which yielded about 180 gallons of wine. Thus, the 800 gallons of wine amounts to approximately four or five acres in production. This was a substantial planting, especially when one considers that it was accomplished by a small number of people engaged in carving a community out of the wilderness. Of course, a yield of one ton per acre is very low by today's standards. Later reports placed the crop at about two tons per acre, which is still low when compared to modern vineyards. This small crop resulted from several factors. Many of the wild American grape species are naturally shy producers of fruit, and the Cape grape certainly had American parentage in its pedigree. A second consideration was the shortage of labor and lack of fertilizer on the frontier. This is evident in Dufour's statement that the difference between the Old World and New World was that while the Old World had too many people, the New World had too few people to tend the vineyards and too few animals for manure. But still, a yield of one to two tons per acre was enough to make the endeavor worthwhile financially.

The year 1809 was a critical period for Firstvineyard. Had 1809 (or 1808 for that matter) been a profitable year, then the efforts at Firstvineyard might have been continued beyond the end of the contract. But in the spring of 1809, a frost took the whole crop. As John James later described it, "My two brothers, who tried to keep the place, found themselves too weak to support it; and one frosty spring having took all their crop; and knowing

47

that those of the colony, who had begun in 1802 on the borders of the Ohio, were successful and had suffered nothing by the frost, they abandoned the place to an American tenant." When this event is compared to the 1,200 gallons of wine produced at New Switzerland in the same year, one can see that the project at Firstvineyard had run its course.

While the frost of 1809 was the last straw, the underlying cause of the failure went back to the beginning. In hindsight John James summarized the plight of Firstvineyard as follows:

> The plan was well laid, if we had perfected it; but in 1799 too anxious to begin, we went into business before all the 1160 [errata, 160] shares were subscribed for, and while there was but very little money collected five acres were planted. ...The failure of the first plantation [except for the Cape and Madeira grapes] caused a relaxation among the shareholders, and not only a great difficulty was experienced in collecting the subscribed money; but the subscription of all the shares was never performed, so that all of our stock was made use of, for paying for the hiring of negroes and other hands, and we were never able to purchase a single share or even to pay for the land: then the whole burden of the establishment rested on our family.

Dufour had weathered the crisis of 1800, when he was criticized by the shareholders for not going to Europe to obtain the vines. But when the European vines began to fail in 1802, the shareholders, lacking Dufour's passion, saw only dying vines and lost interest. Dufour saw not the failed European vines but the surviving Cape and Madeira vines. Herein lay the difference that separated Dufour from the previous grape-growers who worked during the 200 years of failed American viticulture. He took those surviving vines and propagated them to replant the vineyard, seeing in them a hope for the future. Yet without the continued support of the shareholders he could not reasonably justify the continued labor of his family at Firstvineyard. In 1809, his part of the contract had been fulfilled and the last of his family could leave Kentucky in good conscience. So after years of effort and a few tantalizing results, the project at Firstvineyard was abandoned.

Other factors had also worked toward the demise of Firstvineyard. One was the lack of suitable water transportation in the interior of Kentucky. The Kentucky River was subject to immense fluctuations in depth. In times of flood it could rise thirty feet, and during times of drought it could drop so precipitously that boats were left stranded. An anecdote illustrates the unreliability of the Kentucky River as a method of transport. In the winter of 1806, John G. Stuart, a young Kentucky resident, was serving as a crewmember on a flatboat. They loaded their boat at Cleveland Landing near Lexington on February 23–26, and proceeded downriver only one-quarter mile before stopping because of low water. The weather had been very dry and the river depth was dropping. Stuart and his companions were forced to wait for rain to raise the water level. They waited almost two months for rain. On April 16th it rained very hard and the river began to rise very rapidly. The flatboat was able to travel from just below Cleveland Landing to a spot just below Firstvineyard, at which point it was landed with great difficulty because of the high water.

Stuart visited the vineyard to borrow some tools to fix the boat. That evening he returned the tools and "pass'd some hours in conversing with an amiable Swiss Girl." Perhaps smitten, he returned to Firstvineyard the next day and "spent some agreeable hours in the company of the amiable Maria Dufore." The water soon receded, and Stuart and company were finally able to complete their voyage down the Kentucky River. Dufour's choice of the Ohio River over the Kentucky River was a sound one. Once the steamboat arrived on the scene, the difference in commerce between the two rivers was magnified many times over.

Yet another factor that contributed to the abandonment of Firstvineyard was the presence of slavery in Kentucky. At first John James Dufour had looked upon slavery as a way to secure a reliable labor force for his vineyard, and his original plan had called for the purchase of slaves. The money troubles of Firstvineyard had precluded this purchase, so he was forced to hire and train his labor force each season. This went on until his relatives arrived, at which point they worked the vineyard on shares. As the Swiss lived in Kentucky, they came to have a greater understanding of slavery as a system. The deeply religious and hard-working Swiss "chafed under the presence of slavery and desired to escape it." Further evidence of the opposition of the Swiss settlers to slavery is supplied by John James's refusal to settle the colony in either Kentucky or Tennessee, despite repeated offers of cheap lands and longer credit terms. Ultimately, John James could have chosen to settle his colony on the Kentucky bank of the Ohio River, gaining all the advantages of the Ohio River trade. The fact that he chose not to do so underscores the desire of the Swiss colonists to live in free territory.

In the spring of 1809, John Francis and his brother John David finally left Firstvineyard. John Francis loaded his family and possessions on a boat and headed down the Kentucky River to the Ohio River. Upon reaching the Ohio, it was discovered that the water was too high for a safe trip to New Switzerland. Some of the family's friends came down to the boat to help move it. As they reached the mouth of Indian Creek, a storm came up which threatened to capsize the boat. This could have been a disaster, since the boat carried all of John Francis's earthly goods, as well as his wife and 18-month-old son Perret. Luckily, after dumping a few of the heavier items overboard, the boat was saved from sinking and the last residents of Firstvineyard completed their move safely.

There is at least one reference to another group of Swiss vine-growers in Jessamine County, Kentucky. They were supposed to have been located near Crozier Mill on Jessamine Creek. But "after some years of cultivation of the European varieties, [they] abandoned their vines and homes and sought success in more congenial climes." There is no evidence that they had any connection with Dufour and his colony at Firstvineyard. That another group of Swiss vinedressers had settled in Kentucky at about the same time should not be too surprising. At the same time that the Dufour colony left Europe, other Swiss winegrowers were also departing for America to escape the wars of Europe. As David Golay wrote from Bordeaux, France, to his brothers and sisters before his departure:

> Some vineyard workers are leaving on the same ship as we are, to introduce the grape culture in America. The Dufours who preceded us to America are happily disembarking at Philadelphia. They will not be the only ones to propagate the new product. In a few years the country will have wine from its own vineyards, if one can judge by the number of enterprises that are going to be producing wine.

In the interest of attracting more settlers to the colony at New Switzerland on the Ohio River, John Francis Dufour wrote an article in the fall of 1811 that appeared in the (Cincinnati) *Niles' Weekly Register*. In this article, he gives an excellent (although probably somewhat biased) description of the settlement at New Switzerland and the results that were beginning to appear. He wrote:

> New Swisserland is situated on the right bank of the Ohio river, in Jefferson County, Indiana territory, about seven miles above the mouth of the Kentucky river. This settlement was begun in the spring of the year 1803, by some Swiss of the canton of Vaud, formerly a part of the canton of Bern, their principle object is the introduction of the culture of the grape vine in this country. This settlement, or rather the place called New Swisserland, extends

from about three quarters of a mile above the mouth of Plumb creek down the river to the mouth of Venoge creek, known by the name Indian creek, a distance of about four miles and a half fronting the river, and extends back for the quantity of about 3,700 acres of land. . . .

The lower end about two miles along the river, is occupied by thirteen Swiss families, containing sixty-six individuals, of every age—10 of those families have successively come to join the three first who had began the settlement. Had it not been for the difficulties in crossing the ocean, it is believed the whole distance of four and a half miles would have been filled up with as many more of those industrious people.

The improvements of the Swiss are considerable, considering the time when they began, the few hands employed in them, and their inexperience in the way of improving lands in this country. They have now about 140 acres in cultivation, about eight of which are planted in grape vines, now bearing; which offer to the eye of the observer the handsomest and most interesting agricultural prospect perhaps ever witnessed in the United States. There are about 8 or 9 acres more planted in vines, which are not yet bearing; and they continue planting more every year. The crop of wine of 1810, has exceeded the quantity of 2400 gallons, the quality of which has been thought by judges of wine, superior to that of the claret of Bordeaux. Out of the quantity about 120 gallons was white, or yellow wine, made out of Maderia [*sic*] grapes. . . . The precious culture of the vine will be tried in different parts of the Union, and will undoubtedly multiply with rapidity. The Swiss will encourage it with all their power; they give vine slips gratis to whoever will plant them, with directions and instructions for their cultivation.

At the time that this glowing report was printed, a man by the name of J. F. Buchetee was teaching school in New Switzerland. He was sufficiently impressed with the wine culture being developed by the Swiss to write a poem immortalizing it. This long work, titled "Empire of Bacchus," was originally written in Latin. Some time later William Priestly translated it into English. It is written in a florid and overblown poetic style typical of the times. The poem contains many references to Greek Gods, the temperance of wine consumption, and the rain, frost, and excessive heat that were the enemies of wine production. The most interesting part of the poem was the verse naming the heroes who produced the wine:

> Hail, Bettens and Morerod! Blest be each name!
> Sons of Bacchus your names shall endure
> And Siebenthal shall flourish immortal in fame
> And you too vine-rearing Dufour.

It is worth pointing out that Bettens, Morerod, and Siebenthal are the first individuals to receive praise and that Dufour is credited with vine-growing almost as an afterthought.

Residents of New Switzerland were not the only ones impressed by their industrious work. Travelers along the Ohio also observed the strange experiment being conducted by the Swiss. One of the earliest reports comes from Lydia Bacon, a traveler who passed the settlement on September 3, 1811. She wrote,

> Last night our boats were anchored under a very high bank whose summit presented nothing very inviting, so much so, that we hardly thought of taking the trouble to ascend it, but our minds were soon changed by the report of some whose curiosity had led them to reconnoiter a little distance, they returned with some beautiful straw Hats, which they purchased of a Swiss family, whom they found settled a short distance from the River, about 30 families had taken up their residence here, being driven from their own country by the troubles in France they fled to our peaceful shores, & purchasing some land of Government have planted Vineyards, the produce of which; enables them to realize what they had fondly anticipated in an exchange of Countries. Their Wine made from the Maderia [sic] & Clarret [sic] Grapes is excellent. We purchased some. This place is called Veva, it is New Swiss.

Lydia Bacon referred to the wine made by the Swiss settlers as "Clarret." It was very common for early Americans to refer to native wines using European names. This tradition became deeply ingrained in the Americas and still continues to this day (much to the chagrin of wine purists) with the use of terms such as Chablis or Burgundy for American wines.

We have yet another view of the Swiss settlement from the report of David Warden, who was also a traveler on the Ohio River. He passed through the area around the same time as Lydia Bacon, and wrote,

> The culture of the vine has been successfully introduced by a colony of Swiss emigrants, established at New Switzerland. In the year 1811, 2,700 gallons of wine were produced from a surface of twenty acres, and is found to be of a good quality. The grapes which have succeeded best are those from the Cape of Good Hope and the island of Madeira. Those of the country give wine of a tolerable good quality.

Another view of the expanding Swiss settlement and its increasingly famous wine was provided by a traveler named John Mellish. He wrote on September 16, 1811,

We were now in sight of a Swiss settlement on the other side of the river, to which, on account of the head wind, we moved with difficulty; but on our arrival we were very much gratified by the appearance of this thriving colony. We were told that they emigrated to America about ten years ago, and first attempted the business of vine-dressing on the Kentucky river; but not succeeding to their wish, they moved to this place, which they found to answer very well. We found the vineyards in very good order, and the grapes, which were at full maturity, hung in most luxuriant clusters. They were of two kinds, claret and Madeira, both reputed to be of the best quality, and the sample which we tasted had an excellent flavour. The wine consisted of two kinds, of course, claret and Madeira. The Claret was rich in quality, but too acid. It was, however, a very palatable and pleasant beverage when diluted with water. The Madeira wine we found very unpalatable, but we were informed that it wanted age. The person who gave us our information said the colony consisted of about 56 persons, who were all vine-dressers, but they had no connection together in business. Each family was independent within itself. They have farms besides the vineyards, and they make all their clothing, so that the produce of the wine is so much added to their stock. Last year [1810] they sold 2400 gallons at one dollar and a half per gallon; this year they will sell 3000; and they are very sanguine that they will be able to bring the business to full maturity. Their markets are, Cincinnati, Frankfort, Lexington, and St. Louis.

Mellish paints a picture of a vibrant community and a thriving wine industry. The Swiss seem to have been well on their way toward achieving their goal of transforming a corner of southern Indiana into a region known for its grapes and wines.

The Swiss settlers had sought to escape war by moving to America, but in the winter of 1810–1811 conflict broke out in Indiana. Frontiersmen and settlers had been moving into the area in increasing numbers. The great Indian chief Tecumseh had decided to halt white expansion by unifying regional tribes in resistance. This, accompanied by British instigation of area tribes, had caused a steadily escalating number of incidents between settlers and Indians. These events were some of the underlying factors behind the Battle of Tippecanoe (fought on November 7, 1811, near modern-day Lafayette, Indiana) and the War of 1812.

Up to this time the colonists at New Switzerland, being French speakers, had not had trouble with the Native Americans. But they were not unaware of the increasing tensions in the Ohio Valley. They arranged to post a watch and devised a system to spread the news of an Indian attack. One of the settlers, Elisha Golay, became a captain of the state militia in 1812. One of Elisha's first tasks was to construct a blockhouse northeast of

New Switzerland, from which forty or fifty men could defend the community. While the new blockhouse gave an increased measure of protection to the Swiss, the settlers were still apprehensive about their safety.

In the early hours of December 16, 1811, a visiting mail-carrier staying at the cabin of John Francis Dufour was awakened when he felt the cabin shaking. Everyone in the cabin rose quickly because they thought they were under attack by Indians. After waiting for some moments and hearing no more noise, the incident was blamed on the mail-carrier's horse, which was tied to the outside of the cabin. However, when the inhabitants woke up in the morning and felt more shaking, they looked out the window to see that the trees across from the cabin were also swaying and realized that the shocks of the night before had been an earthquake. The tremors were the result of the gigantic New Madrid quake, which rocked the Midwest.

The Swiss colonists on the frontier of Indiana were not the only ones directly affected by the War of 1812. John James Dufour had returned to Switzerland with "the intention of bringing out with him to this Country his father, one of his brothers, his wife & son, & a number of other families accustomed to the culture of the vine." He intended to sell their Swiss assets to pay off the debt on the land they had purchased from the government. However, he became trapped by the continuing wars in Europe and the outbreak of war in America. It was now no longer considered safe to make the voyage across the Atlantic. There was a possibility that the Swiss would not be able to pay off their loan on time and they would lose their land and the improvements they had made.

Fortunately for the Swiss colonists, other people in the western territories were also having problems paying for their land. There had never been much hard currency on the frontier, and what cash there was was used to pay for manufactured goods brought from the East. The American government greatly needed the loyalty of the western territories during the War of 1812. Some in the government in Washington feared that the settlers west of the mountains would find it more convenient to support the British than to repay their loans. The U.S. Congress passed a law allowing for an extension of time for settlers to pay for their land. The law stipulated that anyone who had purchased 640 acres or less at the regular terms would be granted an extension. But this special law did not apply to Dufour and his associates because they had purchased more than 640 acres on special terms.

Confronted with this problem, the colony drew up a petition to Congress, dated December 22, 1812, to ask for another special exception. The lengthy petition described their circumstances, stating that they had

> about twenty acres of vineyard, about six of which are now b[e]aring & in full perfection, & the two or three last crops of wine have given the most evident proofs that the borders of the Ohio are as prospitious [*sic*] to that salutary production as those of most of the rivers of Europe.

They went on to say,

> The frequent alarms from the savages have caused to your Petitioners a great deal of expense & trouble in providing arms & ammunition and other preparations for defense, for they could not think of abandoning their plantations (although the most of their neighbors removed across the river) but were determined to defend them to the last extremity.

The Public Lands Committee, chaired by Samuel McKee, reviewed the petition. Jonathan Jennings, territorial delegate to Congress, wrote a letter to McKee, dated June 10, 1813, in support of the petitioners. He stated that he was familiar with the Swiss settlement. They were poor people as judged by their manner of living, habitations, the uniform opinion of others, and their own declaration. He felt that were it not for their vineyard, their land at auction would not bring the minimum price for which the government was selling land. He said that from his own knowledge they made a considerable amount of wine, but he could not say how much. He concluded by saying that they would have extended the vineyards considerably except that they had not received the funds from Europe to do so.

The petitioners hoped that the government, in consideration of all of their hardships and the efforts they had put forth, would forgive their debt, or, failing that, grant them an extension of ten years which would enable them to continue their work and make repayment. On August 2, 1813, the federal government passed a law granting them an extension of five years to make payment on the debt. Once again, petitioning the United States government had proven to be of great value to the Swiss colonists.

On October 15, 1813, the *Kentucky Gazette* printed a list of laws that had recently been passed by Congress. The above law was described as "An act for the relief of John James Dufour and his associates." The Kentucky Vineyard Society subscribers apparently thought that they were the "associates" mentioned in the law and that they were about to receive some sort of relief. A notice was posted in the *Kentucky Gazette* that read as follows:

> The shareholders of the Vineyard Association are hereby notified to meet at the house of John Postlethwait, on Saturday the 23d day of October, in order to elect five directors agreeably to a law passed last session of the Legislature.

What a bitter disappointment it must have been to the subscribers when they found out that they were not the "associates" mentioned in the act. This incident was the last gasp of the Kentucky Vineyard Society.

On the same page of the newspaper was an advertisement for New Switzerland and the soon-to-be-laid-out town of Vevay.

Vevay

This town just laid out on a liberal plan, is situated in the Indiana Territory, on the bank of the Ohio river, about 22 miles above Madison and eight above the mouth of the Kentucky river—the situation is truly beautiful, being in the centre of the flourishing and very important settlement of New-Swisserland, where the cultivation of the vine is carried on with great success; the soil and climate being well adapted to it. The immense quantity of wine which will be made annually in this settlement and its vicinity, will render VEVAY one of the most important places in the western country. On the Kentucky side there is a flourishing and wealthy settlement. The inhabitants, besides large apple and peach orchards, also begin to plant Vineyards. It is remarkable that for a considerable distance above and below this place, the orchards bear every year. A post office is established here, and the mail from Jeffersonville to Cincinnati passes and repasses every week. Besides these great advantages, this town has that of being laid out on a healthy, rich, high and dry, though level spot.

There is a saw and grist-mill within one and a half miles, and another grist-mill will be in operation this fall, within three and a half miles back of this place.

Lots will be sold at Auction on the third Monday and Tuesday of November next—the terms of payment will be one sixth ready money, and the balance in three annual instalments [sic]. Tradesmen will be encouraged.

JOHN FRANCIS DUFOUR,

September 13, 1813

N.B. First rate Coopers, who could make wine vessels of any size, from 5 to 2000 gallons, would meet with great encouragement.

This same advertisement was also run in the Cincinnati, Frankfort, and Louisville papers. The lots were to be sold from land that belonged to John Francis Dufour.

Also in 1813, an ad was run in the *Niles' Weekly Register* of Cincinnati for Vevay wine. It read,

"Forward."—Daniel Debeltaz, at *Cincinnati,* Ohio, advises tavern keepers and others, that he had received a supply of good red wine, superior to the common *Bordeaux* claret, which he offers at 2 dollars *per gallon.* He further says that he will be supplied with "white and Madeira wines." This wine is produced at *New Switzerland,* Indiana Territory, where the vine-yards are in the most prosperous state. The cultivation is rapidly extending on the shores of the *Ohio,* and has every prospect of soon reaching the demand. How delightful is it to behold the opening resources of our country; and contemplate the time when all that may satisfy our wants or gratify our appetites, shall be found in the growth and produce of the republic! [emphasis in original]

This advertisement illustrates that the Swiss vinedressers at Vevay were selling wine to distant retail markets. While there had been some wine produced in other areas of the country, until then no one had achieved a scale of production that could supply a commercial market. Vevay wine appeared in all of the major western cities, including Cincinnati, Lexington, Louisville, Vincennes, and St. Louis, as well as at numerous inns and taverns in the region. The distribution of wine to this growing market is the main reason that Indiana can claim to have been the birthplace of the American commercial wine industry. The elusive vision of Americans producing American vintages was finally being realized.

During the War of 1812, it became patriotic and fashionable to purchase domestic products rather than imported British products. This was a boon to the vinedressers of New Switzerland and to U.S. agriculture and manufacture in general. Capitalizing on this spirit of domestic production and in an effort to raise money to defray cost of the war, the U.S. government passed a law on August 2, 1813, which required that anyone selling foreign merchandise pay a fee and obtain a license. The law would go into effect January 1, 1814, and remain in effect until one year after the end of war with the United Kingdom of Britain and Ireland. Unfortunately for the vinedressers of New Switzerland, the government also imposed a licensing fee of $15 on anyone who sold wine retail. "Retail" was defined as a sale of less than thirty gallons at one time. We know that at least one member of the colony obtained a license. It is license #13, dated October 31, 1814, and it bears the name of L. Gex Oboussier. Feeling aggrieved, the colony again petitioned the government for relief. This petition carried the same date as Gex's permit. In the petition to Congress, they argued first that the quantity of wine they sold by retail was so small that it hardly amounted to twice the amount of the annual fee. Second, wine was purchased mainly by those who visited them in order to obtain vine slips for the purpose of planting their own vineyards and also by the sick of the community who purchased it so that they could be assured it was pure and free from any mixture. Third, beginning vinedressers who had labored for three years with nothing yet to gain could not afford the license. Finally, they argued that cider and beer had been exempted from the tax. And besides, Congress had previously encouraged the planting of the vines. They concluded by asking "that vinedressers may be authorized to sell by the Small at their own houses wine of their own growth, without being obliged to procure the license except however when any of them should announce to the public their intention of making their business of retailing said wine." There are ten signatures on the petition: four Dufours, two Siebenthals, Philip Bettens, Jean Daniel Morerod, David Golay, and L. Gex Oboussier. The inclusion of Gex's name on this petition is perhaps the only occasion that someone who was not a signer of the covenant of 1802 was involved in official business with the government on behalf of the colony. It demonstrates that Gex, while not an original member of the colony, had become a member of the inner circle. The federal government apparently saw the wisdom of their petition. On February 8, 1815, Congress passed a law declaring that no vinedresser who sold wine of his own growth at his own place would be required to obtain a retail permit.

In 1817, Samuel R. Brown, a resident of Lexington and former member of the Kentucky Vineyard Society, wrote an article about New Switzerland for the *Western Gazetteer* of Cincinnati. He wrote, "They have now greatly augmented the quantity of their vineyard grounds, which, when bearing, present to the eye of the observer the most interesting agricultural prospect, perhaps ever witnessed in the United States. The principal proprietors of the vineyards, are the Messrs. Dufours, Bettens, Morerod, Siebenthal." Mr. Brown described the location of Vevay as being half a mile above the upper vineyards. This is one of the few descriptions of the actual locations of the vineyards. It is interesting to note that while mentioning the Dufours as vineyard proprietors, the description of the location indicates that the vineyards were on property belonging to the Golays, Bettens, Siebenthals, and Morerod.

On September 30, 1818, in a letter to friends in England, a Mr. William Tell Harris wrote yet another favorable review of Vevay and its wine:

> This is the commencement of the vintage, which induces me to protract my stay. The grape chiefly cultivated is the Cape, the wine from which, similar to

[*License to a Retailer of Merchandise, including Wines and Spirits, in the country.*]

No. *13*

WHEREAS _____ of the Town of _____ in the County of _____ in the _____ Collection District of _____ hath duly made application for a License to sell by retail Merchandise, including Wines and Spirits:

NOW KNOW YE, That the said _____ is hereby licensed to sell by retail Merchandise, including WINES and SPIRITS, at _____ in _____ in the _____ aforesaid, during one year following the _____ day of _____ one thousand eight hundred and _____ in conformity with an Act of the Congress of the United States, passed on the second of August, 1813.

Commissioner of the Revenue.

Countersigned at *Jeffersonville*
in the Collection District aforesaid, this
thirty first day of *October* 1814
Allan D. Thom
Collector of the Revenue for the
Collection District of *Indiana Territory*

Gex license. In 1814 the federal government, in an effort to pay for the War of 1812, required that wine retailers obtain a permit to sell wine "by the small" (any quantity under thirty gallons). Louis Gex-Oboussier of Vevay, Indiana, obtained the required permit, and on the same day the vinedressers of Vevay petitioned the government to be exempt from obtaining the permit. Their petition made its way successfully through Congress, and producers selling "by the small" were exempt. (Courtesy of Indiana State Historical Society) claret, would, if allowed to get old, be equal to port; it sells from one dollar to one and a half per gallon. Besides their vineyards, they have extensive peach and apple orchards, from which they draw large quantities of cider and peach brandy.

In 1819, Edmund Dana gave a description of Vevay which showed what an unusual prospect the town presented to the traveler and how much the town had grown since first being laid out in 1814. He wrote,

> Vevay . . . is a pleasant flourishing town, containing 190 houses, a decent brick court house, a jail, printing office, a large distillery, several taverns and mechanic shops. A branch of the bank of Indiana is established here. . . . This land was obtained from the government on an extended credit, for the purpose of encouraging the cultivation of the grape vine; in which employment the Swiss have been more successful, it is presumed, than any attempt on a large scale, within the United States. In 1815, about 100 hogsheads of wine were produced from all the vineyards; some of which belonging to individuals, have singly grown grapes latterly, sufficient to make 1,000 gallons of wine. The Madeira and the Cape of Good Hope have flourished better than any other species which has been tried. The vines of each grow well, but the Cape being much less liable to be injured by early frost, is the least precarious and the most productive. This wine is wholesome and not unpalatable. It is preserved through the summer months without distilled spirits, and grows better by age.

This quote illustrates how industrious the Swiss settlers had been since they first laid out Vevay and what a handsome sight the town now was. The description of the wine shows that it was of good quality. That they did not need to make an addition of spirits demonstrates that finally a grape had been found that no longer required fortification to preserve the wine beyond the first season.

Vevay wine was rapidly gaining a reputation throughout the state. The vineyards became a source of pleasure to people up and down the river. Travelers and writers of the time declared that Vevay was the most successful wine-making area of the country. During court weeks (a frontier event when the circuit court would come to town and hear cases), the judges and lawyers would sit around in the evening and sample the wine of Jean Daniel Morerod, or Father Morerod, as he was then known. During election years, touring politicians would often stop at Vevay in an effort to gather votes. On one such occasion the governor, Jonathan Jennings, was visiting Vevay with his entourage. They all stopped at Father Morerod's home to taste some of his wine. The governor and one or two others from abroad, being unaccustomed to wine, became considerably befuddled, as did some of the "Vevay boys." The way back to town was blocked by a large growth of dog fennel, a yellow flowering weed. The politicians passed through this field wearing white trousers and shirts. In their confused condition they soon emerged and presented to the townsfolk an amusing spectacle of the governor and fellow dignitaries wearing yellow pants and yellow spotted vests.

There is another interesting anecdote about Vevay wine from this time period. In 1818, a canal project was proposed to bypass the falls of the Ohio at Jeffersonville, Indiana. The Indiana Legislature passed an act chartering the Jeffersonville and Ohio Canal Company. The company was organized and a board of directors was elected. Agents were appointed to receive subscriptions of stock, and John Francis Dufour was appointed agent for Vevay. On December 12, 1818, he received a letter outlining a lottery for securing money for the canal. The lottery would give the winning tickets a monetary prize and the rest of the money would go toward the completion of the canal. On April 15, 1818, a letter was sent to John Francis Dufour informing him of the winning lottery numbers. It included this request: "Dear Sir: —I enclose you $15 to purchase some Vevay wine, that which is unmixed by any kind of preparation would be preferred."

On the first Monday of May 1818, construction of the canal was started. Vevay wine was used to toast the beginning of the canal, speeches were given, and a few feet of canal were started at the ceremony. After the gala celebration starting the project, little more was done and the canal was never completed. The few feet dug at the opening ceremonies under the influence of Vevay wine were all there ever was of the Jeffersonville and Ohio Canal.

The years during which John James Dufour was away in Europe proved to be a very important time in the life of the Swiss colony. After the abandonment of Firstvineyard in Kentucky, the Swiss concentrated their efforts on the work to be done in New Switzerland. The rapid expansion of the colony was truly remarkable. In a matter of a few short years, New Switzerland went from a dream in the wilderness to a thriving community that was producing and selling the first American wines. By 1815, the town of Vevay had become a city of 190 houses, complete with all the services that a frontier town could offer. The selling and growing of Indiana wines was still novel enough to attract the attention of travelers, who described it not in the jaded terms that had originally been reserved for American wines but in new terms that spoke of its success and quality. The day that Dufour had been anticipating since his arrival in America had finally come. This was the day that

> the people of this vast continent, [would be able] to procure for themselves and their children, the blessing intended by the Almighty; that they should enjoy, and not by trade from foreign countries, but by the produce of their own labor, out of the very ground they tread, from a corner of each one's farm, wine thus obtained, first handed from the grand Giver of all good, pure, genuine and unmixed by avarice, that it may have the effect on his heart and family intended by the Creator.

The American wine industry had been born.

6. The Vevay Winemakers

JOHN JAMES DUFOUR returned to Europe in 1806 to retrieve his wife and son and settle his affairs in Switzerland. Unfortunately, the continuing wars in Europe and the outbreak of hostilities between England and the United States conspired to keep him from carrying out his plan. For the next ten years, John James remained in Europe tending his family's vineyards, studying wine-making, and ruminating on the cultivation of the grape. It was not until the defeat of Napoleon at Waterloo in 1815 that he was ready to leave his home in Switzerland.

On February 20, 1816, he made his first entry in his account book since 1806. It read, "Deposited with Monsieur Ausset at Vevey for traveling funds to return to the United States L 1200." The next several months were spent purchasing cloth and having it tailored into shirts, pants, and vests, as well as procuring other needed supplies. On June 23rd, John James made his last dated entry in his account book. "Received of Mr Ducret, schoolmaster at Cherney the sum of 1000 livres to deliver to Marie, the widow of J. Dl. Boralley. Received of Judge Vuichoud, for Daniel, the sum of L 33.1.5." This was followed by one more line, undated, which read, "On my arrival I paid the above two sums." It is unclear exactly why John James chose to end his formerly detailed account book in such an abrupt manner, with no mention of his Atlantic crossing or of his daily purchases. Perhaps it is because on his first voyage to America he was using family money in his efforts to establish the family in the New World and needed to account for his spending decisions to his father. Apparently, the second voyage to America did not require the same detailed record keeping as the first.

One other tantalizing mention of his return trip to America can be found in his book *The American Vine-Dresser's Guide,* in which he made reference to having kept a travel journal, from which he quoted the following,

> Tuesday, 2d July 1816: We continued to descend the Rhone with great rapidity. We are passing Coteroties, where a very renowned wine is made. The vineyards are in terraces, with dry stone walls half tumbling; farther down, the

hills become naked and rocky; and there are no stakes to their vines; on both sides of the river are a great many Mulberry trees.

He then launches into a discussion of making silk. We can assume that at the time of writing the *Vine-Dresser's Guide* he had possession of the travel journal since he quoted from it. But what became of the travel journal? This one quote is the only mention of its existence. What a treasure it would be if it were found! One further mystery concerning his return to America is that both his wife and son, for reasons unknown, and contrary to his aforementioned plans, remained in Switzerland.

While still in Switzerland, he certainly learned of the fate of Firstvineyard in Kentucky and the success that the colony was having on the banks of the Ohio. On his return to America, he visited Firstvineyard to see the results for himself. He wrote,

> They abandoned the place to an American tenant, who supposed we had a bad title to the land, obtained a new warrant, and became owner by patent, & let all the vines go to destruction. At my return, which was in 1816, on account of the war which prevented my coming sooner, I found the vineyard grown up with briars, and I had to have recourse to law, to have the intruder ejected.

What legal right John James had to the Kentucky ground is unknown. Had the Kentucky Vineyard Society purchased the property on contract? What happened after the dissolution of the society? All of this is unclear, especially since his son, Vincent, appears to have purchased the same land again in 1828.

It is not surprising that John James settled on the Ohio River after his return from Europe. However, he chose not to live in Vevay among his brothers and sisters; instead, he lived upriver at his original purchase near Markland. Here he founded a farm, which he grandly called "Dufouria," and set about planting an orchard and nursery from which neighbors could procure vine cuttings and tree slips. He also set out a large peach orchard, but, unable to turn a profit on the peaches, he distilled them, making a peach brandy. This went on for a period of several years until he was able to find a buyer for his peaches. Dufour also constructed a small house, which was a long, low, one-story brick dwelling with a frame addition. It was described as a modest dwelling that was much smaller than the homes of his brothers and sisters in Vevay. John James lived alone on his farm, apparently preferring the company of his grapes to that of people.

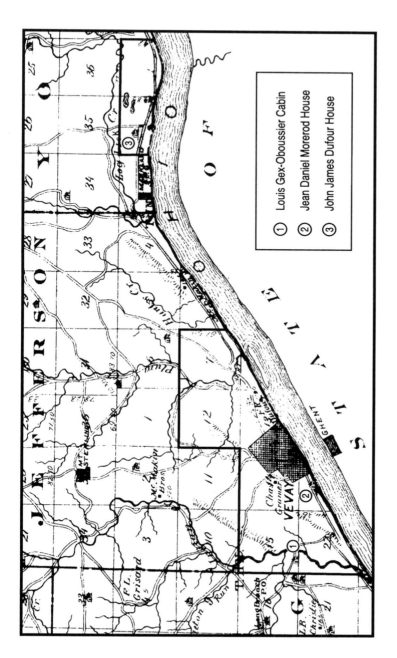

Switzerland County map, showing the location of the John James Dufour House and the boundary lines of Dufour's property, as well as the locations of the Louis Gex-Oboussier Cabin and the Jean Daniel Morerod House.

John James Dufour house. This is an enlargement of a photograph from the 1920s. The house across the newly plowed field is that of John James Dufour. Julie LeClerc Knox described the house as a long, low brick house with a frame addition. The large buildings in the background of the picture were not there during Dufour's time and are gone today. The smokestack behind and to the left of Dufour's house was for the plant that generated steam to operate the locks at the old Markland Dam. (Courtesy of Lilly Library)

Establishing a farm on the frontier took a great deal of effort. Because Dufour was a perfectionist and worked alone, he could not always accomplish the task he set for himself. In *The American Vine-Dresser's Guide,* he describes in great detail the proper methods of planting vines. He explained that to do it correctly a trench should be dug, in the center of which topsoil should be placed; the vines should be planted in this topsoil. However, when he set out his vines at Dufouria, he was unable to do the trenching in a timely fashion. Not wanting to compromise his vineyard, he devised another method:

> I did a little better yet, but not according to good rules, for want of means and help. My vines were planted in holes like any other trees, and when they had made shoots long enough, which happened the third or fourth year, I dug trenches eighteen inches broad and two feet deep [by hand!], one foot of the bottom of the trenches was filled with top earth; stakes were planted in the middle of the trenches in regular rows, as true as could be, two feet nine inches apart, the rows being six feet three inches, then the vines being dug to the bottom without damaging any of the roots, were carefully laid down on the top of the earth which had been put in the trenches to fill up the half of their depth, and a shoot raised by the side of each stake, where it was made fast by a willow, and two inches of top earth thrown on the trench to cover the vines running horizontally, the trenches were left open the remainder of the year.

This description shows just how much effort Dufour was willing to put forth for his vines.

The trenching described above must have been challenging for the aging Dufour, especially since he had only one healthy arm. But he was willing to take whatever steps he felt necessary, no matter how difficult, to ensure the success of his vines. The irony is that after completing this task, Dufour decided that it had done little to help his vines and probably was not worth the work.

The conditions that Dufour found at Vevay in 1816 were heartening. The colony was producing wine on a scale never before seen in the United States. The fame of the colony had spread as travelers commented on the pleasant prospect of the vineyards and wrote to their friends about what they had witnessed. There seemed to be no practical limit to the potential success of the colony.

One of the most notable and successful vintners in the Indiana wine industry was Jean Daniel Morerod. Aside from the fact that he was involved in Napoleon's Italian campaign prior to the battle of Marengo, little else is known about what he did before he came to America. As has already been mentioned, Morerod had followed his love, Antoinette Dufour, to America. In the spring of 1802, Jean Daniel and Antoinette were married at Firstvineyard. What Jean Daniel lacked from the want of money he made up for with ingenuity. To enhance his wedding day he made wedding shoes for himself and his bride; he also carved her a wedding comb from a cow's horn.

Shortly after the wedding, the new bride and groom, along with the Bettens, moved to New Switzerland to begin the work on the colony. At first, both families lived together in a squatter's cabin. Life was not easy on

Morerod house. This is a 1920s photograph of the
Morerod house, titled "Social Center of Swiss Colony,
Vevay." The house was completed in 1817 and has
been wonderfully restored. One of the famous
Morerod casks is still to be found in the cellar of the
house today. (Courtesy of Lilly Library)

the banks of the Ohio, and they faced many hardships and privations. Both
families were poor, and neither one owned a cow. They borrowed milk every
other day from a friendly neighbor by the name of Maguire. Since coffee
was expensive they only prepared it on the day they had milk to put in it.
On the days they did not have milk, they took the cloth in which the coffee
was pounded and inhaled the lingering aroma.

After several years, the improvements Morerod and Bettens made at

New Switzerland began to be noticeable. Each had planted several acres of vineyards, which bore their first crop in 1806 or 1807. Jean Daniel Morerod was the owner of the land immediately to the west of the holdings of the Dufours, and his property bounded the future town of Vevay on its western side. Morerod built a handsome two-story brick house facing the Ohio River, which was completed in 1817 after three years of work that included making all the bricks on the property. The house still stands on the edge of Vevay. The original road to the place has been abandoned due to erosion of the riverbank, so now the house is approached from the rear. The cellar under the house contained Morerod's famous casks. One cask was able to hold 500 gallons, and the other could hold 700.

At some point, Jean Daniel Morerod came to be known as Father Morerod, reputedly because of his good nature and kindness. Apparently, he took in orphans and befriended the poor and homeless. It is interesting to note that it was Morerod who was often visited by important people and that it was his house which became a meeting place. He seems to have had the ability to get along well with people and appears to have been less cantankerous and more likeable than John James Dufour.

If any one personality deserves to be known as America's first successful commercial wine maker, it should be Jean Daniel Morerod. He is said to have made the first wine in the colony, and he left three detailed account books covering the years 1809 to 1851. He began recording wine sales in 1811 and continued to do so in his own hand until 1835. The account books are a record of the people who bought wine from him on credit as well as the number

Morerod portrait. According to L. H. Bailey, author of "Sketch of the Evolution of Our Native Fruits," this is a portrait of Jean Daniel Morerod. Bailey visited Vevay in the 1890s and interviewed the descendents of Father Morerod and the Dufours.

of days that various people worked for him. The books demonstrate that for the majority of Morerod's life, he made a substantial part of his income by selling wine. It is also notable that he was selling wine to many of the original settlers. We can assume that those buying wine on a regular basis were not themselves wine producers. John Francis and John James Dufour were two of his most regular customers. Amie, David, and Daniel Dufour also bought wine from him, and occasionally Jean Francis and Francis Louis Siebenthal did as well. The scarcity of entries in Morerod's account books for the Golays and Bettens suggests that they were themselves wine producers. Louis Gex-Oboussier is also absent in the records, except for one purchase of thirty gallons of wine, which suggests that the Swiss had a small bulk wine market between producers.

In June of 1821, a traveler on the Ohio River stopped at Morerod's farm. His description of Morerod and his wines was flattering:

> We stopped at Vevay a Swiss settlement established about 18 yrs. since & went to the vineyard of Mr Morcroid [an attempted phonetic spelling of Morerod] who very politely shewed us his establishment, Cellar &c he has only Four acres in vines from which he makes about 800 Galls. yearly the vines were procured from Philadelphia whither they were brought by a Frenchman from the Cape of Good Hope the wine is like Claret & very fine we bought some at a Dollar p[e]r Gall: & I never desire to taste better he promised to let me have what setts [sic] I wanted at 1/4 Dollar p[e]r 100 & gave me some information respecting their culture he has now a fine Establishment altho' when he arrived at Vevay he had but 12 Sous piece in the world & The settlement is very thriving there are about 40 acres under vines.

Father Morerod was also mentioned in the national press. The success of the Vevay winemakers was related in a series of articles dealing with wine-growing in America, published in 1819, first in the *National Intelligencer* of Washington, D.C., then reprinted in the *American Farmer* of Baltimore. The author of the article signed it, "A Friend to the National Industry." In the second installment of the series, the unnamed author paraphrases a letter written by a Mr. Dufour of Vevay. The article mentions Father Morerod but mistakenly places him in Glasgow, Kentucky, where another Swiss gentleman by the name of J. F. Buchetti had settled in 1814 and was also growing grapes. (This was in all likelihood the same J. F. Buchetee, although the spelling is different, who had been the schoolteacher in Vevay a few years earlier and who wrote the poem "Empire of Bacchus.") This error aside, the article provided useful information about Vevay to the national public and proves the growing fame of the Swiss

Vineyard terraces. 1920s photograph of the vineyard terrace at Vevay, Indiana. Morerod and one other grower terraced the hillsides to plant grapes. These were said to be the best vineyards of Vevay. (Courtesy of Lilly Library)

settlement. The author of the letter stated that Father Morerod's large 800-gallon cask was full of the last year's vintage, which was to be kept for eighteen months to two years.

The fourth installment in the series of articles in the *American Farmer* appeared in December of 1819. The unknown author underscores the importance of the Swiss efforts:

A measure of manifest importance to the thorough investigation of our capacity and actual inceptions in the vine and wine business, is now proposed to be suggested to all persons of experience in the culture of the grape vine, and the manufacture of wine, in those parts of the United States where the vine cultivation has been attempted, on a great or small scale. The respectable gentleman who superintends the vineyards as our American Vevay, has happily led the way.

The "friend of the industry" was probably John Adlum. He had planted a vineyard in Havre de Grace, Maryland, east of Baltimore, but then moved to Georgetown outside of Washington, D.C., around 1814, where he established another vineyard. Adlum made wine from the Alexander grape and liked the results. The Alexander (or Tasker's) grape and the Cape grape are thought by many to have been the same variety. In 1809, Adlum tried to persuade Thomas Jefferson that the Alexander grape should be pursued above all other varieties. This was four or five years after John Francis Dufour had taken the Cape wine samples to Jefferson for his analysis. Adlum has been called the father of American viticulture. Perhaps this title should have gone to John James Dufour or even to Jean Daniel Morerod. But Adlum lived in the East near the larger metropolitan areas and newspapers, and as a result he drew more attention than did Dufour and the Swiss colony west of the mountains.

Even international notoriety came to Father Morerod. An 1813 report that appeared in the *Schweizerische Monathschronik* of Zurich, Switzerland, reported that "Jean Daniel Morerod was the most successful proprietor whose vineyard in that year yielded over seven hundred gallons of wine. He had begun with eighty saplings, in 1812 he had 1200 vines and sold 200 gallons of wine, each for about two piasters."

While Jean Daniel Morerod was perhaps the best-known vintner of Vevay, he is not the only one that deserves remembrance. Another notable personage of Vevay was Louis Gex-Oboussier (his own last name was Gex but he added his wife's maiden name at the end of his name in an old Swiss tradition). He was not one of the original signers of the Swiss covenant, but he was one of the earliest Swiss settlers to join the colony after the Indiana lands were purchased. He bought 319 acres of land from John James Dufour that came from the land that John James had bought just to the west of their original purchase in order to make the lots perpendicular to the Ohio River. Gex planted vineyards on his arrival and became a wine producer. He wrote a series of letters to relatives and friends in Europe that offer an interesting picture of life in the colony. At first, things seemed to be much to Gex's liking. Shortly after his arrival in 1803, he wrote to Jean Mennet in Antwerp about life on the frontier. Gex recommended to his friend that should he ever leave Europe he would find much opportunity in the fertile lands of the Ohio River Valley. In 1804, he wrote another letter to Mr. Mennet in which he outlined the concept of the newly organized Northwest Territory. He also suggested that his friend live in Kentucky saying, "If [one] wishes to come, and live leisurely, buy 200 or 300 acres across from [New] Switzerland in Kentucky, where one can hold Negroes. . . . A family of Negroes would cultivate land so [one] would only need to supervise." Perhaps the struggle to establish his farm had begun to sour Gex on life in the wilds of America. Tragedy struck sometime in the year of 1806, when Gex's wife died. The loss seems to have hurt him very deeply and was compounded in 1808 when his brother-in-law died accidentally while descending the Ohio River. In 1809, he wrote another letter to his friend in Antwerp. In this letter he makes some very pointed complaints about America, saying,

> I made for Perdonnet early in 1808 a notice on this territory and our colony, and proposed to make a copy for you and brother Felix, and would have sent it, but Perdonnet wished to make it public and had it printed in the *Journal De Commerce* the 13th and 16th of June, and you have probably read it. It contains only the truth and can give you a more correct idea of our country than many of the works published on America. The beginnings are so hard and so costly for Europeans to come, as I did with ideas so false as those I had received from the correspondence of my friend Dufour.

Gex went on to complain about the heavy expenses and about the debt he owed on his land, which he was unable to repay. He closed his letter by recommending patience and hoping for peace. Apparently, the optimism with which John James had written about America had been misleading to Gex.

In the next few years, things improved somewhat for Gex. In 1812, after being a widower for six years, he remarried. Like several other members of the colony, he married one of the Golay daughters. Her name was Marriane. She had been married before, but had left her husband, Henry Bornand; in December of 1811, she was granted a divorce by a special decree from William Henry Harrison. Gex's marriage appears to have been as much a marriage for financial convenience as for love, since Gex referred to the marriage as "caused by the needs of my establishment." In 1812, Victor Dupont, a friend of the Golay family, visited Vevay. Of the visit he said,

Upon entering the home of Mrs. Oboussier for whom we had some cargo, I saw a woman who got up from sitting near a corner by the fireplace and who threw her arms around my neck! Thinking that it was a custom of the land, I went ahead and let her do it and I was hugged by a dozen small girls and boys who were around the room, when she identified herself: it was Mrs. Bornand, today Mrs. Oboussier, wife of the head man of the town, himself with a yellow and dried up appearance at 50 years, but a great philosopher.

In 1815, Gex sold wine to Joseph C. Breckinridge of Kentucky, who was the father of the future vice president, John C. Breckinridge. The invoice shows the shipment of two chests to be delivered by keelboat. One chest weighing 228 pounds contained 75 bottles of wine and the other chest weighing 185 pounds contained a keg of 14$\frac{1}{2}$ gallons.

The invoice read:

JCB No. 1 @ 228, one chest with

27 bottles extra, cape claret	(in the top part)	.85	$22.95
24 bottles madeira	in the middle	1.00	$24.00
24 bottles old cape, claret	in the bottom	.60	$14.40
No. 2 @ 185 one chest with keg in			
14 $\frac{1}{2}$ gallons new cape claret		1.75	$25.37 $\frac{1}{2}$
	Together		$86.72 $\frac{1}{2}$

That Gex received up to $1 per bottle is testament to the quality of the wine; unimproved land was then selling for $6 an acre. Perhaps to assuage Mr. Breckinridge about the cost of the wine, he stated that "Mr. Morerod sell[s] his wine at two Dollars when he has the trouble to bottle it & pack it up and .25 less when he sell[s] in kegs." However, in light of the detailed records that Morerod kept, this statement appears to be confusing if not outright misleading. Morerod's records show that he never charged more than 50 cents per bottle. The local residents of Vevay probably brought bottles to the winery to be filled directly from the barrels. In this way, the bottles were continually recycled and wine could be sold for 37 to 50 cents per bottle. The Tarrascon brothers, who operated a general merchandise and shipping business in Pittsburgh, were one supplier of bottles. The bottles were ordered by post and shipped down the Ohio River to Vevay.

Henry Clay, famed Kentuckian and former Firstvineyard shareholder, visited both Morerod and Gex when he was in Vevay. Perret Dufour related an interesting anecdote about one of Clay's visits to Vevay. Clay purchased twelve bottles of wine from Gex and returned to Kentucky, where he stored it in the cellar. When the governor of Kentucky and several friends were visiting, Clay decided to bring up a bottle so his friends could taste a little of the bounty of the west. When the bottle was opened, it was found to contain whiskey. Thinking that some mistake had been made, Clay brought up another bottle for tasting. This, too, was found to contain whiskey, as were all the subsequent bottles that were tried, until eventually it was found that all twelve bottles contained whiskey. The mystery was solved when it was discovered that Henry's son, James B. Clay, had been sampling the Vevay wine unbeknown to his father. He replaced it with whiskey, which apparently James did not care for, until eventually all the Vevay wine had been consumed.

The Golays were another wine-making family of Vevay. They had arrived from New York in 1804. Like the others, they grew grapes and made wine. David Golay wrote to his brother-in-law, Abraham Louis Reymond, in July of 1815. He said that his son Louis was "the manager of a vineyard for the benefit of a rich individual who pays him well." He went on to say that "we are making excellent wine which amounts to 27 Batz wholesale and 36 Batz retail. I would like very much to sent you a case of bottles."

Little is known about the grape-growing and wine-making of the Siebenthals and Bettens. Francis Louis Siebenthal set up shop as the town blacksmith until the year 1820 or 1821. One of his items of production was something that resembled a two-pronged potato hook that the Swiss vinedressers used to remove the weeds from around their vines. Even less is known about the Bettens family, although it is assumed that they were grape-growers and winemakers as well.

Jacob Weaver was another vinedresser, and although he is less well known than some of his compatriots, he left us some record of his daily life. He moved to Vevay from New York some time around 1814. He married Charlotte, another of the Golay daughters. He purchased land along Plum Creek at the far eastern edge of the colony, but soon found that his land was prone to flooding; when the Ohio River rose, it was under ten feet of water. In 1815, Weaver moved his family to a 40- or 50-acre farm at the western end of the colony, along Indian Creek, three-quarters of a mile back from the Ohio River. At first, Weaver helped one of his brothers-in-law on his farm, since his own land had not yet been cleared. In May 1816, Weaver moved to the place of his father-in-law, David Golay, who had recently died, and took over that farm. That same spring, Weaver and his brother-in-law Lewis Golay rented a vineyard on shares, for which they paid one-half the wine for rent. Unfortunately, Mother Nature was not kind to them. As he wrote a family member back in New York:

> On the 15th of May we had a very sevear [*sic*] frost which almost totily [*sic*] destroyed some of our vineyards for this season. I had a lose [*sic*] on the vineyard I had rented at the least calculation of about from 200 and 50 to 300 dollars but you must understand that I have not to pay this out of pocket for I had taking the vineyard on shares this lose [*sic*] was out of my share but I have rented the same place again for another season to try my luck once more.

On December 12, 1817, he wrote to his father in New York describing his farm as follows: 17 acres of cleared ground, 2 acres of grape vines, 10 loads of hay, 50 bushels of oats sowed, 1 bushel of flax seed, 10 bushels of sweet potatoes, 350 bushels of other potatoes, 150 bushels of corn, 50 bushels of wheat, 46 bushels of buck wheat, 2 acres of pasture, and 1 acre of calf pasture and yards. He also described for his father the livestock that he was raising. He had 2 milk cows, 6 young cattle, 3 sheep, and 14 hogs. From his acreage of grapes, he got about 260 gallons of wine. The diversity of Jacob Weaver's farm is typical of farms for the period. The farmers needed to produce much of their own food and fiber as well as cash crops such as grapes and wine.

While the vineyards were proving to be a good economic base for the community, not everyone in Vevay was involved in grape-growing. As it turned out, the brothers of John James Dufour did not necessarily share his all-consuming enthusiasm for the grape. John Daniel helped lay out the town of Vevay. He also helped secure the county seat at Vevay and helped to fund the construction of a courthouse and jail. In 1824, he was the chairman of a convention that nominated Andrew Jackson for president of the United States. In the absence of a touring preacher, John Daniel sometimes filled in, and tradition has it that he read a good sermon. A letter he wrote in 1815 to the Massachusetts Missionary Society provides an interesting anecdote about John Daniel's religious nature. It was a thank-you note for sending him Bibles printed in French. But apparently he was not too impressed, because he had noticed several typographic errors as well as binding errors which caused some words and lines to be cut off. He wrote a letter to the Missionary Society saying he regretted "that a book so sacred as the New Testament had not been printed with greater care." There is little to suggest that he grew grapes or made wine.

Another Dufour brother who made a name for himself outside of the vineyards was John Francis. He and his brother David had been the last to leave the Kentucky project and therefore came late to Vevay. Before John Francis arrived, he had paid someone to clear part of his land and plant a cornfield and a few vines. When he moved to Vevay in 1809, he built a cabin that was 20 by 14 feet and settled in among his kinsmen. In 1810, he became the first postmaster, and the first post office was located in his cabin. Even though he was the third oldest Dufour brother, he rapidly assumed a leadership role in the community. John Francis also gave land so that Vevay would have a courthouse and donated the lots that became the town market, the school, and the Baptist church. In 1816, John Francis established Vevay's first newspaper, *The Indiana Register,* by paying off a mortgage on a printing press. In 1817, he was named the president of the Vevay branch of the State Bank of Indiana, and in 1824, he became associate judge, which granted him the power to perform marriages and preside over circuit courts. John Francis was elected state representative for Switzerland County in 1828. This ambitious and influential Dufour built several homes, each one nicer and larger than the previous one. These homes included the "ferry house," long considered the most architecturally interesting building in Vevay, as well as a picturesque stone cottage overlooking the city. He also owned a fine brick home in Vevay on Market Street that was called the first "pretentious" home in the village. All of these activities left little time for tending grapes, and John Francis is remembered not as a vintner but rather as a successful politician and town-builder.

Each year the notoriety of the colony grew. The newspaper articles emanating from the *Indiana Register* generally glowed with enthusiasm and the confidence of ensured success. In July of 1816, an article from the *Indiana Register* was reprinted in the *Niles' Weekly Register* of Cincinnati. The article included an interesting description of Vevay:

> *Vevay* was laid out in the fall of 1813—but was a *forest* in 1814. In that year it was selected as a suitable place for the seat of justice for Switzerland county. It stands on the Ohio, 22 feet above the highest freshet [this is an allusion to the beneficial presence of a second bank above the river, which discouraged flooding], 45 miles by land, 70 by water, below Cincinnati, and contains *seventy-five* dwelling houses, besides shops, &c. and has a brick court-house, jail and school house. A brick market house is contracted to be built, and preparations are making for building a house of public worship. It has 8 stores, 3 taverns, 31 mechanics of different professions, with shops, &c. 2 lawyers, 2 physicians, a carding machine and a public library of 300 vols. Receives a mail

three times a week, and has several mills in its neighborhood. The site is said to be beautiful and it promises to become the centre of the *wine business* of the west, the grapes raised here being of a very superior quality. One gentleman [probably Morerod] calculates on making the present year 1,000 galls. of wine, which sells at 2$ per gallon.

This description gave the reader the impression that Vevay would be one of the important cities of the West, one that would be known around the country for its wine production.

In August of 1817, yet another mention of the Swiss at Vevay appeared in the *Niles' Weekly Register*. It opened with a promising description of that year's crop:

> The Vineyards in the vicinity of that place, have the brightest prospects of rewarding the labors of the vine dressers. The luscious fruit is in great perfection; and it is cultivated extensively by the Swiss settlers—whose numbers will probably be greatly increased by the late emigrations. It is pleasing to learn that these cultivators of the vine on the Ohio, find it a very profitable business.

The article went on to contrast the good crop at Vevay with the less fortunate efforts of a non-Swiss grower, at "another point on the Ohio."

> Since the latter end of May, we have had rain almost every day and our grapes (that weathered the frost) are rotting very fast. I still expected to save about 100 gallons, but the weather continues wet and seems to get worse and worse—I am afraid there will be none left—it appears as if the elements have conspired against us since we planted the vine; or else the god Bacchus, unlike the king of Portugal, is determined not to transplant his empire from Europe to America.

Contrary to the glowing report in the *Niles' Weekly Register*, Jacob Weaver declared that 1817 was not a good year for grape-growing in Vevay. He wrote that they had "frost up to the 15–16 and to the 20 of May but frost was not as sevear [*sic*] as it was the 15 of last May when it destroyed cheaf [chief] of our vineyards." He went on to say that the vineyard he tended had suffered considerable damage but that what remained looked as good as could be expected. In another letter, dated December 12, 1817, he wrote that he "also lost considerable of grapes by the wet which made them drop before they were ripe." Perhaps the *Niles' Weekly Register* story was too rosy in its outlook regarding the Vevay vintage of 1817.

When John James Dufour returned to America, he found the Swiss colony at the peak of its success. The amount of wine produced, as well as the quality of the product, placed Vevay, Indiana, at the center of the American wine industry. The varied efforts of the individuals involved contributed to the success of Vevay. John James Dufour had provided the vision and tenacity that established the colony on the banks of the Ohio River. His work in Kentucky with the Cape grape had assured that the colony could successfully grow grapes and produce wine. The actual work of growing grapes and making wine fell to the families of Morerod, Golay, Siebenthal, Bettens, and Gex. There were others, such as Weaver, who came later and established their own vineyards or worked the existing vineyards on shares. The Vevay wine industry grew rapidly between 1810 and 1820. Travelers, residents, and the national press all agreed that the Swiss in Vevay, Indiana, were the superior example of grape-growing in America.

7. Trouble in Paradise

FROM THE FOUNDING of the Swiss colony at Vevay in 1802 through the return of John James Dufour in 1816, the Indiana venture was crowned with success. Starting with two families in 1802, the colony increased in size every year, reaching 1,800 people in 1815. The number of buildings in the town of Vevay had increased from a couple of squatter's cabins in 1802 to 75 dwelling houses in 1816. The amount of wine produced had also steadily increased. The first few years saw very little production because the vines took time to mature, but by 1808 the vintage was 800 gallons and that of 1809 was 1,200 gallons. The crop of 1810 exceeded 2,400 gallons, and in the bountiful year of 1818 7,000 gallons of wine were produced. At its peak, Vevay produced approximately 12,000 gallons of wine annually. At that time there was no other region in the United States that could claim such a successful wine industry. However, the success would prove to be short-lived.

In the years following the War of 1812, life on the western frontier changed rapidly. The war with Britain had been ardently supported in the West because it removed the threat of British expansion and the threat of Indian attack and supplied an immense economic stimulus. The war also brought about increases in prices, wages, and crop values. A wave of patriotism swept over the United States during the conflict, and it became one's civic duty to buy American products. This brought about an increase in American industries. When the war was over, the British calculated that while they had lost the military battles, they could win the economic war that was to follow. They set about flooding the fragile U.S. economy with manufactured goods, willing to take a loss for a few years in an effort to crush the new American industries and regain their lost markets. In a few years, many of the American cities that had become industrial centers were brought to their knees. Pittsburgh went into a decline that would last nearly a decade, and Lexington, the former toast of the West, would never regain its former status as the premier city on the frontier. The fact that the western industrial cities were markets for Vevay wine did not bode well for the colony of vinedressers on the Ohio River.

Perhaps worse than the dumping of British goods in America was the inflationary pressures that had been set off by the war. Prior to the war, the West had typically been cash starved. Money was printed by the eastern banks, and the currency that managed to cross the Appalachian Mountains quickly returned east when the settlers bought manufactured goods.

Two solutions to this problem appeared in the West. First, a barter economy was developed. This sufficed for the daily transactions in which chickens, corn, hogs, or land could substitute for money. However, this was not sufficient for a developing urban economy. The second solution was to establish western banks. Banks suddenly sprang up in town after town throughout the frontier. Pennsylvania authorized forty-one banks in 1814, Ohio had created twenty-six by 1818, and Kentucky set a record by establishing thirty-three banks in a single session of the legislature. And while it is hard for us to imagine today, all of these banks had the power to print currency. The currency-starved West soon was awash in money. The confusing proliferation of banks made it difficult to compare the values of the different notes. Money that was good in one city might not be good in another, and much of the money had insufficient capital behind it and was essentially worthless.

Inflation became the new economic reality. Land values, which had been fairly stable because of the large amount of land available, increased rapidly. A speculative land boom spread across the West. Cities such as Louisville and St. Louis which had been in the middle of the wilderness twenty years earlier were now urban centers that commanded urban land prices. For example, a lot outside of St. Louis that sold for $30 an acre in 1815 sold for $2,000 in 1819. That this increase in value was unnecessary and dangerous occurred to some of the more perceptive western citizens. As a citizen wrote to the Lexington paper, "Everywhere within the state has property of this description [city lots] at some time or another within the last few years been pushed up to the most enormous prices justified by no present uses to which it would be applied nor profits which it could yield."

In 1818, the directors of the Bank of the United States decided something had to be done to curtail the dangerously large amount of currency without backing. The solution was to contract the money supply by ordering western banks, specifically the Cincinnati banks, to call in their loans. This measure burst the financial bubble. The Cincinnati banks were unable to back all of the money they had printed, and soon banks started closing. As bank after bank failed in 1819, the West went from a situation of surplus currency back to one of currency shortage. Now deflation was the economic challenge. This had an immediate effect on the western manufacturing cities as well as on the prices of agricultural goods. Capital became harder to secure, and cities such as Lexington and Pittsburgh, which had enjoyed nothing but prosperity, were faced with economic ruin. Their products steadily declined in value.

Agricultural problems were initiated by the end of the Napoleonic Wars in Europe. The cessation of hostilities released a flood of manpower that allowed the Europeans to once again grow enough food to feed themselves, and European agricultural markets for the western farmer dried up. As the American urban centers faltered, the price of farm products dropped rapidly, and many farmers found it unprofitable to harvest their crops. The vinedressers at Vevay, caught in an economic tailspin, could do nothing to change these underlying economic factors.

Thomas Nuttall, director of the Harvard Botanical Gardens, ventured down the Ohio River in November of 1818. He lodged for a night with a hospitable Frenchman three miles above Vevay. The Frenchman engaged him in a conversation and displayed a blend of bitterness and premonition about the Swiss wine-growing experiment. Nuttall's host informed him that

> he had emigrated last summer (1817) from Grenoble, and had purchased land here at the rate of 10 dollars per acre, including the house and improvements which he occupied. He complained how much he had been deceived in his expectations, and that if he was home again, and possessed of his present experience, he would never have emigrated. He did not give a very favourable account of the settlement of Vevay, and he and others, particularly a Swiss whom I called upon, informed me that the wine here attempted to be made was of an inferior quality. It sold for at 25 cents the bottle, but soon became too sour to drink, and that instead of obtaining the northern vines for cultivation, those around Paris, they had all along tended the southern varieties. So the vineyards of Vevay, if not better supported, will probably soon be transformed into corn-fields. The wine which they have produced is chiefly claret, sometimes bordering on the quality of Burgundy, for the preservation of which their heated cabins, destitute of cellars, are not at all adapted; we do not, however, perceive any obstacle to the distillation of brandy, which could be disposed of with great facility and profit.

The letters of Jacob Weaver also reflect the uncertain economic times in the West. In September 1818, he informed his father that "wine is got to be very cheap it has fall[en] from 4 shillings per bottle to 2 shillings per bottle [50 to 25 cents]." At this same time, corn sold for 60 cents per bushel.

In January 1819, Weaver complained about the lack of money, saying that it was harder to purchase land now that the land office only accepted Bank of the United States currency. In 1819, the price of corn had decreased to 40 or 50 cents per bushel. By July of 1820, corn was only worth from 25 to 37½ cents per bushel, and the economy was getting worse. Weaver said,

> Our country is very extensive and produces in abundance. Since there is no foreign trade at present, the market is glutted. Worst of all, no money is to be had so you must sell on credit or not at all. When a farmer goes to a store to buy anything, he [the storekeeper] won't take credit. There is but little demand for the farmer's products.

In November 1821, Weaver mentioned the precarious situation of banks in Indiana: "No money. All the banks in our state have failed but one [including the bank at Vevay]." The last of Weaver's letters were written in 1824. The price of corn had fallen to 10 to 15 cents per bushel. Wine was a meager 50 cents per gallon when sold by the barrel, and stores would no longer accept goods in trade.

Many of the vinedressers in Vevay felt the sting of economic decline. In October 1818, Louis Gex ordered bottles from the Tarrascon brothers of Pittsburgh but was informed by letter that "the claret bottles are missing." The letter implied that something had happened to the factories (the letter is not specific) and that "the market is without window glass and porter bottles and one could not possibly have items less profitable." Wine-making on the frontier was seldom easy, and during times of economic hardship it was sometimes impossible to obtain supplies.

Gex wrote a letter in September of 1823 outlining complaints similar to Jacob Weaver's. Gex felt that the bank closings coupled with poor laws passed by the state legislature had worsened the situation. He wrote, "Farmers can only raise own food and clothing. Little silver suffices only for salt, boots and other necessities, which one can only obtain for cash in hand." He closed the letter by saying that in the twenty years that he had been in America, he had not bought one yard of material. His work clothes were homemade, and his Sunday suit was the same one that he had brought from Europe many years before.

Father Morerod, the largest and most successful Vevay producer, seems to have weathered the financial crisis somewhat better than his compatriots. In 1812, Morerod was selling wine for 37½ cents per bottle. There was no change in price through 1821, but in 1822 the price dropped to 25 cents per bottle.

The effect of this sudden deflation, the closing of the banks, and a lack of currency all had serious repercussions for the Vevay wine industry. The market for corn had almost disappeared. Farmers could no longer make money selling it, yet they continued growing it. The excess corn was distilled into whiskey, because this was one of the most effective ways to store and move excess grain. The surge in whiskey production helped to drive down the price of the wines of Vevay. Both products sold for about 50 cents per gallon by the barrel, and it became increasingly more difficult to sell the Swiss wines.

However, the Swiss at Vevay did not let the financial crisis rob them of all their pride and joy. There would be one last hurrah, one more moment of national publicity, and a few more toasts when the Marquis de Lafayette arrived on his American tour. Lafayette had been instrumental in helping the cause of American independence, for which patriots across the nation remembered him fondly. Because Lafayette had been the youngest American general, he was one of the few heroes still alive at the time. In 1824, when he decided to return to the land that he had helped free, he was received with great fanfare. The tour was an immense success, and everywhere Lafayette went, great crowds gathered to honor him. He traveled throughout the nation visiting every state and most major cities.

When the Swiss at Vevay found out that Lafayette was going to visit Cincinnati, they decided to meet him. John James Dufour led a large delegation of Vevay residents, including the Vevay artillery company and their cannon, "Old Betts," to Cincinnati. Some of the residents of Vevay who did not join the delegation predicted that the Swiss would be little noticed amid the throngs of admirers trying to see Lafayette. On May 19, 1825, Lafayette arrived in Cincinnati. He was met by a large crowd at the edge of the river, which included such notables as Ohio's Governor Morrow, William Henry Harrison, a committee of prominent Cincinnati residents, and the Cincinnati artillery company. A demonstration of rapid-artillery firing was performed, and Lafayette judged the company from Vevay, commanded by John James's son Vincent, to be the finest artillery company that he had seen in America. Lafayette's secretary, Levasseur, later wrote,

> As we crossed the public square, we saw the gunners stationed at their park of artillery. Their elegant and martial uniform, was that of the French artillery. We were informed that this was the Vevay Artillery Company. It was, in fact, composed almost entirely of Swiss, among whom a great number had served in the artillery of the French army. Their maneuvers appeared to be executed with a precision and rapidity altogether remarkable.

When Lafayette retired to prepare for dinner, the Swiss followed him. As his secretary described it,

> We had hardly returned to Mr. Febiger's, in whose hospitable house we lodged, when we saw thirty or forty persons arrive, who entered the drawing room, and requested permission to speak to Lafayette. "We are citizens of Vevay," said an old man at their head, who spoke to me in French, and for whom all the rest seemed to possess great deference. "We were induced to hope that the friend of liberty, would come and visit our little town, and that we should have the pleasure of showing him our vineyards, and inducing him to taste the wines of our vintage; but his passage through Kentucky deprived us of this happiness. Nevertheless, we could not miss seeing the man whose name was dear to us even before we left our country, and we resolved upon coming here to salute him."

Lafayette was unable to come down to the drawing room when the Swiss arrived, so he sent his son to greet them. George Lafayette was received with great tenderness, and the Swiss repeated their story to him. Just as the colonists were describing the condition of their vineyards, the marquis appeared. Levasseur wrote,

> The general arrived, and immediately the Swiss of Vevay having formed a semicircle to receive him, the most aged among them, whom I had heard called Father Dufour, advanced and welcomed him by an address full of feeling. When he had finished speaking, all these inhabitants of Vevay threw themselves into the arms of the general and tenderly embraced him. They had brought with them some wine of their vintage, which they presented us, and we joined them in drinking to the prosperity of their new and the regeneration of their old country.

> It must be confessed that the wine of Vevay is by no means exquisite. Nevertheless, it is quite a pleasant drink, and according to my taste, the best of the wines made in the United States.

At midnight, at a signal given by the Vevay artillery, Lafayette took his leave of Cincinnati. The trip from Vevay had been more successful than the naysayers had predicted. Not only had the Swiss artillerists had special notice taken of their martial proficiency, but the Swiss vinedressers had received a personal audience with Lafayette and their vintage had enjoyed praise.

While the 1820s were particularly hard on the Swiss wine colonists, it was the time in which John James Dufour completed one of his greatest achievements, the writing and publishing of *The American Vine-Dresser's Guide*. In 1801, Dufour had promised Congress that he would "use every exertion by his example to render the Culture of the Vine familiar to the people of the United States" if it would grant him a concession to purchase land. This promise had yet to be fulfilled. The contractually minded Dufour would fulfill this promise. To do so he started writing a book.

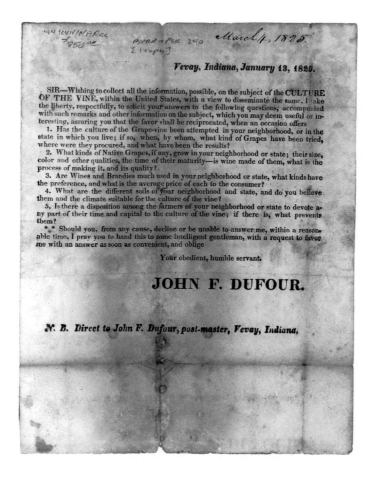

John Francis Dufour broadside. John Francis, publisher of the Vevay newspaper, printed this circular to help his brother John James gather information for his classic book on grape-growing and winemaking. It is unknown how widely the flyer circulated and what responses were received. (From the Broadside Collection of the Indiana Historical Society)

In January of 1825 John Francis Dufour published a questionnaire to assist his brother in his research. The one-page circular requested the reader to direct responses to John F. Dufour, postmaster, Vevay, Indiana. It contained five broadly worded questions about grape and wine production. The first entry asked if the culture of the grape had been attempted in the neighborhood or state of the reader. The second question asked what kinds of native grapes grew in the area and what their traits were. Third, the circular asked if wines and brandies were often consumed in the area and what their average prices were. The fourth question dealt with the suitability of the soil for the growing of grapes. The final question dealt with the disposition of farmers in the area "to devote any part of their time and capital to the culture of the vine; if there is, what prevents them?" It is unknown how widely the circular was distributed or how many responses were received. It does show that Dufour was attempting to gather all the available knowledge and write the most complete essay on American grape-growing and wine-making up to that time.

The complete title of Dufour's book was *The American Vine-Dresser's Guide, Being a Treatise on the Cultivation of the Vine, and the Process of Wine Making, Adapted to the Soil and Climate of the United States.* S. J. Browne of Cincinnati published the book in 1826. It is a strange book, written in a thoroughly scientific vein by a Swiss immigrant who was not a native English speaker. In the preface of the book, John James wrote:

> It will be found something like presumption in me, to write a book in a language, to which I am a stranger. . . . But as I had, and yet have to answer so often, verbally and by writing, queries about my avocation, I have attempted to write down, and give to the public at large, the answers to any questions which may be made about the cultivation of Grape-Vines, in the United States.

The project may have been presumptive on John James's part, but so was everything else he had done in his life. No one had ever written a true textbook on growing vines in American conditions. In his preface John James acknowledged

> the grand book of nature, from which most all I have to say has been taken, for want of other books, and even, if I had them, among the many I have read on the culture of the vine, but few could be quoted, for none had the least idea of what a new country is.

THE

AMERICAN

VINE-DRESSER'S GUIDE,

BEING A TREATISE

ON THE

CULTIVATION OF THE VINE,

AND

THE PROCESS OF WINE MAKING;

ADAPTED TO THE SOIL AND CLIMATE

OF THE

UNITED STATES:

BY JOHN JAMES DUFOUR,

FORMERLY OF SWISSERLAND, AND NOW AN AMERICAN CITIZEN,
CULTIVATOR OF THE VINE FROM HIS CHILDHOOD, AND FOR THE
LAST TWENTY FIVE YEARS, OCCUPIED IN THAT LINE OF
BUSINESS, FIRST IN KENTUCKY, AND NOW ON THE
BORDERS OF OHIO, NEAR VEVAY, INDIANA.

Then said the trees to the vine, come thou, and reign over us:
And the vine said unto them, should I leave my wine, which cheer-
eth God and man, and go to be promoted over the trees?
Judges, c. ix. 12 & 13 vs.

Cincinnati:

PRINTED BY S. J. BROWNE,
AT THE EMPORIUM OFFICE.
....
1826.

Title page of *The American Vine-Dresser's Guide*. Dufour became ill while on a trip to Kentucky to distribute the book to his friends. He died in the spring of 1827.

The books that had been written were treatises on European techniques, European conditions, and European vines. Dufour would write a book about American grape-growing that was actually about American conditions. After all, who was more qualified to write such a volume if not John James? Was it not Dufour who had established the first successful commercial vineyard? As he wrote, "The Kentucky Vineyard Society, may be with great propriety considered as the beginner, the true introducer of the cultivation of the grape vines into the United States." Thus armed with years of experience, his characteristic self-assurance, and powerful claims to his previous success, John James began writing.

There are so many amazing facets to the *Vine-Dresser's Guide,* so many unexpected discoveries and so much keen observation, that it is hard to believe that it was written 200 years ago by a man on the edge of the frontier. John James opened the book with a preface outlining some of his experiences and establishing his authority on the subject. In the first chapter, he gave a very general history of wine and grapes in the Old World and contrasted that information with what he had observed on his travels in America. In Chapter 2, Dufour outlined failed attempts he had seen in America and the difficulties he had surmounted at Firstvineyard with the discovery of the Cape grape. He was concerned that his pet grape, the Cape, was being unduly criticized; he wrote, "I will also try to save the character of our Cape grapes from being made merely wild grapes, because some are now found in the woods; and, to put any one in the way to distinguish wild from tame grapes, I will give the description of the botanical characters of the blossom of both sorts." He concentrated on the differences in the blossoms of wild and imported grapes. The botanical knowledge of the day led him to believe that if a grape had perfect flowers (containing the parts of both sexes, which made it capable of self-fertilization), it was European. The Cape had perfect flowers, therefore it had to be European. To Dufour, the scientific proof of his observations always took precedence over opinions. The fact that Dufour's grape was a cross, and that crosses also have perfect flowers, does not lessen the sharpness of his logic and observation.

Also in Chapter 2, Dufour discussed the problems that the Swiss had to overcome to successfully produce wine in America. The first challenge was the making of the wine. Yet that was not all:

> To that may be added another obstacle, that the first vine dressers of a country have to encounter; it is the prejudice against home-made, of a people who are

used to imported wines only, which are, or ought to be of the best sort, and of the strongest, naturally or by mixture, with spirits, to support the transportation; the home grown wine which is to appear first among such a people, must resemble exactly the one he is used to, to engage him to pay for it: Such was our case at first, but we gradually found a market for all we made; I saw a great many; who would not taste the Swiss wine, because it was not as strong as imported Madeira, . . . but having drank of it a few times for company sake, they have become great lovers of it; so that, by the by, consumption having pretty well kept pace with the product, old American wine has always been scarce.

But Dufour was optimistic about the future, writing, "The time will come, when country-born varieties will equal our most sanguine expectations."

Dufour wrote his book so that it introduced all the general knowledge that had been learned in Europe. For example, Chapter 5 is a description of fifty European grape varieties, and Chapter 7 is a discussion of European methods. But, unlike other authors, who assumed that the techniques of Europe would work in America, Dufour realized that trying to grow grapes in America was a totally new undertaking. He listed the European methods so that he could contrast them with the methods that he had worked out for American viticulture. This is one of the factors that make the *Vine-Dresser's Guide* different from the works that had come before and from many that would come after.

Much of the book is devoted to the ideas that Dufour had formulated in his detailed observations and experiences while growing grapes. His profound use of the power of observation resulted in his ideas being years ahead of their time. For example, he was a proponent of using fertilizer for vineyards, despite the objections of some of his contemporaries, especially European authors. Furthermore, he detailed good times to fertilize, such as in the spring when the rain can leach the nutrients into the soil. He also described what should go into good dung and how one went about maintaining a dunghill.

Even more innovative was Dufour's description of the diseases and pests that plagued American vineyards. These foes of grape-growing had yet to be described and had remained unidentified for 200 years. John James approached the problem of grape afflictions in the same observational manner that he approached everything. Liberty Hyde Bailey, the author of the excellent book *Sketch of the Evolution of Our Native Fruits*, published in 1898, wrote that Dufour's disease descriptions were "the first explicit account of the vine diseases." Dufour's descriptions were as follows:

The different diseases that I have seen affecting the vines, are not numerous. They may be denominated, 1st. The Mildew, called Charbon or Tache, by the French, whose meaning is, by *Charbon,* burnt to a coal, or like a coal; and by *Tache,* a black speck: 2d. Unripeness of the young wood, which causes it to be frostbitten: 3rd. Short jointed, called Sorbatzi, by the Swissers: 4th. Exhaustion, by overbearing.

Of the four diseases discussed, the most important discussion was about mildew. As Dufour wrote,

The Mildew or *Charbon,* is the most severe disease that sickeneth grapevines. One of the first symptoms is a mouldy and black dust that appears some time on the under surface of the leaves in the months of July and August, and grows gradually more intense. Black specks then appear on the young parts of the shoots, and on the fruit, as if made with a hot bit of iron: the leaves then crisp and fall, the fruit becomes black, and dries, and what fruit seems to escape the sickness, will not ripen well, and remain uncommonly sour; the young shoots will be extremely brittle, and the pith black.

Bailey wrote about Dufour's discussion, "It is very likely that two diseases are confounded in this description. The account of the leaves suggests downy mildew; but the description of the affected shoots is more likely that of the black-rot." Even though Dufour had combined the effects of two diseases, it was still the first attempt to describe the afflictions that were the major enemies of American grape production. A concerted scientific effort was not made to understand these diseases until they started showing up in Europe in the mid- to late 1800s.

Dufour was also a pioneer in the field of girdling vines, a technique which was first reported in 1817 in a French article by Lambry. The practice consisted of cutting a small band around the fruiting canes in an effort to increase production. Dufour made his first experiment at what he called "belting" in 1818 or 1819 on a pear tree. An instrument had been invented in France to do the girdling efficiently, and shortly thereafter one of the devices was sent to Vevay. Several of the Vevay vinedressers had these instruments made in Cincinnati. That Dufour's book was read by few people and was not republished until 2000 (by Editions La Valsainte, Vevey, Switzerland) is evidenced by the statement in *General Viticulture,* published in 1962 by the University of California Press, which declared, "The earliest record of girdling in the United States appears in the report of the state horticulturist of Massachusetts for the year 1887."

Other helpful advice that Dufour gave about growing vines still applies today. In Chapter 19, Dufour explains that plowing between rows is a good way to keep down weeds, which he correctly felt stole nutrients from the vines. He also advised that when planting on a hill, the vineyard should follow the contours and be laid out across the hill rather than straight up and down, which would contribute to erosion. He recommended that vineyards should occupy the tops of knobs or hills because they are less likely to suffer frost damage than vineyards located on a plain. When it came to pruning, Dufour warned his readers that if they were paying their vineyard workers by the pound of grapes, they would be likely to underprune, which would cause overcropping and exhaustion of the plant. In Chapter 10, Dufour detailed the ideas behind trenching and explained how to drain wet ground.

Illustration from Dufour's book, which offered advice on everything from planting, pruning, harvesting, and storing grapes to all aspects of wine-making.

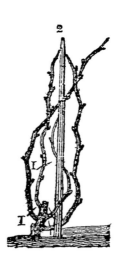

Dufour presaged the creation of our modern grafted varieties. The joining of European vines onto hardy American rootstocks was one of the methods that saved the European wine industry from destruction during the phylloxera epidemic in Europe in the later 1800s. Dufour attempted the grafting of "cultivated (European) vines" onto native American grape root stock but had little success. While he may have inadvertently and unknowingly found a solution to the as-yet-unidentified phylloxera problem, his grafted vines were still subject to mildew and did not survive. But the fact that Dufour saw the utility of this approach is voiced in this quote: "My principal object in grafting vines, was to ascertain if those which are subject to the mildew in new planted vineyards, would escape it, if grafted on species which were not subject to it." Even though Dufour's grafts were not successful, the idea was clearly outlined; Dufour was years ahead of his time.

The oddest chapter of the book has to be Chapter 8, which was devoted to the production of mulberries and silk. Here one sees the last gasp of the age-old European idea that America could produce the "holy trinity" of wine, silk, and olive oil. Apparently, Dufour believed that there was a possibility that American vinedressers could emulate those of Lombardy, who grew their vines intertwined with mulberry trees, which provided the food for silkworms. The fact that silk was difficult to produce and incredibly labor intensive did not deter Dufour. It did not seem to trouble him that in order to incubate the eggs of the silkworms, he had to place them in a flat snuffbox and keep it in his armpit for three days. He closed the chapter by saying "But, as we live in an epoch of new discoveries, it is worth while to make the trial;—and I see no reason why it should not succeed."

Dufour addressed wine production with the same careful eye for detail that he had applied to grape-growing. He offered sound advice about the different methods that should be used to produce good wine. For example, he recognized the importance of sanitation: "Cleanliness is as necessary with wine as with milk." He explained how one could construct a home-made hydrometer with which to measure the sugar content of wine or must. He also recommended sulfur to help prevent oxidation of the wine and to stop or prevent fermentation. Dufour understood the role that the skins played in wine coloring and the role that the stems played in adding tannin. He knew the techniques to make white wine from red grapes, which is done by gently crushing and pressing the red grapes and fermenting them immediately without letting them sit on the skins. He discussed the merits of different types of fining agents which are used to clear wines. He mentioned using egg whites and isinglass, both of which are techniques that are still in use today. He also understood that oxygen had a negative effect on wine, which could be avoided by keeping the contact to a minimum: "The more the wine is kept from the contact of the air, the better." If all of this advice had been followed, it should have prevented many of the problems that plagued winemakers. As John James stated, "It is easier to prevent sickness in wine than to cure it. A good cellar, extra cleanliness, often visiting, and racking, and keeping always full, will most surely prevent disease."

The Vine-Dresser's Guide was the first truly American wine text, written by someone who was familiar with the conditions and problems present in America and directed at overcoming these problems. As Thomas Pinney wrote in his excellent history of the American wine industry:

> A Vine-Dresser's Guide . . . may fairly claim to be the first truly American book on the subject. The works of Bonoeil, of Antill, of Bolling, and of St. Pierre are of course much earlier, but none of them has anything to say about an extensive experience of actual vine culture in this country. Adlum's book, though in some ways genuinely American, and earlier than Dufour's by three years, is far more derivative. Dufour had earned his authority.

The revolutionary ideas contained within the book show what a keen intellect the man possessed. As *Putnam's Magazine* wrote in 1854, "And the day must come when among our national benefactors, few will rank higher than the names of Adlum, Dufour, Longworth and Fisher, our pioneers in Grape culture in this country." And in the same article, "The results of Dufour's journeyings and experiments are embraced in a volume which, even to this day, is a textbook for the cultivators in the west." The fact that many of the techniques he described are still in use today demonstrates the soundness of his advice.

With the publication of the *Vine-Dresser's Guide,* John James Dufour completed the last accomplishment of his interesting and distinguished life. He may have intended to return to Switzerland for his last years, but his wife, who still resided in Switzerland, died in 1823. Since 1796 they had been apart more than they had lived together. Perhaps that is the way they preferred it, but he still must have been saddened to hear of his wife's death.

This bad news was followed by another difficult situation. John James had always been a serious person, honest in word and deed throughout his life. Thus, it must have been particularly hard when, in October of 1826, he found himself in court facing his brother, John David, over a debt of 84 dollars. John James was able to produce receipts for the amount in question and the suit appears to have been dropped. Still, it could not have been a pleasant experience for either brother, and doubtless the lawsuit helped to further embitter the aging pioneer.

On February 9th, 1827, at the age of 64, John James Dufour died on his farm above Markland. Had he lived a few years longer, he could have promoted his masterpiece on grape and wine culture. Without John James to promote the book, it did not sell widely, so that at the time of his death, he still had 205 copies in his home. The estate also included "a set of copper plates, copies for writing." They were valued at 40 cents. The plates were probably for the illustrations in the *Vine-Dresser's Guide*. One hundred and seventy six copies of the book were held by a retailer in Louisville, and four copies were with another in Lexington. In his estate, the books were valued at 40 cents each. John Francis Dufour, executor of the estate, requested of the court that the books be sold individually rather than at public auction, as they would bring more money that way. At the final settlement of the estate in August 1832, Daniel Vincent Dufour, the sole heir, received ninety-eight copies of his father's book.

Vincent was apparently much affected by his father's death and for a time was considered insane. He used to lie for hours beside his father's grave, and at one time he even threatened to kill himself. He never adjusted to life in America, and it was evidently with some relief that he returned to Europe in an effort to collect a family inheritance.

John James was buried in a large vault with bronze doors, upon which was carved the ghastly epitaph,

> Remember man as you pass by
> That as you are now so once was I;
> But as I am soon you must be;
> Prepare for death and follow me.

The old vault apparently caused so much curiosity that over the years it was repeatedly broken into, until eventually the roof was set on fire. The whole structure was torn down and the eight bodies reburied with simple headstones (the vault was also the final resting place of some of Daniel Vincent's children). The small graveyard became more and more overgrown with weeds, until eventually the burial ground could only be approached by wading through tall grass and briars. Julie LeClerc Knox wrote that his tombstone said:

> John James Dufour
> Born in Canton Vaud, Switzerland
> Died 1827, age 64

Apparently, at a later time, in a cemetery about three-fourths of a mile away (near the center of the northwest quarter of section 2, T. 1N, R.2W) but still on the original farm, a stone was placed which read:

John James Dufour
1763–1827
loyal, Courageous Leader
Swiss Family Founders of
Vineyards and Vevay 1802
Friend of Jefferson. Buried
Here on His Old Land ENTRY

As the years passed the location of his gravesite became questionable, and even his descendants became unsure of his final resting place.

The death of John James Dufour highlights another factor in the decline of the Vevay wine industry. The original Swiss settlers had come to America with the express purpose of founding an American wine empire. By the 1820s, several of the original settlers had died or moved away. Francis Louis Siebenthal died about 1824 from a disease contracted while delivering produce down the Mississippi River. David Golay, who rejoined the colony in 1804 after his aborted stay in New York, cultivated his vineyard and farmed until his death in 1815, just as he was starting to reap his first success in America. Louis Gex-Oboussier moved from Vevay in 1826, having given up his farm a few years earlier, and resettled in New Harmony, Indiana. Amie Dufour, the youngest of the Dufour brothers and sisters, moved to Vevay by 1812 but did not remain there long. He soon moved to New Orleans and then to Vermillionville, Louisiana.

Father Morerod lived the longest of the Vevay grape-growers. He lived in Vevay with his wife Antoinette until his death in 1838; she lived there until she died in 1857. Father Morerod's will provides an interesting counterpoint to John James's epitaph. In it he requested,

> And though it may appear singular to some it is my will and pleasure, that no costly clothing, nor a costly coffin, be buried to rot with my body but if I should die at home I wish my body to be wrapped up in a plain white sheet and put in a plain coffin made of pine or other cheap boards the cost of which shall not exceed two dollars and that the difference in price between this equipage of mine and that usually afforded in Vevay to travelers, to that place whence no one returns, be dealt out to those who shall meet at my house to accompany my body to the grave, in the best wine that may then happen to be in my cellar.

What a pleasant farewell to this kindly old winemaker. It was also a farewell to the Vevay industry, which declined after the death of its most successful vinedresser.

Was Father Morerod actually laid to rest in an inexpensive coffin and the money saved used to serve his finest wine to his mourners? An article written in 1894 cast some doubt upon whether Father Morerod's last request was carried out or not.

> In his will was expressed a desire that the old custom of his native land be carried out as far as practicable at his demise. His associates had long since began to look upon this as not only nonsensical, but a heathenish custom, yet out of pure regard for his wish, a few gathered in a private room and drank wine.

We will never know the truth of the matter. By the turn of the century, attitudes about wine had changed across much of America. Wine was no longer a mealtime beverage or a natural and pleasant part of life. At least one of Father Morerod's granddaughters had become "a tireless worker for the WCTU." This attitude would persist for a number of years. Indeed, even Julie LeClerc Knox, in her 1942 genealogy of the Dufour family, felt the need to account for Dufour's life work. On the first page of Chapter 1 she reminded the reader (in all likelihood another Dufour descendent) that "it must be remembered that wine, at that time, was considered more or less a necessity, especially in France, where it still is, as water was too impure for drinking. However that is as it may be, and Jean Jacques need no apology."

For John James Dufour, the establishment of American vineyards was the greatest quest of his life. But for the rest of the immigrants, growing grapes was suitable only if it helped turn a profit or increased the community's welfare. The industry grew until the decline in wine prices meant that the settlers had to expend more effort on their grapes than was justified by the rewards. As a result, they were attracted less and less to wine production. In the mid-1820s, when the next generation was starting to come into adulthood, the financial crisis was at its height. With no end in sight to the economic troubles, many of the vineyards were pulled out and corn and potatoes planted in their place. The remaining vineyards ceased to have commercial value. Father Morerod's wife, Antoinette Dufour, survived him by twenty years, and during that time her children cared for her. A descendant wrote, "Long after the vineyards were abandoned as a business, enough of them were left to please her, accustomed to seeing them as a reminder of Switzerland."

As the vineyards declined, the town of Vevay also declined in importance. An Austrian traveler on the Ohio, Karl Postel, described the conditions he encountered at Vevay in the mid-1820s:

The vines however have degenerated, and the produce is an indifferent beverage, resembling anything but claret, as it has been represented. Two of them [Morerod and ?] have attempted to cultivate the river hills, and the vineyards laid out there are rather of a better sort. The town is on the decline; it has a court-house, and two stores very ill supplied. The condition of these, and the absence of lawyers, are sure signs of the poverty of the inhabitants, if broken windows, and doors falling from their hinges, should leave any doubt on the subject.

In 1830, three years after the death of John James Dufour, two books about grape-growing and wine-making were published. Both contained references to what the Swiss at Vevay had accomplished in America. The first was by William Robert Prince, a fourth-generation nurseryman from Long Island, New York. His book was dedicated to Henry Clay for his support of the development of natural resources and his patronage of industry. The dedication read in part, "But, Sir, the additional circumstances, that you more than thirty years ago, united with many of our fellow citizens in forming an association for promoting the cultivation of the vine in our country." This association was, of course, the Kentucky Vineyard Society. Dufour seemed to be fading from the picture already. Near the end of Prince's book, he made the tantalizing statement that a second volume would be published. He said that it would contain writings and letters from several gentlemen. One gentleman in the list was "L. Gex Esq." This could be none other than Louis Gex-Oboussier, former Vevay resident newly removed to New Harmony. Unfortunately, Prince never wrote the second volume.

The second book of interest published in 1830, titled *American Manual of Grape Vines and the Method of Making Wine,* was written by Constantine Rafinesque. He was an eccentric character who wrote on many features of the natural world. He taught at Transylvania College in Lexington, Kentucky, and later worked in John Adlum's vineyard in Georgetown, Maryland. In his book he listed the "principle wines already made." Four of the wines in the list were from Indiana. They were:

#1 Vincennes, pale red, light

#2 Vevay, red, acid

#3 Vevay prime, brown, sweetish, fine

#17 Harmony, red, acid, good

Rafinesque castigated Legaux for his mismanagement of the Philadelphia

Vineyard Society but gave him credit for diffusing the Cape and Madeira grapes throughout the country by declaring them to be Vinifera varieties. He contends that no one would have tried them had he not engaged in this bit of deception. This brings up an interesting point. Whatever the varieties were named, Dufour would have tried them. He noted that they were the only vines that grew decently in Legaux's vineyard. Because Dufour held the Cape grape to be European, based on the botanical evidence of the time, it has been written as recently as 1985 that "his observation ignores the reality of hybridization between species in which perfect flowers dominate. Whereas other winegrowers could accept American blood in wine grapes as the wave of the future, foreign-born Dufour was filled with disdain at the idea, and he may have been the world's first grape-variety 'racist.'" But this is far from the truth. In reality, Dufour's observations were correct, but science had yet to catch up with him. His actions demonstrate that he actually was one of the first grape-variety "egalitarians." He realized at Firstvineyard in Kentucky that it wasn't the pedigree of the grape that mattered but rather the performance in the vineyard, and this is the exact advice that he gave to the Philadelphia Vineyard Society in 1806.

In 1846, a third book appeared. This one was titled *The Cultivation of American Grape Vines and Making of Wine* and was written by Alden Spooner. He gives us a good view of the Swiss vineyard of Vevay at that time:

> They turned attention to our native vine, first to the Cape grape, and subsequently to the Isabella and Catawba. After forty years of experience they consider our climate and soil inferior to those of Switzerland for producing saccharine matter and consequently wine. They say that, in this country, 12 pounds of grapes are required to make a gallon of wine, and, in the old country, 10 pounds. At one time they had 40 acres under cultivation; now only 5. They say they can cultivate other products to greater profits.

In the 1840s, hay became Vevay's important cash crop, and several individuals became wealthy and famous hay dealers, including U. P. Schenk, who built a remarkable mansion in Vevay. Vevay also became known for its author Edward Eggleston, who was one of Indiana's most renowned sons in the late nineteenth century. His novel *Roxy* offers an interesting description of Vevay in the 1840s. It is a love story whose main characters were patterned after real Vevay residents. The vineyards and wine industry played little active role in the book. Yet there are several scenes in which people are sneaking around the vineyards and hiding between the rows of vines. The description of the old Swiss settler named Jacques Dupin was probably based on the recently deceased Father Morerod. As Eggleston wrote, "He came hobbling out of his room into the sunlight. He was a picturesque figure, with his trousers of antiquated cut, his loose jacket, and his red yarn cap pointed at the top and tousled." Eggleston has this character speak in heavily accented English with snippets of French thrown in. Despite the presence of some vineyards even into the 1840s, it becomes clear in *Roxy* that the vast majority of the residents had little to do with vine-rearing by this time.

In 1895, an unusual visitor toured Dufour's old haunts. This was well-known Cornell University horticulturalist Liberty Hyde Bailey. Bailey had an interest in grapes and grape cultivation, and he wanted to write about the American grape and wine industry. To do this, he set out on a tour of new and old vineyard sites, much like Dufour's tour before he planted Firstvineyard. The resulting volume, published in 1898, is one of the most well-researched and complete portraits of early American viticulture and is still superior to many of the more recent works. He visited the site of Firstvineyard, taking pictures and making sketches. He visited Vevay, he talked with the descendants of the original vinedressers, and he read Dufour's book. His descriptions of the former vineyard sites are good. Bailey described the remains of Dufour's Kentucky effort:

> The traveler who visits this spot to-day finds an open glebe stretching from the Kentucky River to the hills. Upon this lowland he will see a clump of bushes and poke-weeds, and a few stones, marking the site of the old log house, which perished about 1845 to 1850. Near by is a broken hollow pear tree, three feet in diameter, which tradition says was brought from Europe by the Dufours. This tree, which bears a Summer Bell pear, still gives an annual crop of its indifferent fruit. Just beyond is the hillside where the plantings were made, and the remnant of a stone wall marks one of the boundaries of the vineyard.... This hillside, where once the vine was planted with prophetic hope, is now a sheep pasture; and only tradition remains to recall the struggles and disappointments of a noble band of pioneers, though fruitless to themselves, was fraught with blessings for the years to come.

Bailey gave this description of the decline and abandonment of Vevay's vineyards:

> Grape-growing, as a business, has long since perished at Vevay. The vines took sick and would not bear; or if they bore, the fruit rotted before it was ready to harvest. Only one variety, known as the Cape grape, gave any important return. On the 27th of May, 1832 or 1833, a killing frost ruined

Firstvineyard. This photograph, taken by L. H. Bailey, shows Firstvineyard as it appeared in the 1890s. According to Bailey the old house perished around 1845 to 1850. The vines were planted on the hillside just beyond the remnant of a stone wall.

most of the remaining vineyards, and the Catawba, which was just becoming famous, was set in the place of the old varieties. But even this took the disease, and grape-growing there soon entered into a decline, from which it never recovered.

Despite the early recognition of Vevay's place in wine history by authors such as Bailey, the succeeding generations of authors who wrote on the subject quickly forgot Vevay, until the story of Dufour and the Swiss became a footnote to the history of wine-making in the United States. But Dufour's significance is being rediscovered. In addition to republishing his book in 2000, Editions La Valsainte of Vevey, Switzerland, has translated it into French, and that version includes some additional information and photographs.

The decline of the Vevay wine industry was largely caused by factors beyond the colony's control. The drop in the price of agricultural products and the glut of cheap whiskey guaranteed that the vinedressers would have a difficult time in the 1820s. The children of the original settlers had not grown up in the wine culture of Switzerland. Unlike John James, they did not have the vision to build an American wine empire. Their choice was between a declining way of life based on the vine or any one of the numerous opportunities that America had to offer. It is not surprising that they abandoned the vine. Not even the publication of the groundbreaking *Vine-Dresser's Guide* could change the unfavorable economic conditions. Ultimately, it was not the quality of the wine or lack of perseverance but simple economics that spelled the end of the Vevay efforts. The industry had been successful as long as the West could support it. The Swiss effort at Vevay ended as it had begun, a revolutionary idea that was years ahead of its time.

8. New Harmony

JOHN JAMES DUFOUR was not the only European visionary to lead a colony to Indiana to plant the vine. The attraction of cheap land in America coupled with religious and political freedom was a powerful draw to those in the Old World. Europeans looked across the Atlantic and dreamed of the day that they could settle the frontier, their heads filled by overblown reports sent back by speculators. Germany at this time was suffering from both war and economic depression, and a great number of its citizens were looking for the chance to start a new life. One of them was George Rapp. He was the son of a vine planter and shared Dufour's vision of a better life in the New World, but that is where the similarity ended.

Johann Georg Rapp was born in Württemburg in 1757. Rapp supported himself from the proceeds of his vineyard; one year he made 300 gulden. He might have been a vinedresser his whole life had he not possessed a religious zeal which caused him to speak out against the state church. In 1785, Rapp delivered a personal confession of faith that outlined why he chose to separate himself from the official church. The confession was delivered to the town council of Iptingen, which was the religious and political body ruling over his hometown. In it he criticized the decadence of the Protestant church and clergy and the lack of harmony among men. The immediate result of this confession was that Rapp was labeled an outcast, but he must have struck a chord with fellow Württemburgers. By 1791, Rapp had become the unofficial leader of a folk church and was attracting enough attention to displease the authorities. In June 1791, Rapp was ordered to stop preaching because he was not a prophet. The tension between Rapp and the authorities increased until 1803, when he was summoned to Maulbronn to undergo a lengthy questioning. He was not punished as a result of this summons, but he decided that the religious persecution and the threat of Napoleonic conscription in Germany made it an undesirable place to live. Rapp decided to go to America and found a utopian community in the wilderness.

Rapp arrived in Philadelphia on October 7, 1803, and began searching for a spot to settle a colony. At first Rapp investigated western Pennsylvania, but eventually he chose a spot by the Muskingum River in Ohio. He planned to buy land there when more followers arrived. He returned to the East Coast and stopped for a time in Baltimore, where he preached to the large German population. On July 4, 1804, the ship *Aurora* landed in Baltimore with 300 of Rapp's followers. Rapp at once tried to secure land for his flock. On July 10, 1804, Samuel Smith, a Baltimore acquaintance, wrote Rapp a letter of introduction to President Jefferson. The letter read:

> Sir/ Permit me to have the honor of presenting to you Mr. Peter Hoffman, a merchant of this City, of the first respectability, Independence & political Rectitude—he Visits you in Company with Mr. J. G. Rapp—who has immigrated at the head of a large Number of persons lately Subjects of the Duke of Wirtemburg [*sic*], in whose behalf he will present a Memorial & State their wishes—I have on Looking at the law passed in favor of "Dufour & Associates" in 1802, been led to hope that Congress would pass a similar Law on Behalf of those people—Their making a Settlement so far in land will unquestionably Enhance the Value of the public Land—I Need not offer Observation on a subject So well understood by you—but take farther the liberty to pray you to give some Attention to the Views of those people & the Observations of my good friend Mr. Hoffman & have the honor to be Your Obedt servt
>
> S. SMITH

It is interesting to note that Rapp had heard of the exception made for Dufour's purchase and that he desired similar treatment for his colony. Jefferson replied to Rapp on July 12, explaining that it was not in his power to grant such a request even though he was favorable to the proposal. Jefferson informed the Germans that the only way to obtain such assistance was to get legislation similar to Dufour's passed through Congress.

George Rapp's position was complicated by the arrival of more of his followers throughout the summer of 1804. These immigrants were immediately commented upon in a German newspaper from Lancaster, Pennsylvania. The article gave a good description of the immigrants and their reasons for coming to America:

> The cause of the great emigration from Württemburg is said to be chiefly the following: Since the Christian religion during the French revolutionary war became very decadent, many people separated from the churches and have united with each other and everywhere have received the name Separatists, and because of their religious attitudes have been hard pressed and persecuted by the government. Under penalty of high fines they were forbidden to hold

separate services among themselves, and this brought on their decision to leave their fatherland rather than give up the religious principles which they have adopted, and to cross the great world ocean and come to this country, as a place of refuge, where each man is granted general freedom of conscience. Since as yet their religious principles are not exactly known to us, we can at present give no report of these. We are assured, however, that they firmly believe in the trinity of God, that they show themselves to be quiet, industrious, peaceful, and virtuous, and that they incidentally, plan to concern themselves with agriculture and viniculture.

George Rapp went to Philadelphia and then to Pittsburgh while he looked for a parcel of land large enough for his colony. He apparently gave up on purchasing land in Ohio, since it was so far removed from other settlements. Instead, he decided to make a purchase in Butler County, Pennsylvania, about twenty-six miles from Pittsburgh. He agreed to pay $10,217.74 for the land, and on December 22, 1804, he made the first payment of $3,405.91. The ground was suitable for Rapp at the time because he was desperately in need of a home for his arriving colony. Unfortunately, the purchase caused some disagreement among his followers, since some had already moved to Ohio and purchased small parcels of land there. The result was that several of Rapp's wealthiest followers left the community before its inception and eventually sued Rapp to recover the money they had invested in the society.

Within a matter of days the colonists started heading to their newly purchased ground. By January 14, 1805, thirty-one families had relocated to Pennsylvania. They immediately began the difficult task of clearing the ground and constructing homes. Thus the town of Harmony, Pennsylvania was established. It was to be the home of Rapp and his brethren until the second coming of Christ, at which time the moral Germans residing in the wilderness would be saved and the immoral millions of the world would perish in fire and brimstone.

Despite the difficulties that surrounded the purchase of land, the work of establishing a colony continued. On February 15, 1805, the Articles of Association that were to formally found the Harmony Society were drawn up and signed. The gist of the document was that the society would be formed by a communal effort of its members. When members entered the society they had to surrender their private property and work toward the greater good of the society. In exchange, they were to be cared for in sickness and health, preached to and administered by Father Rapp, and provided with all the necessities of daily life. If they should desire to leave, a stipend would be given to them upon their departure in exchange for the work they had performed while in the society.

Construction continued at a rapid pace and very quickly a town began to emerge from the wilderness. But as construction continued it became obvious that there were some problems with the land and that this might not be the ideal location. First, the amount of ground available for the expansion of the community was limited, since most of the neighboring ground had been purchased already. Second, the land was not suitable for the cultivation of grapes because the winters were too severe. As Rapp wrote, "The land where they live presently is too small, too broken & to cold for to raise Vine." Finally, the Harmonists were having problems within their flock, most of which were caused by the decision to purchase land in Pennsylvania instead of in Ohio.

In an effort to rectify the problems facing the colony, the Harmonists presented a petition to Congress, as Jefferson had suggested, which outlined their need for land in a different area. Rapp was most interested in land in the Northwest Territory because it prohibited slavery. One site he looked at was on the northern bank of the Ohio River, opposite where the Kentucky River empties into it. This was very near New Switzerland, and one can only wonder what would have happened had the Harmonists settled there. The petition emphasized that they would establish vineyards, and was obviously based on Dufour's petition of 1802. George Rapp traveled to Washington to garner support for the bill and be present when it was debated. Unfortunately for Rapp, when the bill came up for debate Congress did not pass the measure, and no special concession was made to the Germans. This was largely due to the fact that unlike Dufour, who had gained the support of Albert Gallatin, Rapp had failed to secure the necessary political support in Congress. Also, at this time, many Americans looked with distrust upon the large influx of German immigrants. To further complicate matters, Rapp's group was looked upon as a religious cult.

After the failure of the legislation that would have enabled the Harmonists to move farther west, they had no choice but to make the best of their site in Pennsylvania. During 1805, the colonists completed forty-six log cabins, a large barn, a grist mill and three-quarters of a mile of millrace. In 1806, they built a two-story stone-and-timber inn, an oil mill, a dyer's shop, and a tannery. They also cleared 300 acres of land for corn and fifty-eight acres for pasture. By 1807, they had completed work on a brick storehouse, a sawmill, and a brewery. They cleared 400 acres for grain and planted four acres in vineyards. The year 1807 also marked the start of the exporting of Harmony products; the community sold 600 bushels of grain and 3,000 gallons of whiskey in that year. The sale of whiskey may seem a little strange for such pious people, but the Harmonists could justify it since they did not indulge in the beverage but only sold it to generate badly needed cash. The rapid expansion of the town continued into 1808, when the Harmonists built a brick meetinghouse, a brick dwelling house, stables for cattle, a frame barn, and a 200-foot-long bridge over Connoquenessing Creek. In 1809, they completed a fulling mill (for making wool cloth), a hemp mill, another oil mill, a gristmill, and a brick warehouse which contained an arched wine cellar. By 1811, the society numbered about 800 persons, all of whom were employed in the building of the community.

The events of the outside world were starting to encroach on the Harmonists during the years 1812 to 1814. The land around them had all been sold and many more settlers were moving into the region. The people moving in were often jealous of the success of the Germans, and a feeling of ill will toward them started to grow among their neighbors. In 1814, several Harmonists had been drafted for the militia that was being organized for the war against England. The colonists refused to serve, just as they had refused to serve in the Napoleonic Wars, and were fined $1,348. They only paid $640, and probably were not even required to pay that much, as the fines were later ruled illegal, but the matter served to further aggravate the problems between the German colonists and their neighbors. Another factor that pushed the Harmonists to seek a better location was the lack of year-round water transport in that part of Pennsylvania. Connoquenessing Creek was not a suitable avenue for shipping, which forced the Harmonists to pay for twelve miles of overland transportation to the Ohio River. One Harmonist outlined the problems in Pennsylvania:

> There we built a city named Harmonie where we lived for ten years happily and in peace, but since that region has quite a few inhabitants and no more land could be purchased except at very high prices, and since we could not further expand, and also because the climate was not quite suitable to us because the winter was somewhat too long which made the raising of sheep and viniculture somewhat difficult, therefore we agreed to leave that place and seek a region which with respect to culture, trade, and situation would offer more advantages for factories of various type.

Rapp proposed moving the colony from Pennsylvania and justified it by quoting scripture:

> And to the woman were given two wings
> of a great eagle, that she might fly
> into the wilderness, into her place,
> where she is nourished for a time,
> and times, and half a time, from the
> face of the serpent.

There was little debate over the need to move from Pennsylvania; the question was where and when. In the spring of 1814, George Rapp and a few companions started down the Ohio River to look for a new site for the community. On April 20th, the travelers visited Limestone, Kentucky, and by April 25th they had made it to Jeffersonville, Indiana, which lies across the river from Louisville, Kentucky. They liked the land that they had seen so far (the trees had already started to leaf out), but it was really too hilly for their needs. George Rapp believed that the Wabash River in Indiana might be the ideal site for his colony, saying, "By the way, my spirit will not be at rest until I have been to the Wabash. According to all appearances that will be our place."

On May 2nd, George Rapp saw the land along the Wabash River and liked it well enough to make a purchase. On the 9th of May he bought 2,435 acres of land on contract in the vicinity of modern-day Posey County. Later in 1814 he purchased an additional 5,370 acres. On May 10th, Rapp wrote a letter to his followers in Pennsylvania which described the land he had seen and acquired:

> So we set our course for the Wabash, and after we had crossed the prairies below Vincennes, we got to the White River. There the good land began; so good, you cannot believe what rich and beautiful land lies there. . . . So we went up the channel [of the Wabash] and the hill declined. There above the channel we came upon better land, so that the brethren thought and are convinced there could be no better land. There we have now purchased close to 7000 acres, in part out of the office and in part from settlers. Some of this still is to be bought which we plan to do tomorrow when we leave here.

Rapp went on to point out the obvious advantages that this site would have over the location in Pennsylvania:

> The Wabash is a large stream of water, it is considerably larger than the Allegheny. Throughout the year there will be no hindrance to shipping to New Orleans. The place is 25 miles from the Ohio mouth of the Wabash, and 12 miles from where the Ohio makes its curve first before the mouth. The town will be located about 1/4 mile from the river above on the channel on a

plane as level as the floor of a room, perhaps a good quarter mile from the hill which lies suitable for a vineyard.

In short, the land on the Wabash had year-round water transport, it had a climate and area suitable for growing grapes, and it was far enough on the frontier that the Harmonists would have few neighbors. These were the qualities for which they had been searching.

The Harmonists wasted no time in starting their Indiana venture. On June 20, 1814, Frederick Rapp, the adopted son of George Rapp, who had been left behind to run the village of Harmony, Pennsylvania, wrote in his memorandum book, "The first people of the Harmonie left for the Indian territory in 3 boats which contained 40 wagon loads of goods. In cash I gave them four thousand dollars to take along." The great exodus from Pennsylvania had begun.

At about this same time the Harmonists received an interesting letter from a Swiss vine-grower named John Francis Buchetti, who had a vineyard in Barren County, Kentucky. This is the same vintner who had once taught school in Vevay. The letter connected the efforts in Kentucky, the Harmonists, and the Swiss at Vevay:

> Having heard through many channels of your vineyards, I take the liberty of dirrecting [*sic*] to you this letter in order to know whither I might get slips of the species you have, which as I understand, have been imported from the Rhine and are doing well in this country.
>
> But, before, I must let you know that I am a Swiss vinedresser having settled a Large vineyard in the above said County and State and intending not only to carry it into full Effect but also to provide myself with as many sorts of vines as possibly I might find.
>
> I got but 3 kinds on which I may rely upon and these are; the Cape, Madaira [*sic*] and Chassloss; the others are still uncertain and in all are about 10 thousands.
>
> Gentilemen, [*sic*] I write you this with all speed to pray you to be so good as to let me know the soonest possible whither I might get any slips from you of every kind you have of which I am in need of and mostly of those you think the best excluding the Cape, Madaira [*sic*] and Chassloss.
>
> Write me also the price of your slips per hundreds or Dozens, so that I might have time enough and to convey you money and you to send them to my address—(via Louisville)—so that I might have them for against March 1815, which is the season of planting them. . . .

> My Country people on the Ohio . . . and I do whatever we can to promote and e[n]courage the vine culture in these parts, in order to Banish, as much as we can, the pernicious evil of distilled spirits, which destroies [*sic*] more lives in this state than the Sword of war.
>
> In our Settlement on the Ohio [the Swiss at Vevay] the Crop of the year 1813 was about 7000 gallons of wine all made out of the Cape, out of about 19 acres in vines. Now there [are] nearly 40 acres planted in both young and old which will bear in 2 years. I wish to have large details about your vineyard and wine &c &c.
>
> But I fear of being too long. I will send you another time further particularities about ours, for, as we are of the same trade and coming mostly of the same country, I do wish to hold with you a constant Communication in letter respecting the Vine-Culture &c &c.

The letter nicely illustrates that growing grapes on the frontier was still a novelty and that the few individuals who were engaged in it knew of each other and carried on correspondence. The fact that Buchetti requested European varieties from the Harmonists shows how the hope of finding a successful European grape in America still dominated people's efforts despite repeated failures.

In June of 1814, the Harmonists started advertising their Pennsylvania lands for sale, as well as all the buildings in the town of Harmony and the many improvements that they had made in ten years. The ads were placed in the major newspapers of Pittsburgh and the (Cincinnati) *Niles' Weekly Register*. It took some time to sell their Pennsylvania holdings. At first, the property was offered for sale at $200,000 for the whole community. The Harmonists got no offers, so they postponed the sale and lowered the price. By January of 1815, Frederick Rapp had lowered his asking price to $135,000, which he pointed out was approximately equal to the proceeds which could be generated by the property in one year. This generated some interest, but still the property did not sell. Finally, on May 6, 1815, a Mr. Ziegler from Bethlehem, Pennsylvania, bought the property for a rock-bottom price of $100,000, half of what the Harmonists had originally asked.

The society did not wait until their lands in Pennsylvania had sold before they commenced the work of building their Indiana settlement. The first boatloads of people left on June 20, 1814, and were joined by more colonists on September 20th and 21st (which included Father Rapp, as George was fondly called by his flock). On October 30th and 31st, a great quantity of goods and supplies were sent down the river. These supplies included four barrels of old high wine, one barrel of old brandy, three barrels of common brandy, and one barrel of currant wine. The wine that had been produced in Pennsylvania was too valuable to leave behind. On November 1, 1814, an additional 103 Harmonists left Pennsylvania, and on the 14th, 85 more departed for the Wabash. In December, Frederick Rapp left Harmony with another eight families, 125 head of sheep, and two flatboats. In January 1815, Frederick traveled back to Pennsylvania in order to continue directing the Harmonists' move. On March 18, Frederick dispatched another six flatboats and one keelboat to New Harmony. On April 5th, one transport, one keelboat, and three flatboats departed. On May 9, Frederick and the last group of Harmonists left Pennsylvania after completing the sale of the ground and making the final preparations.

The journey from Harmony, Pennsylvania, to the society's land in Indiana proved to be fairly easy, and most groups completed it without mishap. Along the way the Harmonists remarked on the beauty of the country they were moving into and the sights they saw along the river. Of course, the sight of grapes and vineyards in southern Indiana gladdened the Harmonists, since it was partly the lack of suitable climate for vineyards that had helped propel them westward. In September of 1814, George Rapp, on his second trip to New Harmony, sent two of his company to visit the Swiss at Vevay:

> I sent Fleckhammer and Gerber to the Swiss with compliments, so their superior named Mr. Morerod sent me a bottle of wine, which was good, one year old. He also sent some grapes. He would like vines of all kinds, a dozen each. Their vineyards are still green and the brothers said they were full of grapes but only of one kind, the black. He still has some wine in the cellar. They have an extraordinary settlement, with good soil on the Ohio.

This is high praise from the dour Rapp, who rarely seemed to admire the efforts of people outside his community. In November or December of 1814, George Rapp mentioned the Swiss again when he wrote of the delivery of vine slips requested by Morerod at Vevay: "The vines have been delivered to the Swiss. The brethren were very well treated. They have a lot of wine in the cellar, from three different years. They [the brethren] also brought along vines."

The Harmonists were also pleased to note vines in other areas of Indiana. Jacob Baker, a trusted lieutenant, saw a large grapevine in

Vincennes and wrote, "Today at Judge Park's in General Harrison's garden I ate ripe peaches and am taking some home, and to my astonishment I saw such a grapevine there which apparently will produce 2 bushels of grapes." Rapp also remarked on the prospects of growing the vine on his newly purchased lands: "I expect to make enough wine after a while. The region and location for it is excellent."

While the departure from Pennsylvania went fairly smoothly, setting up a community in Indiana did not go as well. The first boatload of Harmonists to arrive had the most difficult task, since they had to carve a settlement out of the surrounding virgin forests. When they landed in the Indiana territory, it was high summer and the bottomlands that the community had selected proved to be an excellent breeding ground of fever and illness. Many of the first to arrive fell ill shortly after disembarking. A letter written back to the Harmonists still in Pennsylvania described the tragedy that was unfolding:

> Forschner is sick and his boy, and Dürr also Kepler and Jacob Langenbacher died, and during the winter we shall be able to do nothing. Only Weingärtner is steady, and Bezenhöfer. . . .
>
> I have no more farmers. Waldman will probably not come through, his fever through neglect has changed to a chest fever and cough and he often almost chokes. Launer is the same, perhaps even worse, and will die. Läuble changed from fever to dropsy and has enough to do. Several more are in such condition. In the case of Feucht it has changed to a devouring fever so that no one can stop him and he no longer wants to use his reason. Likewise Kreil and Kohler. I cannot do a thing any more, if Christoph [the society's doctor] does not come the people will die through the winter.

There was little that the settlers could do as they watched their numbers diminish from disease. The only hope was that the season would change and that the change in weather would bring about better health.

Despite the difficulties caused by the intense heat and swampy ground, the Harmonists persevered and continued the work of building their settlement. They cleared land and built cabins to house the daily arriving colonists. In December 1814, the vine cuttings arrived in New Harmony; George Rapp wrote to Frederick saying that they were in good condition and had arrived healthy. He also stated that there were enough vine plants in New Harmony and that no more need be brought from Harmony unless they were "special." By the 10th of March, 1815, the Harmonists had finished planting their orchard and were two days away from having their vineyard plantings finished. They had also succeeded in building fifty-seven cabins and were about to start clearing land for corn. It is illustrative of the importance that the Germans placed on wine production that they planted their vineyard so early.

The Harmonists were an industrious people, and the settlement continued to grow throughout 1815 and 1816. Frederick Rapp described the progress that had been made by 1816 in a letter to a friend:

> Our town lyeth on a handsome plain about a quarter mile from the wabbash [*sic*], high enough, that we never have to fear any inundation, between the town and the river, layes the rigest [richest] land that ever can be, but gets comonly [*sic*] over flowed in the Spring, from the river, which runs off again in good time, so that enough Corn, hemp, & tobacco can be raised theron, this bottom is from ¼ to ½ mile wide then begins a second bottom from 1 to 3 miles wide, on which our town is situated, and contains the beutifulest [*sic*] lands wheron Corn wheat Rye & all kinds of small grains can be raized [*sic*], . . . a beautifull chain of low & round hills, which land affords very good soil and is exellent [*sic*] for pastures or Vineyards. We have . . . [now] this six months every day from 40 to 50 hired hands employed to Cleare [*sic*] those small hills for sheep pasture, we pay from 6 to 10 Dlls. Per acre for clearing . . . we have now between 7 & 800 acres under fence and this year are expecting a good wheat harvest, we also have a vineyard, and I am in hopes this climat [*sic*] will be very suitable for raising wine, every family of us has a convinient [*sic*] loag [*sic*] house good houses we have none but two, but will now make a begining to encrease [*sic*] them, materials for building we have sufficienty [*sic*] enough.

In July 1816, Frederick Rapp wrote a letter to an acquaintance in Germany requesting a shipment of vines. The letter provided a brief description of the new vineyards as well as a list of the vines to be sent:

> Last year we built a vineyard here and have the best prospects for good success because the climate is mild and the weather regular and the soil of first quality, only we have too few kinds of vines and no prospects of getting more than from Germany. . . . Therefore I ask you to be so kind as to obtain the following vines for us and to see to it that they are well packed: 500 Roth-Elbe, 500 Weiss Elbe, 50 Schwarz Elbe, 500 Weisse Silvaner, 50 Schwarze Silvaner, 500 Süss Welsche, 300 Rothe-Gud Edel, 500 Feldleiner. Roth und Schwartz, 500 butzscheeren, 500 Muscadeller Roth. Schwartz und Gelb, 100 Fischschwänze, 500 Fiderer, 500 Grabstök, 500 Affenthäler, 500 Hudler, 500 Süss Rothe, 100 Cläscner, 500 Riessling, 500 Schwartz-Welsche, 100 Mährländer, and if several other kinds might be available which you would consider it good, we would be pleased to receive some of them.

From the list of grapes it appears that the Harmonists wanted to try all of the popular varieties of Germany in their American plantings. Of course, all of the Vinifera varieties would be doomed to die shortly after their planting in America, since none of them possessed the necessary resistance to native diseases. It is interesting to note that the Harmonists were still planning to plant European vines in America, even after they had communicated with the Swiss at Vevay and Buchetti in Kentucky, all of whom had noted the paucity of varieties that did well in America. Apparently the Germans assumed that the Swiss had not tried these varieties or that they had lacked the skill to grow them. For whatever reason, it doomed the Harmonists to repeat the failures that so many grape-growers had experienced before them.

The New Harmony vineyards were planted in orderly terraces and formed a pleasant backdrop to the community. One traveler wrote that in 1816 the Harmonists had twelve acres of vineyards planted. Frederick Rapp described the crop of 1818: "The Vines able to bear are full of great Clusters of grapes." Mr. Courtney, an English visitor, described the settlement in 1819: "They have cleared, fenced and cultivated about 1400 acres of heavy timbered land, planted orchards and vineyards, and have now in store wine from their second vintage." Another English visitor, William Faux, described the vineyards in a report he sent back to England: "They have a fine vineyard in the vale, and on the hills around, which are so beautiful as if formed by art to adorn the town. Not a spot but bears the most luxuriant vines, from which they make excellent wine." The Harmonists imported more grapevines from Germany in 1822, and these vines were planted by March of 1823. Frederick Rapp wrote to an acquaintance in Boston, "Our Orchards well sat with the best kind of every specie of fruit trees are very productive; the culture of Wine succeed somewhat better here then [*sic*] in Penns. yet by far not as well as in the old Countries." The problems with Vinifera vines and disease probably prompted this statement. William Herbert wrote in 1822, "Their little town, seen from the neighboring hills, which are covered with their vineyards and orchards, has an exceedingly pleasing appearance." Karl Bernhard, the duke of the German state Saxe-Weimer, wrote in 1825 about the fate of some of the vineyards: "I went to the orchard on the Mount Vernon road to walk, and beheld, to my great concern, what ravages the frost had committed on the fruit blossoms, the vines must have been completely killed."

With the planting of vineyards the Harmonists could look forward to producing wine from their own grapes. But they were not limited to grapes for wine-making. In June 1816, George Rapp wrote that the Harmonists "had a great number of currants and are making wine of that which is there." In September, Rapp wrote that they had four barrels of costly wine in the cellar, although he gives no indication of the type or where it was produced. In October 1816, Elisha Harrison, a second cousin of William Henry Harrison, wrote to the Harmonists requesting wine, peach brandy, and Percico French brandy. Apparently he liked the wine and spirits because he made another order in December. This time he requested that it be delivered on credit until he could sell it at a neighboring tavern. In 1817, the Harmonists shipped a barrel of wine to Nathaniel Ewing, a storekeeper and merchant in Vincennes.

The Harmonists continued efforts to expand their wine market. In 1820, Frederick Rapp wrote a letter to a Vincennes merchant saying that he would like to have payment for whiskey in the form of Nashville, Bank of Tennessee, or Kentucky money. However, he was willing to sell wine in exchange for Indiana paper (which was more risky considering Indiana bank closings) because he wanted to introduce their wine to the Vincennes market. The Harmonists also sent their wine as gifts to public officials and friends of the society, such as Frederick Graeter, justice of the peace of Knox County, who in 1822 received a "small barrel of Harmonie Wine." In April of 1823, the Shawneetown store manager's wife wrote to the Harmonists, explaining that they had accidentally sold two kegs of wine that were supposed to be given to someone else. In June 1823, Frederick Rapp had twelve half-barrels of wine shipped to Pittsburgh in order to test the market there. He instructed his acquaintance in Pittsburgh to sell the wine in the barrels but if that proved impossible to sell it for $1 a gallon. He added this perceptive note, "It must however be considered that the first introduction will measurably affect future Sales." On November 22, the Shawneetown agent wrote, "The wine goes quite rapidly by gallons and quarts, ought to get some more soon, perhaps one barrel of each." The end of November 1823 found Frederick Rapp trying to sell wine in the Cincinnati market by sending it to a friend who lived there; he wrote "that if it should meet with good Encouragement, I would always send you more."

The net result of the Harmonist wine-marketing efforts in the Ohio Valley must have been disappointing. The goods that the Harmonists produced, such as woolen cloth, clothes, shoes, flour, and even whiskey found ready markets on the frontier. Wine was a different matter. The same problems that had confronted the Swiss at Vevay also posed problems for the Germans. First, wine was time-consuming to produce, and the best markets for their product were the major eastern cities, which were far removed from Indiana. Second, the financial crisis caused by speculation and the bank failures that hit the Swiss so hard also affected the Germans. The fact that the wine was difficult to sell is amply illustrated by Frederick Rapp's willingness to take Indiana money for it; he would not take that currency for his whiskey.

The quality of the Harmonists' wine is hard to judge. As usual, there are varying accounts about its desirability. It seems to have often been fortified with spirits, which would have displeased Jefferson and the wine purists. George Rapp wrote in December of 1814, "I want to mix this year's wine with whiskey." A merchant at Louisville requested that Rapp send some "high wines, (highest proof) gin, (highest proof) & Apple or peach brandy." Ferdinand Ernst, a visitor to Harmony in 1819, wrote, "The vineyards here, covering about 8–10 acres, give a good wine, which, however, seems to be mixed with sugar and spirits." The addition of sugar and spirits may have made the wine less "pure," but it pleased a certain segment of the population on the frontier. For example, another visitor described the Harmonists' wine by saying, "The flavour appeared to me preferable to that produced at Vevay, of which I had formerly partaken." William Newnham Blane, a young Englishman, toured through New Harmony and tasted some of their wine in 1822, saying, "They . . . made considerable quantities of pleasant tasted wine."

The Harmonists did not produce the wine merely for export. They also produced wine for their own consumption, using it mainly as a medicine. As an Englishman remarked, "They brew beer and make wine: the latter is kept for the sick and to sell." A fellow German wrote to Frederick Rapp,

> The doctor on the Wabash advised him when he lay sick with fever, to give Port wine preference to all medicine, and the history of Pennsylvania, written by Prout, says that the first settlers made wine from Fox grapes, which when a year old was found to be very similar to Port wine. If you should find such on the Wabash, not one vine ought to be spoiled, and a test ought to be made. Our good Father in Heaven has always provided an antidote beside poison, only it is too bad that we are not attentive enough. A gallon of brandy is put into a barrel wine in Portugal. Since these grapes take no more trouble than to be cut, it is too bad that this gift from God is not respected.

The Harmonists also served wine on special occasions, such as when entertaining important visitors or marking a notable accomplishment. As Gertrude Rapp (Father Rapp's daughter) wrote, "At noon we ate dinner with our entire family in the Brother House No. 2. Nathaniel and Horlebaus were also invited. I had a glass of wine served to everyone who belonged to it." The visit of philanthropist and industrialist Robert Owen also marked an occasion noteworthy enough to merit wine, as his son Dale Owen wrote, "At Rapps we tasted some excellent wine made at Harmony, the best from wild grapes, which when kept several years improves remarkably." The measured use of wine by the Harmonists is a reflection of their European culture which prescribed wine in moderation for all civilized people.

By 1824 the Harmonists had decided that it was time to move on. Once again they had developed problems with their neighbors, and once again the land around them was being settled. In the spring and summer of 1824, the Harmonists started looking for a new location for their enterprise and advertising the sale of New Harmony. The advertisements listed all the many improvements that the Harmonists had made in their ten years of occupation: "There are about 2000 acres of land in a high state of cultivation, 15 acres thereof are in vineyard, and 35 acres are devoted to an apple orchard containing about 1,500 bearing apple and pear trees all of choice fruit." The asking price was $150,000 in ten years or $125,000 in five. Robert Owen purchased New Harmony on January 3, 1825. The Germans left behind all that they had built, 219 graves of people who had died in Indiana, and this inscription scrawled on a wall in chalk: "In the 24th of May, 1824, we have departed. Lord with Thy great help and goodness, in body and soul, protect us."

When the Harmonist sold their community, they decided to settle in Pennsylvania again. This signaled an end of grape production as a focus of the colony. The other industries that the Harmonists undertook were much more profitable than their forays into grape-growing and wine-making. While vineyards would still be planted at their third community, Economy, they would not be looked upon as the basis of the colony. They brought most of the wine that they made at New Harmony with them to Pennsylvania. As a visitor to Economy wrote, "Incidentally, with the good German dinner we drank excellent wine, which had been grown on the Wabash and brought from there; the worst, as I noticed, they had left in Harmony." The Indiana wine was served to important visitors or on special occasions, as a traveler remarked, "We came, finally, to say farewell to old Rapp, and to have a last look at this extraordinary man. In the style of ancient hospitality, the old man had his Wabash wines brought forth, he offered them to us, wished us all a good trip, and thus we parted."

At about the time that the Harmonists were abandoning their property to Robert Owen, a familiar character came to live on the Wabash. Louis Gex-Oboussier moved to New Harmony from Vevay. He had been attracted by the utopian ideas and writings of Owen. In a letter written to Robert Owen in 1825, Gex is mentioned: "Of many of those for whom you advertised we have already sufficient numbers and excellent workmen. Mr. Gese [Gex] from Vevais [Vevay] will join when the river rises; an excellent Vinedresser." There is also an interesting anecdote that probably refers to Louis Gex-Oboussier:

> From the mills we went to the vineyard, which was enclosed and kept in very good order. I spoke to an old French vine-dresser here. He assured me that Rapp's people had not understood the art of making wine; that he would in time make more and much better wine, than had been done heretofore. The wine stocks are imported from the Cape of Good Hope, and the wine has a singular and strange taste, which reminds one of the common Spanish wines.

It does seem characteristic of the old Swiss winemaker to know he could do it better than the Germans and to mention the ubiquitous Cape grape. In 1890, a list of names of families that still resided in New Harmony included Gex.

One of Robert Owen's first acts was to tear down the distillery and declare prohibition for the New Harmony settlement. This has been said to be the first known American example of prohibition of liquor traffic by administrative edict. Frost and disease caused damage to the grapes, and the end of New Harmony as a wine-producing community soon followed. As a visitor wrote in 1832, "The vine was formerly cultivated, but it is now quite neglected."

Ultimately, the Harmonists' experience in Indiana was remarkably similar to, yet notably different from, the Swiss efforts at Vevay. Both groups experienced the difficulties of being on the frontier, problems caused by an unstable money situation and a lack of urban markets for their products. Both groups petitioned the government for help, but (and this points out an important difference) the Germans were denied their request largely because of their religious nature and their lack of assimilation into the American culture. They never seemed to fit in with their American neighbors and moved several times, partly due to friction with the surrounding communities. The Swiss, however, fit in amazingly well, quickly adopting American customs. They celebrated the Fourth of July, volunteered for the militia, organized the county seat, and were elected to positions of power in the community. The Swiss adapted so well that their children and grandchildren lost touch with the Old World wine culture, and some even joined the national movement for prohibition. Yet another difference is that financially the Harmonists appeared to be more successful than the Swiss at Vevay. This was because of their shared labor system and their more diversified industries. But in the end, it was the Swiss, because of their dedication to the vine, who had a significant and lasting influence on the progress of grape-growing and wine-making in America.

9. Indiana Wine, 1827–1919

WITH THE DEATH of John James Dufour and the departure of Father Rapp, Indiana lost the visionary leaders who had done so much to make the dream of American viticulture a reality. The Indiana wine industry went into a period of decline and relinquished its position as the premier wine-producing area of the country. In the 1830s and 1840s, wine production began to increase again in the Ohio River Valley in the vicinity of Cincinnati. This was primarily due to one man who had inherited Dufour's vision and who had become the new promoter of the American wine industry: a wealthy Cincinnati businessman named Nicholas Longworth.

Longworth got into the wine business almost by accident. He had been born in the East to a father who had ardently supported the losing side in the American Revolution. The American government seized his father's New Jersey property after the end of the conflict, and the family moved west to Cincinnati. Shortly after arriving in 1803, Nicholas began studying law; six months later he was a practicing attorney. He won his first case and for payment received two copper stills. Having no use for the stills, he traded them for thirty-three acres of land outside of Cincinnati. This was the first of his many land purchases in the Cincinnati area. The Cincinnati land boom came at the perfect moment for Longworth. Soon he was making more money as a land speculator than as a lawyer. In a matter of years, the unknown frontier lawyer became the second wealthiest man in America.

Longworth's wealth allowed him to devote more time to his personal interests, one of which was horticulture. Longworth liked to dress in gardener's clothes while working on his property; sometimes he was mistaken for one of his own employees. He had his first vineyard planted in 1823, four miles below Cincinnati, by a German named Amen. The vineyard was planted with the Cape grape, the same one that Dufour had done so much to promote, and it was largely because of Dufour's success that Longworth made his first trial. The knowledge that Dufour had so painstakingly gathered throughout his life was of great value to Longworth. He acknowledged his debt to Dufour in an interview later in his life saying, "At the commencement, I planted largely with the 'Cape' grape, as this was the only grape found to succeed at Vevay." Cincinnati would be the inheritor of Dufour's efforts. However, Nicholas repeated the mistakes of every other vineyard planter when he imported thousands of European grapevines from Madeira, France, and Germany. Needless to say, they all failed. In 1825, Longworth received cuttings of the Catawba grape from John Adlum. This grape was to become the focal point of the Cincinnati wine industry.

Knowledge was not the only valuable export from Vevay that helped begin a flourishing wine industry in Ohio. In 1827, one of the Siebenthal sisters married a Swiss man by the name of John Emanuel Mottier. Shortly thereafter, they moved from Vevay to the Cincinnati area. John was a vinedresser, and he continued his profession in Cincinnati. By the 1840s, Mottier had made quite a name for himself, and his vineyards and their produce were well known. In an article that appeared in the *Western Farmer* of October 1840, Mottier and his vineyard were mentioned:

> On Wednesday the 16th ult. rode down with a small party to . . . [a vineyard] owned by Mr. Longworth, but leased to Mr. Mottier, who is his own *Vigneron*. It is kept in fine order, everything neat and businesslike. There are about seven acres planted, only about two-thirds of which, however, is yet in bearing. The varieties found to suit best are the Catawba, Isabella and Black Cape.

The article describes Longworth's approach to the economics of growing grapes. He developed a form of sharecropping by which he supplied the land and vines in exchange for 50 percent of the harvest. Most of his growers were from the large German immigrant population in Cincinnati. It was a system that served him well until his death in 1863.

An 1842 newspaper article mentioned Mottier:

> He is an enterprising man of Swiss descent who understands the practical details of the business of cultivating the Grape and manufacturing of wine. At this time he has about six acres of ground occupied for this purpose.
>
> Every thing connected with his establishment wears an imprint of regularity, neatness and judicious arrangement—and the annual returns I am assured are certainly of so great an amount as to amply repay him for his labors. . . .
>
> Mr. M. makes wine principally, I believe from the Catawba Grape that is pure, and when of proper age is more suitable for the sick than almost any that is imported.

Mottier proved to be successful as a grower and winemaker, as this quote from the April 1844 issue of the *Western Farmer* illustrates:

> Mr. Mottier, who has a flourishing vineyard near town, has sold every gallon of his American wine. His crop last year from about four acres (now in full bearing) was 1,000 gallons. He has also two or three acres more coming into bearing. His sales, during the last eight months, exceed 2,500 gallons, including some of his previous crops, at 75 cents to $1, per gallon, chiefly at the latter price. He has made and sold since he commenced business nine years since, 8,000 gallons. He uses no brandy in the preservation of his wine, which is thus the pure juice of the grape.

In June 1844, Mottier wrote an article for the *Western Farmer* about viticulture. His advice was practical and covered everything from planting to pruning. The purpose of the article was to promote grape culture and fill gaps in the general public's knowledge, as Mottier wrote: "It seems that there is a great interest beginning to be excited in this neighborhood about planting grape vines; and, thinking that the proper mode of cultivation is very little understood, I will proceed to describe the way I conceive to be the best."

The 1840s were a period of unparalleled growth in the Cincinnati wine industry. Longworth's wine was being sold throughout the Midwest, especially his sparkling Catawba, a naturally carbonated, champagne-style wine. The famous American poet Henry Wadsworth Longfellow was moved to compose a poem called "Catawba Wine" after drinking the sparkling Catawba. Longworth continued to expand his operations; in 1850 he completed his second wine house. This mammoth building, 40 feet by 120 feet and four stories tall, had a basement that was 23 feet below the surface of the ground. Longworth was able to do all of his wine operations from this building.

The Cincinnati Horticultural Society held a competition in 1845 to judge the wine then being produced in the Cincinnati area. Mottier and the other major Cincinnati producers, including Longworth and Longworth's son-in-law Dr. Flagg, entered the competition. Mottier did very well and his wines received much praise, with notes such as "Very good, resembling old Madeira," "Good high flavored," "Best new wine, will be superior with age," "Good for new wine, with age will be of the best quality," and other positive comments. Of course, it was noted that Mr. Longworth had entered the greatest number of wines from his several vineyards and that he had been engaged in growing grapes longer than anyone else in the region. The article in *Western Farmer* about the competition closed by saying, "the

committee are of [the] opinion, that the period is not dista
wines of the Ohio will enjoy a celebrity equal to those of the i

The Ohio River had finally become America's Rhine, the ce
production whose bluffs and banks were crowned with vineyarc
there were 350 acres in production, by 1852 more than 1,200 ac   ... by
1859 more than 2,000 acres. A portion of this acreage extended down the
river into Indiana. The U.S. census for 1859 recorded that Ohio had
produced 568,617 gallons of wine, which was the greatest quantity for any
state in the nation and represented approximately 35 percent of the national
total. The Cincinnati producers were enamored with the thought that their
valley was "America's Rhine" and used the phrase with such regularity that
it became an unofficial motto of the region.

In 1850, Dr. Robert Buchanan wrote a wine text. He was a Cincinnati
resident and longtime friend and supporter of Longworth. His book, entitled *Culture of the Grape and Wine Making,* was a popular text that went
into multiple editions throughout the 1850s. But the art of grape cultivation
had improved little since Dufour's publication in 1826. Buchanan gave
much of the same advice that Dufour had given, such as the value of
trenching, the proper distance between vines, the advantages of planting on
hillsides, and the necessity for and methods of pruning. Knowledge of how
to identify diseases, an aspect of Dufour's work that had been very advanced
for its time, had made little progress in the interim years. Buchanan and his
compatriots had new names for the diseases and could recognize the onset
of some of them, but they still did not know the underlying causes and had
found no practical solutions. The efforts of the Cincinnati growers to
overcome these diseases were varied and exhausting. Buchanan's discussion
of the disease known as the "rot" is illustrative of this process. First,
Buchanan gives a description of the disease and the time period when it was
likely to hit. Then he states, "The cause is supposed to be an excess of water
about the roots of the vine, in any clay subsoil retentive of moisture." He
notes a palliative measure: "Vines planted in rows eight feet apart, in one
instance, were found not to be affected with rot, but very slightly." He also
mentions that the growers tried "'special manures,' . . . having tried with
success, a mixture of guano, gypsum and wood ashes," as well as "covering
the whole surface of the vineyard with shavings, leaves or coarse grass."
Unfortunately, although growers tried each of these methods, none of them
were successful. As Buchanan wrote, "Various modes of prevention have
been recommended, but none yet tried have proved effectual." Despite the

passage of thirty years, the Cincinnati growers were in the same position as Dufour. All they could do was describe the diseases and discuss plausible solutions. But there was an interesting difference between Dufour's approach and that of the Cincinnati growers. Dufour believed that vine-dressers should use the hardiest grapes available and then deal with their particular characteristics in the wine-making process. Buchanan and Longworth believed in using the best-tasting grape, no matter how it behaved in the field. Each approach had its merits and problems.

This difference in approach was the basis for an article that appeared in 1858 in a publication titled *Cozzen's Wine Press*. The article was titled "The Last Words of John James Dufour." It was written by the editor of the magazine and began with a description of Dufour and his efforts at Vevay. He said that Dufour's treatise was still a textbook for the cultivators of the West. He also said that Dufour "was an *original thinker;* adapting new methods to new conditions of soil and climate; brave in theory and practice, and, of course, successful. But like all other originals, somewhat bound by those bird-cage wires of prejudice which environ every man who has a world of his own." He went on to say, "Dufour, with that loyalty and love for his favorite grape, held strongly to his faith in the Schuykill Muscadell (or Cape) as the chief wine grape of his adopted country, until his younger rival, Longworth of Cincinnati, advanced the standard of proscription, and put forth 'Catawba' as the watchword."

The editor explained that this rivalry was touchingly portrayed in a letter he had received from Mr. Robert Buchanan of Cincinnati. He believed that the letter would put the matter of which was better, the Cape or the Catawba, to rest. The editor then quoted from the letter as follows:

> The poor old vigneron (Mr. Dufour) . . . after a long and active life, the latter half of which had been devoted to his favorite scheme of establishing wine growing in the United States on a permanent basis, was aware that he had pruned his last vine, and must prepare for another world. He called his doctor to his bed side, and inquired how long he probably might live; upon being told perhaps a few hours, "then," said he, "I must get some doubts off my mind that have long perplexed me. Longworth and I have often disputed about which was the best native grape—the Cape (Schuykill), or the Catawba. I advocated the former, he the latter variety. Both of us were confident in our own opinion of being in the right, and many a glass of wine from each grape was tasted over and over again without final decision. This lasted for years. At length I began to admit that the delicate 'bouquet' and the flavor of Catawba was superior to the Cape, but insisted that the Catawba would not keep, but would sour in a year or two. Longworth then gave me three bottles, and told

me to test that, saying the wine would keep well, and improve by age, for he had tried it. One bottle I opened in six months. It was good. Another was opened in a year; it was better, and perfectly sound. The last I buried near a large stump in my vineyard; and now, doctor if you will allow me to send my son for it, and draw the cork, I shall be able to decide that question, and depart in Peace." The bottle was searched for and found, the cork drawn, and a glass of the wine presented to the old gentleman, who was propped up in bed that he might taste it. It was held to the light for him, and he tasted it two or three times. "Ah, doctor," said he, his countenance brightening up, "Longworth was right. Catawba *will keep*. It is good wine—it is *very* good wine." This was the last worldly act of a worthy and useful man, whose long life had been devoted to doing good to his fellow men, and to acts of kindness and benevolence to the community in which he lived. I give you this story as I got it, with an assurance from the narrator that it is true.

The editor then closed by saying, "True? Who can doubt it? It is as touching and simple as a parable." It is indeed a touching and well-written little story, but it is without doubt untrue. The letter is an obvious promotion of Longworth and the Catawba grape at the expense of Dufour, who had been dead for over thirty years and could take no exception to the obvious inaccuracies. The Catawba grape was released by John Adlum in Washington, D.C., in 1823. Longworth obtained some Catawba cuttings and samples of the wine from Adlum in 1825. He could not have gotten a crop of grapes and made wine from the vines that he had planted in 1825 before Dufour's death in 1827. But could he have given Dufour some of the Catawba wine he received from Adlum? Perhaps, yet Buchanan wrote that Longworth and Dufour argued the merits of the two varieties "for years," and that Longworth gave Dufour the three bottles to try the experiment as Longworth had already done. Obviously these trials would have to have taken more than two years. It would not have been in Dufour's character to agree with the opinion of an upstart rival with little grape-growing or wine-making experience. The improbable tale was simply a quaint marketing scheme to promote the Catawba over the Cape.

Even though he told apocryphal tales about Dufour's last words, Buchanan still recognized Dufour's significance, as he wrote in his text on wine, "Still, the vine-growers owe to Mr. Dufour and his associates, a debt of gratitude, which should not be forgotten." Dufour was still listed in the pantheon of Cincinnati wine heroes, albeit always after Longworth.

With the advent of the American Civil War in 1861, some of the factors that had made wine-making in Cincinnati so successful were to change. First, the cheap pool of German immigrant labor upon which the wine industry had been founded dried up due to the manpower requirements of the war. Second, the continuing problem of rot and mildew, to which the Catawba was so susceptible, wreaked havoc on the Cincinnati vines. Harvests started to fall off as these diseases became established in almost every vineyard. Longworth wrote this anecdote about the problems of rot: "I will name a circumstance at the vintage of 1846, at my vineyard, under the charge of Mr. Myers a skillful vinedresser, which he pointed out to me. He expected to make 2000 gallons of wine: the rot came, and he made 35 gallons only." The loss of a whole crop could not be sustained for very many years in a row, even by the wealthiest vintners.

Other perceptive vintners attempted to replant their unhealthy Catawba with vines that were more resistant. Mottier, following the philosophy of Dufour by relying on the hardiest varieties available, replanted his vineyard with the newly discovered Delaware, which was very resistant to the rot and mildew combination. He esteemed this grape higher than all others and remarked that it "stood perfectly, without the least appearance of disease, although surrounded by Catawba which was almost entirely destroyed." Unfortunately, many growers felt the Catawba made a better wine, so they refused to plant the Delaware. Dr. Meltzer Flagg wrote in 1870 about the Cincinnati industry's demise,

> None of it [American wine] has yet made for itself a respectable market in the large cities outside of the neighborhoods where it is grown; and through the country generally American wine is but little known and poorly esteemed by habitual wine drinkers. Very different from this was promised by the enthusiastic pioneers in grape culture of thirty years ago. Alas, there is a lion in the path! There are two; one called "Mildew," and the other and lesser one "Black rot.". . .
>
> The result of the first six or eight years' experience showed that, with good cultivation, a yearly average of four hundred gallons to the acre could be counted upon. Success most brilliant seemed assured. . . . But a blight came upon our vines, and a mildew on our hopes. To-day the forty vineyards which Longworth planted are being cut up, root and branch. The large wine house he built in Cincinnati is converted into an oil-refinery, and the half million of dollars he embarked in the undertaking has sunk and gives no account of itself. The great valley whose slopes he hoped to see adorned like those of many a river in the Old World—as fragrant at blossom-time, and as purple and joyous at vintage—has become, for the vine, a valley of desolation. When [Longworth] died, in 1863, the doom of his hopes was sufficiently evident, though not as yet fully accomplished; but to the last he refused to despair, and it was well enough he should pass away without knowing how nearly had failed the great work of his life.

The Cincinnati industry was never able to overcome the losses occasioned by the vine diseases, the Civil War, and Longworth's death. By the 1870s and 1880s, the wine industry had moved north to Lake Erie, eastward to New York, and farther west to Missouri and California. In 1869, both California and Missouri produced more wine than Ohio, and by 1879 California produced 183,746,304 pounds of grapes, compared to Ohio's 19,693,603 pounds of grapes. The Ohio River Valley had been the Rhine of America for only thirty years.

In the time period between the decline of the Cincinnati industry and the advent of prohibition, Indiana continued producing grapes and wine. In the Ohio River Valley, grapes were grown near Cincinnati and as far west as Jeffersonville, Indiana. Regions that had formerly been thought too cold for the cultivation of the grape, such as the northwestern counties near Lake Michigan, were planted when it was discovered that the Great Lakes region had a favorable climate. Grapes were also planted in the interior of the state, far from either the Ohio River or Lake Michigan. Many of these plantings were made possible by the introduction of new varieties that were developed by dedicated amateur American grape-growers. The most popular variety was the Concord grape. It made its first appearance in the early 1850s and in 1865 received the Greely prize as the best all-round variety. It was widely planted throughout the eastern United States after the Civil War. Other popular varieties of this period included the Clinton, Delaware, Ives, and Norton. Literally hundreds of varieties came and went during the late 1800s as the eternal search for the perfect vine continued.

The agricultural census of 1860 estimated total Indiana production at 102,895 gallons of wine. Most of this production was still centered on the Ohio River Valley. Patriot, Indiana, a small river town between Vevay and Cincinnati, was receiving some notoriety for its wine production. An article in a Missouri paper in 1860 discussed the vineyards at Patriot:

> The vineyard of Mr. Chase, at Patriot, in this county, produced about 3,000 gallons of wine last season, and a considerable quantity of brandy. And we believe the vineyard of John Allen deceased, at the same place, is larger than Mr. Chase's. In this county in a good season, we presume not less than ten thousand gallons of wine and brandy are made, and the quantity is yearly increasing.

Picturesque America, an early travel book filled with woodcuts of scenic American destinations, displayed a view of the vineyards of Patriot, Indiana. Beneath the woodcut, a flattering caption read,

Patriot, Indiana. Vineyards were planted on the banks of the Ohio River from Cincinnati to Jeffersonville in the mid- to late 1800s. Patriot, Indiana, was said to have made up to 10,000 gallons of wine per year.

Below Cincinnati are the vineyards, stretching up the hills along the northern shore. Floating down the river in the spring and seeing the green ranks of the vines, one is moved to exclaim, "This is the most beautiful of all," forgetting that the mountains of Virginia and the parks of Kentucky have already called forth the same words. The native Catawba wine of the West was first made in Cincinnati, and the juices of the vineyards of the Beautiful River have gained an honorable name among wines.

Bellevue, in Kentucky, and Patriot, in Indiana, are charming specimens of river-scenery, the latter showing hill-side vineyards.

The 1880 agricultural census presented a slightly different picture. Grape production was about the same—the state produced an estimated 99,566 gallons—but the production centers had shifted. The area around Terre Haute went from an estimated 585 gallons in 1860 to a substantial 32,250 gallons in 1880. This was largely due to an increase of Italian immigrants to the area and to the introduction of the new grape varieties.

The Little Italy Festival in the town of Clinton, north of Terre Haute, traces its heritage back to this era. The northern counties of Indiana, especially those near Lake Michigan, experienced a similar increase in grape production in the 1880s.

An 1890 report on grape production rated Indiana a distant sixth, with 3,850 acres. California was rated first, with 155,272 acres, followed by New York, with 43,350; Ohio, with 28,087; Missouri, with 10,000; and Virginia, with 4,100. Of the grapes raised in Indiana, 5,390 tons were used for table grapes; only 1,347 tons were made into wine. A surprising 2,425 people were estimated to be employed in the vineyards. These statistics represent a grape and wine industry that had spread across the state but was of diminished importance nationally.

In the late 1800s, grape-growing increased substantially in northern Indiana. The 1860 agricultural census estimated that the counties on the northern border of Indiana produced 2,400 gallons of wine. The 1880 census showed that the same region had produced 5,031 gallons of wine. In addition to the grapes that were used for wine, significant quantities of grapes were sent to market for use as table grapes and in juice, jellies, and jams. In the agricultural census for 1899, northern counties were as heavily planted in grapes as the counties along the Ohio River; the state essentially had two grape-growing areas. Northwestern Indiana continued to produce grapes and make a small amount of wine until prohibition, at which point the surviving vineyards raised grapes for table use, juice, and home winemaking.

In 1890, an Indiana vine-grower named J. Lacksteder, who lived on the Ohio River near Leavenworth, wrote a letter to Hermann Jaeger of Neosho, Missouri. Hermann Jaeger was an unusual character, a grape breeder from Missouri who greatly enhanced our selection of grapes. Jaeger, among other individuals, was instrumental in shipping American vines to the French for the grafting and breeding of phylloxera-resistant vines. Despite his efforts on behalf of the French wine industry, the onset of local dry laws and black-rot fungus in Missouri ruined him. Unfortunately for Jaeger, while he was regarded as a hero in France, he was relatively unknown in America. One day he and his team of horses left home and never returned. His impact on the wine industry can be seen by examining grapevine genealogies. Many of today's most popular French hybrids have a Jaeger vine in their parentage. Jaeger's reply to Lacksteder's letter shows us the thinking of the times. Lacksteder felt that adding manure would help prevent grape diseases such as rot. Jaeger replied that the application of manure would make vines healthier in general but that ultimately it would not cure any disease. He correctly felt that there were only two ways to avoid disease, "Planting only the few varieties that resist Rot sufficiently, or using copper remedies." The first remedy was the one that Dufour had proposed as early as 1806. The second solution was relatively new, having been invented in 1885—a mixture of copper and lime that went by the name of Bordeaux mixture. It is unknown if Lacksteder followed Jaeger's good advice, but the letter illustrates several things. First, it shows that the Ohio River Valley was no longer the cradle of innovation. Second, it illustrates that even at this late date there was quite a bit of ignorance about grape culture. But most important, Jaeger's mention of copper remedies and hardy grape varieties signals the future direction for the eastern wine industry. At last there were beginning to be answers to the problems that had plagued eastern viticulture for 300 years.

During the time between the Civil War and prohibition, Indiana ranked among the top ten states for grape-growing, and wine was made across the state from these grapes. Unfortunately, the records of many of these ventures have been lost. In many regards, other than the size of the operation, there was often little that distinguished home wine-making from commercial wine-making. Government permits were not generally required, so there is no way to check state or federal records. However, we can be certain that at least one winery existed in Elizabethtown, Indiana. The authors had heard of the existence of this winery through various people from that area but had found no hard evidence. Recently, one of the authors happened to be visiting with Ben and Lee Sparks, who once operated Possum Trot Vineyards near Trevlac, Indiana. There on a shelf on the wall of the former tasting-room stood an old wine bottle clearly embossed with the words "P. E. Wills's celebrated wines, Elizabethtown, Ind." Ben said that he purchased the bottle in Elizabethtown from a descendent of the original owner of the winery. There is probably more Indiana wine history hidden in our attics and cellars.

Wineries were scattered across southern Indiana. According to Dr. Donald MacDaniel (owner of the now-closed Treaty Line Winery in Connersville, Indiana), Oldenburg, Evansville, Vincennes, and New Alsace all had wineries prior to World War I. Unfortunately, the physical remains of these wineries have largely disappeared and many of the older residents who knew of these wineries have died and taken their knowledge with them.

This wine bottle was displayed in the former tasting-room at Possum Trot Vineyards (now closed) near Trevlac, Indiana. The hock-style bottle is embossed with the following: "P. E. Wills's celebrated wines, Elizabethtown, Ind." Ben Sparks, owner of Possum Trot Vineyards, told the authors that he purchased the bottle from a descendent of the owners of the Elizabethtown winery.

The final portion of Indiana's early wine history ends with the enactment of prohibition. National prohibition did not suddenly appear one day out of the blue. Rather, it developed slowly in local areas over a long period of time. In the early 1800s, the idea of temperance began to grow in response to widespread abuse of distilled spirits. By midcentury the moderate goal of temperance had turned into a full-fledged movement for prohibition of alcohol. As the movement grew, the drys agitated for increased restrictions on alcohol. In 1851, Maine became the first state to vote itself dry. In 1855, the Indiana legislature passed a prohibitory state law, but it was later declared unconstitutional by the state supreme court. The drys continued to push prohibition and the issue was bitterly debated in Indiana throughout 1856, but the state remained wet. During the Civil War, the prohibition movement lost its momentum, but in 1881 and 1883 the issue was brought up again. It failed to pass in both the House and the Senate. In 1907, the courts in Indiana decided two cases with potential national prohibition implications. One, the case of *Soltau v. Young*, decided that the saloon-licensing statute in Indiana was illegal. The second case, known as the Sopher case, came to the same conclusion. The drys had hoped that they would be able to declare liquor sales unconstitutional on a national level by winning these Indiana cases. But neither case ever reached the U.S. Supreme Court.

In 1908, through the efforts of Governor J. Frank Hanly, the Indiana legislature passed a county option law. This law was hardly a victory for the drys, because even if a county did vote to be dry, its neighboring counties that remained wet continued to supply the demand. The law was repealed in 1910, when the temperance Republicans were defeated in the general election. The efforts of the prohibitionists seem to have been counterproductive. In 1911, there were 18 percent more saloons than there had been in 1893. Indiana went from a peak of seventy dry counties in 1909 to twenty-four in 1912 and thirty in 1914.

Despite setbacks in Indiana, the prohibition movement continued to gain momentum at the national level. The drys continued to agitate by making inflated claims about both the dangers of alcohol and the Eden of prohibition. In the end, the national prohibition debate tipped in the favor of drys. The Eighteenth Amendment, which called for total prohibition, was ratified on January 29, 1919. It had a grace period of one year. This allowed time for producers to deplete their inventories, but in actuality it allowed the public one year in which to stock up. On October 28, 1919, Congress passed the Volstead Act, which defined an intoxicating beverage as anything over one-half percent alcohol. Thus, when prohibition actually began on January 29th, 1920, beer and wine were illegal as well as whiskey and rum. The enactment of prohibition, an effort to perfect the nation, erased the work of generations of grape-growers and winemakers across the country.

The leaders who founded the United States understood the proper place of wine in the life of the nation. Ben Franklin once said that "God loves to see us happy, and therefore He gave us wine." Thomas Jefferson argued that the tax on wine ought to be low so that the common man could afford it and drink it in the place of ardent spirits. Many of the settlers who landed on our coast brought the vine, intending to enjoy its blessings. People such as Dufour and Longworth spent their fortunes and indeed their lives trying to solve the riddle of eastern American grape-growing and wine-making. The Ohio River Valley became the Rhineland of America and faded away. Missouri, New York, and California rose as the new wine regions of the nation. And then Americans, in a moment of wishful thinking, decided that they really were not very interested in their much-deserved wine heritage after all.

10. The Modern Indiana Wine Industry

THE EIGHTEENTH AMENDMENT of 1919 struck a terrible blow against American wine culture and the fledgling American wine industry. Prohibition supporters had claimed that the passage of the amendment would help curb crime, end urban poverty, and start America on the road to a moral recovery. When the general population realized that prohibition had strengthened organized crime, done nothing to address poverty, and encouraged millions of normally law-abiding citizens to break the laws and work against law enforcement officials, it became obvious that the reality of prohibition had fallen far short of the promised benefits. After the stock market crash and the advent of the Great Depression it became even harder to justify the continuance of prohibition, especially since alcohol taxation had traditionally provided the federal government with a significant portion of its revenue. When James M. Moran, prohibition commissioner, informed Congress that effective enforcement of prohibition and the Volstead Act would cost at least $300 million, the financial argument against prohibition became more persuasive. The death knell of prohibition came when wealthy individuals such as Pierre Dupont, John D. Rockefeller, and Henry Ford decided in favor of repeal. These industrialists, formerly supporters of prohibition, became mortal enemies of the law because of the government's increasing taxation of the wealthy in an effort to recoup funds that the government had previously obtained from alcohol taxes. Thus, there was little surprise when Franklin D. Roosevelt came out in favor of repeal during the presidential campaign of 1932. As Roosevelt's bid for the presidency gained steam and his campaign song, "Happy Days Are Here Again," was heard at campaign rallies, it became obvious that prohibition was in trouble. A few months later, Roosevelt's victory confirmed the country's changing opinions about alcohol. Congress repealed the Eighteenth Amendment with the passage of the Twenty-First Amendment in December of 1933, and finally, the disastrous events of 1919 could be redressed by the American wine industry.

However, depressed economic conditions and a general decline in wine knowledge among the public did not bode well for a quick return to quality wine production for the American wine industry. Many of the better-quality wine grapes in California had been replaced with grapes that shipped well. These varieties had been sent east in boxcars during prohibition to supply the rather large home wine-making industry that had developed. Even though many of the best wine grapes had been replaced by lesser-quality vineyards, these vineyards still provided California with the basis for a renewal of the industry.

The eastern wine industry also began to revive. Ohio, according to the 1938 Internal Revenue Service records, had the most wineries of any state east of the Mississippi, with 138, and produced 1,580,501 gallons of wine. New York had 123 wineries and produced 4,988,381 gallons, which made New York the major eastern wine-producing state. Indiana's northern neighbor, Michigan, had 14 wineries. Even Illinois, which had never been a major wine-producing state, could count 10 wineries. Some interest was expressed in restarting the Indiana wine industry in Vevay, Indiana. The National Grape Growers Association sent representatives to Vevay to investigate the possibility of reviving "its ancient industry." It was believed by some that "the soil of Switzerland county, where Vevay is located, is particularly adapted to the growing of grapes and berries suitable for making the finest of wines." But nothing came of the visit by the representatives. Despite the nearby successes, Indiana had no wineries, and the state, once a leader, was now not even a follower.

The primary obstacle to the reestablishment of a successful Indiana wine industry was the Liquor Control Act that had been passed in 1935 to govern the sale and distribution of alcoholic beverages. This law had been written from a temperance viewpoint and was designed to discourage alcoholic consumption. The law set up guidelines for the formation of a state alcoholic beverage commission that was to be in charge of all alcoholic beverage law enforcement. The main flaws in the law from the viewpoint of prospective vintners were rules that prevented wineries from selling directly to the public. A winery was required to obtain a class "C" permit which dictated that "a winery permit shall not authorize the holder thereof to sell to consumers, or to retailers." Wineries could only sell wine to wholesalers, who in turn sold to retailers, who then sold to the public. Breweries and distilleries were also limited to the three-tiered system, but the system was not as severe a restraint on them. Their production was based on the use of grains, which were bulk commodities and were readily available. Breweries and distilleries were not dependent on vineyards and could increase production more quickly than wineries.

The three-tiered system was not conducive to restarting the Indiana wine industry. It would have been nearly impossible for an Indiana winery to be large enough at the start to offer the volume and pricing necessary to enter its wines into the distribution system. The only reasonable option for a vintner under the 1935 law would have been to bring in bulk wine from California and bottle it for sale to a wholesaler; and in fact this was done. However, this would not have been a true "Indiana wine" because no Indiana grapes were used and no regional wine character developed. It is obvious that in 1935 the state legislators were not concerned with restarting the Indiana wine industry. Until the restrictive laws of 1935 were changed, there would be no rebirth of the Indiana wine industry.

Although Indiana failed to restart a commercial wine industry after prohibition, there was some wine being produced in the state. Throughout this period there were any number of farmers and backyard grape-growers who produced a jug of wine for the family's consumption and perhaps sold a bottle or two. This was largely due to the success of the new grape varieties (Concord, Niagara, Delaware, and many others) that were introduced in the mid- to late 1800s, allowing any individual to easily grow a few vines. These were the same varieties upon which the new wineries in New York, Michigan, and Ohio based their industries after prohibition. The ease of raising these new grapes, coupled with the trend established during prohibition toward home production, encouraged Hoosiers to make their own wine. But, judging from some of "Grandpa's special recipes" that are still in existence, an iron gut may have been a prerequisite for the consumption of some of these "country wines." The grapes could often be very acidic, especially if not fully ripened, and therefore the wines were finished sweet to balance the tartness. To keep this residual sugar from fermenting in the bottle, a high alcohol level was needed in the final product. Therefore a large quantity of sugar was added to the fermenter and the wines were allowed to work until the yeast could go no further, usually 14 percent or higher, and some unfermented sugar remained in the wine. These strong wines did little to help develop an appreciation for wine as an everyday mealtime beverage.

While Indiana languished, events were taking place in the eastern wine industry that would offer hope. First, the drinking trends of Americans started to change. This was due to several factors. One was the mass introduction of GIs to European wine-drinking culture during World War II. Another factor contributing to changing tastes was the emergence of several American wine writers. In 1933, Phillip Wagner, a Baltimore newspaper editor, wrote the first American wine text in English, *American Wines*. Another young author and enophile was Leon Adams. In 1942, he wrote a very influential book, *The Wine Study Course*. He followed this with other works on wine, all of which helped increase knowledge and educate the public's palate. In the late 1960s, there was a general trend toward consumption of drier wines, and in 1968, the sale of table wine exceeded the sale of dessert wines for the first time since prohibition. Wine was slowly regaining its position as a beverage of moderation, a drink to be consumed with meals and in pleasant company, not the domain of the brown paper bag and the town drunk. These changing consumption patterns demanded that there be more choices and greater quality in the world of American wine.

The final ingredient necessary for the success of the eastern wine industry was near at hand. A new class of grapes that was uniquely suited for the eastern American wine industry had been developed in France. The history of their development spans two continents and several generations of grape breeders. In the mid-1800s many Europeans were interested in experimenting with new grape varieties, and for years American vines had been taken to Europe. Apparently one or more of these vines contained the root louse phylloxera, and this pest was introduced into Europe. The American grapes had evolved with phylloxera and had tough, resistant roots, whereas the European grapes had weaker roots that succumbed to phylloxera attacks. The effects on the European vineyards were devastating, and whole plantings were wiped out in a matter of years. By the 1880s, many vineyards on the Continent had been lost, and there seemed to be little hope for the European wine industry.

But help was on the way from an unlikely source. The often-slandered American grape varieties provided a solution to the problem. Two methods for fighting phylloxera presented themselves. One method involved the grafting of European vines to resistant American rootstocks. This method was effective and was popular with winemakers because it maintained the traditional character of the wine. The other method for combating the pest was to cross select European and American varieties to breed resistance to phylloxera into the offspring. These new grape varieties were known as direct producers, since they produced directly from their own roots, which the grafted vines did not. They also became known as the French hybrids. The hybridizers started with the most promising American varieties that had been developed or discovered by the early American grape-growers, such as Hermann Jaeger of Missouri and Thomas V. Munson of Texas. The French grape breeders made thousands of crosses, which resulted in hundreds of new grape varieties. Most of these varieties were abandoned as unfit for wine production, but eventually a pool of grapes began to emerge which had obvious wine-making potential. These grapes had the cold-hardiness and disease resistance of the American varieties, coupled with the more delicate flavors of the European varieties. The new hybrid vines quickly gained in popularity, and the French planted them with great enthusiasm. The growers liked them because the vines were more disease resistant and the grower did not have to go through the time-consuming and expensive step of grafting. At the peak of the popularity of the direct producers, there were nearly 1 million acres planted in France alone. Eventually, the popularity of direct producers led to tighter laws against their planting and increasing attempts by the French government to discourage their use in wine. This was largely a political battle among the different wine regions of France. Southern France was opposed to hybrid grapes, since direct producers allowed more acreage to be planted in the north of France, which hurt the wine economy of the south. The restrictions led to a decline in the use of the French hybrids, yet as late as 1978 there was more wine produced in France from the hybrids than the entire volume produced in California for the same year.

The French work on hybridizing provided important benefits for the American wine industry. The vision of John James Dufour was finally realized 100 years after he confidently predicted that the secrets of grape-growing would be discovered:

> The Wise Creator has endowed the seeds of every sort of fruit, with the faculty of producing varieties, almost *ad infinitum:* at the same time, he has permitted students and learned men, to raise a corner of the veil of nature, and to peep into some of its secrets—among which they have observed, that it is by the mystery of the fecundation of one plant by another of the same family—like the crossing of breed among animals, that that miracle is performed. The time will come when country-born varieties will equal our most sanguine expectation.

It was the introduction of the new French varieties into America after prohibition that provided much of the excitement for the rebirth of the eastern wine industry.

A group of devoted eastern wine enthusiasts began the difficult work of importing, planting, and promoting the direct producers. The task would not be easy because the varieties were completely new and had not developed a reputation with the wine-drinking public. World War II isolated France from the United States and cut off the supply of vines for a period of time, but the cessation of hostilities in 1945 made the new grape varieties available once again. Individuals in the United States and Canada, including luminaries such as Adhemar De Chaunac, Charles Fournier, and Phillip and Jocelyn Wagner, began importing grapes and testing them in their own vineyards. Agricultural research stations and universities also got in on the act; institutions in the state of New York provided much of the work. Penn State, Ohio State, and Michigan State also offered assistance on the project. The efforts of these dedicated individuals, as well as the academic work supplied by the universities, slowly made the public more familiar with the direct producers and eventually caused them to be tried in Indiana. The rebirth of the Indiana industry would be based on these grapes.

The increasing knowledge of wine by the public, including a growing interest in locally produced wines, prompted several eastern states to pass laws more favorable to winery operations. The first state to pass a law favoring small wineries was Pennsylvania in 1968. The Pennsylvania law was influential in that it provided a model for the passage of similar laws in other eastern states. One important aspect of the Pennsylvania law was the recognition that wineries were different from distilleries and breweries. It emphasized the relationship between wine and agriculture by stipulating that the wine was to be made from Pennsylvania grapes, which would provide a regional character to the wines. The Pennsylvania law also set up a volume limit of 50,000 gallons. But most important, the new Pennsylvania law allowed direct sales from the tasting-room to the public visiting the winery. Following the example of Pennsylvania, other eastern states passed laws favorable to winery operations within their borders.

Indiana was still governed by the restrictive 1935 Liquor Control Act. But in the early 1970s, a new generation of wine visionaries emerged on the Indiana scene. These men realized that the legislative situation was completely unfavorable toward wineries and that only by getting the statehouse to address the inequities in the law could Indiana ever reestablish a wine industry. The improving attitudes toward wine in the East gave Indiana winemakers hope.

Perhaps the earliest Indiana wine enthusiast to plant French hybrid grapes was Dr. Donald MacDaniel, an optometrist from Connersville,

Indiana. Dr. MacDaniel had become interested in the French hybrids after reading about them. In 1958, he contacted Phillip Wagner at Boordy Vineyards and had him send some of these new varieties to Connersville. That spring, Dr. MacDaniel planted the grapes and began his experiment in Indiana wine production. His wines were well received by friends and neighbors, and soon wine-making and grape-growing became an increasingly important hobby for him.

Dr. MacDaniel was not the only person interested in wine-making. Bill Oliver, Sr., an Indiana University law professor, had also started making wine at home. In the winter of 1964–1965, he was a visiting professor at Cornell. While attending a cocktail party, he heard French hybrids mentioned and decided that it would be feasible to grow them in the Midwest. From this chance occurrence, Oliver's interest grew until he became convinced that he could grow grapes in Indiana and make Indiana wine. Bill and his wife Mary began producing wine from grapes bought in Ohio and Kentucky that were stomped by the feet of neighborhood children. Oliver's production soon grew until it was overflowing the basement of their suburban home. It became evident to Professor Oliver that his hobby could become a successful business if only the laws were more favorable to the small producer.

Jack and Joan Easley of Indianapolis also became intrigued with grape-growing and wine-making. Mr. Easley was the attorney for the Indiana Toll Road, which runs across northern Indiana. While performing his duties for the Toll Road, he took note of the Michigan orchards and vineyards that lay just across the border. Mr. Easley had heard of the French hybrid grapes through the efforts of Phillip Wagner and thought that they could be successfully grown in the Midwest. As home winemakers, the Easleys, like the Olivers and Dr. MacDaniel, were producing Indiana vintages in their own basement. They too, felt that Indiana could have a real wine industry if only the laws could be changed.

Ben Sparks, a retired naval aviator and Commander USN from Brown County, was yet another home winemaker. He had developed a taste for wine while serving in the navy. However, he found that his tastes were exceeding his budget (he was putting four sons through college), so he too began producing his own wine. A mutual friend introduced Ben Sparks to Bill Oliver, and soon the two wine enthusiasts were pooling their efforts. Ben supplied a large homemade trailer and the two of them traveled to Alexandria, Kentucky, and purchased grapes from a French hybrid vineyard.

The grapes were brought back to Bloomington, divided up, crushed, and put into the cellars of the two winemakers.

The efforts of these different individuals continued throughout the 1960s and into the 1970s. In 1966, Bill Oliver planted a vineyard of French hybrids. He selected a hilly site northwest of Bloomington and planted ten vines each of thirty-five varieties. In 1971, the Easleys planted a vineyard at Cape Sandy along the Ohio River. Because there was no assistance to be had from the academic or agricultural institutions of Indiana at that time, they hired Garth Cahoon of Ohio State University to help in the layout of the vineyard. Joan cared for the vineyard through the 1970s and 1980s. Ben Sparks also began planting a vineyard at about the same time. Dr. MacDaniel continued making wines at home from his French hybrid planting. These home winemakers and grape-growers had learned of one another's activities. It soon became evident that they had a similar view-point, namely that an Indiana wine industry was feasible if the laws were changed. Dr. MacDaniel had legislation drawn up based upon the Ohio winery laws, and at the same time Bill Oliver had legislation drawn up based on the Pennsylvania small winery act. Both men had legislators ready to carry their respective bills. Bill Oliver, with the help of some of his former law students, several of whom had become legislators and knew the right people in the right places, submitted his legislation first and it passed on April 8, 1971, as Public Law No. 77. The law was much more favorable than the previous set of rules governing Indiana wine. The restrictions prevent-ing sales directly to the public and to retailers were removed. The excessive fees that had characterized the old system were reduced. The new law specified that a "small winery" was one that produced not more than 50,000 gallons per year, did not make wine above 14 percent alcohol, and used "grapes, other fruits, or honey produced in this state." One difference from the Pennsylvania law was that under the Indiana law a small winery, "by filing an affidavit with the commission stating that grapes, grape juice, other fruits or fruit juice, or honey produced in Indiana is not obtainable, may apply for a permit to import these products." The last barrier to the reestab-lishment of the Indiana wine industry had been breached. Though decades behind many of the eastern states, Indiana was now well situated by geogra-phy, climate, and politics to join the ranks of wine-producing states. Indiana wine could once again grace Indiana tables.

The passage of the small winery act immediately spurred the opening of several Indiana wineries. In August of 1971, only four months after the law passed, Dr. MacDaniel opened Treaty Line Winery. The winery was housed in an old stone-and-timber barn on a 165-acre farm near Connersville. The opening of the winery and the planting of several acres of French hybrid grapes generated a high level of curiosity. Soon visitors were enjoying wine-tasting in the restored farmhouse and picnics on the grounds with the first bottles of commercial Indiana wine seen in many years. After the opening of Brookville Reservoir in 1974, the winery was ideally located for people who wanted to experience Hoosier hospitality and enjoy Indiana wine and the great outdoors.

Bill and Mary Oliver opened Oliver Winery on May 1st, 1973. It was located just north of Bloomington on State Highway 37. Professor Oliver hired a winemaker from California, increased the plantings in his vineyard, and began production of his own line of Indiana wines. With the backing of a group of investors, he planted a second vineyard just a mile or so west of his first planting. At first, the winery was open only on Fridays and Saturdays, but the popularity of his honey wine, Camelot Mead, encouraged Professor Oliver to expand the hours and the winery. Camelot Mead proved to be a sensation, and the Olivers even considered national distribution of Camelot Mead. There are few visitors to Indiana wineries who have not heard of Oliver Winery, and today they are the largest operation in the state, producing a full complement of award-winning wines.

Other wineries were quick to join the ranks of Indiana vintners, and by 1975 there were seven wineries in operation. Villa Medeo Vineyards Winery, owned by Mike and Liz Mancuso, was located in the beautiful Ohio River town of Madison. Jack Easley and family opened Easley Enterprises Inc., which included a winery in downtown Indianapolis and a vineyard at Cape Sandy on the Ohio River. Alvin Meier opened Swiss Valley Vineyards in 1974 in Vevay, Indiana, continuing the long wine-making tradition in that area. Carl Banholzer opened Banholzer Winecellars Ltd. in Hesston, Indiana, just south of the Indiana-Michigan border. Golden Rain Tree Winery, Inc. started operations in Wadesville a few miles west of Evansville, thus bringing back Father Rapp's southwestern Indiana wine tradition. The state was witness to the opening of wineries from the Ohio River to the Michigan border. Wine had finally returned to Indiana.

The Indiana State Fair has proven to be a special source of encouragement for the state wine industry. Like all state fairs, the Indiana State Fair started with farmers entering their agricultural products and competing against each other for the largest pig, finest cow, or best pumpkin. Over the years it has come to embrace almost every agricultural product grown in the state. Since wine is an agricultural product, it was only a matter of time until it too became a category at the state fair. Dr. Charles Thomas of Indianapolis was one of the initiators of the wine competition, and he entered many of his homemade wines in the early competitions. Today, Dr. Thomas is the owner of Chateau Thomas Winery, which is located just west of Indianapolis. It comes as a surprise to many that the Indiana State Fair wine competition is now the third largest wine competition in the country and has become an international event. Dr. Richard Vine is honorary chairman of the competition, and Ellen Harkness is coordinator. The judges are made up of wine writers, wine consultants, wine educators, vintners, grape-growers, and restaurateurs. In 2000, there were 2,505 entries competing in various categories. Of these, there were 191 entries from Indiana wineries, of which 142 were awarded medals. Every year the number of wines competing has grown, as has their renown, and the future seems truly bright for the Indiana State Fair wine competition.

One important obstacle to the newly reestablished industry was a lack of knowledge about grape-growing and wine-making techniques specific to Indiana. The little information that was available to these early producers was difficult to find and not necessarily applicable to Indiana conditions. Ben Sparks realized that Indiana needed a trade organization to further the exchange of knowledge. He had been to the Ohio Grape Wine Short Course, conducted by Ohio State University, and he felt that Indiana should have a similar program. Ben and his wife Lee were perhaps the earliest promoters of the Indiana wineries as an industry, and it was not uncommon to see Ben dressed in his lederhosen passing out stickers that said "Indiana wine—a grape idea" at wine events and meetings. In 1972 and 1973, the Sparkses began putting together the apparatus of the Indiana Winegrowers Guild, which was to be a trade organization representing both the grape-growing and wine-making interests. They wrote the by-laws of the guild and defined its goals as "the betterment of the conditions of those engaged in viticulture in Indiana, the improvement of the grade of wine grapes grown in Indiana, and the development of a higher degree of efficiency in viticulture throughout the state." The Indiana Winegrowers Guild was incorporated on July 20th, 1975. For $50, Ben's son, John Frank Sparks, designed the guild logo, and Indiana's wine trade organization was established.

The American wine industry and the federal government have been in the process of setting up delineated American viticultural areas (AVAs) since 1978. The viticultural areas are based on physical features that affect the growing conditions of the areas. Any interested person can file with the Bureau of Alcohol, Tobacco, and Firearms to establish the boundaries of an area. The filer must satisfy the following criteria:

1. Evidence that the area is known by the proposed name.

2. Historical or current evidence that the proposed boundaries of the viticultural area are correct.

3. Evidence that the geographical features of the area produce growing conditions that distinguish the proposed area from surrounding areas.

4. A narrative description of the boundaries based on features which can be found on United States Geological Survey maps of the largest applicable scale.

5. A copy of the appropriate U.S.G.S. map(s) with the boundaries marked in any prominent color.

To date, one American viticultural area has been established in Indiana. John Garrett, owner of the Villa Milan Vineyards in Milan, Indiana, proposed in 1983 that the Ohio River Valley be designated as an American viticultural area. Several months were spent in fulfilling the requirements and on October 6, 1983, the Ohio River Valley was declared a viticultural area. Its 26,000 square miles of land in West Virginia, Ohio, Kentucky, and Indiana make it the largest viticultural area in the country. At the time of its inception it only had fourteen wineries. The designation has been a useful tool for promoting grape-growing and wine production in the Ohio River Valley, and the valley has enjoyed an increase in the number of wineries.

One cannot talk about this period of Indiana wine-making without mentioning the monks at St. Meinrad Archabbey in St. Meinrad, Indiana. The Abbey of Eindiedeln in Switzerland established St. Meinrad in 1854. Two Swiss monks selected the southern Indiana site to help minister to the growing German-speaking Catholic population and to establish a seminary to educate priests. In 1991, Russ Bridenbaugh, wine writer for the *Indianapolis News*, visited the monks at St. Meinrad. Mr. Bridenbaugh toured the vineyard with Brother Dominic. The vineyard was laid out on a hilltop about a mile from the archabbey itself, near the Monte Cassino Chapel. This was the second vineyard of the archabbey, the first having been on the campus. The oldest vines in the vineyard date from 1954. They were of the Concord variety and their gnarled trunks gave testimony to their longevity.

They shared their hilltop perch with Steuben, Foch, DeChaunac, Leon Millot, and even the remnants of a Vinifera planting, of which only three struggling Merlot vines remained. The Vinifera vines had been the inspiration of Brother David, who had studied with Dr. Constantine Frank in New York. Brother David brought great improvements in viticulture and wine-making to St. Meinrad. Mr. Bridenbaugh tasted a 1980 Chardonnay made by Brother David. He described the rare bottle of wine as being "quite intriguing, and still very palatable. It was a bright gold color and smelled of very ripe grapes with a unique flavor I found sharing equal parts of wildness and domestication."

Brother Dominic explained to Mr. Bridenbaugh that wine was served every night at the archabbey for supper and every day at mass. Leon Millot was his favorite wine-making grape, but he added that the deer also liked these grapes. He wryly remarked, "We've tried about everything except shooting them, so I suppose they will have their share." Brother Benjamin headed the wine-making operation housed in the old meat-packing building. He said that they made about 8,000 bottles per year, all of which was consumed by the 140 monks at the archabbey. The bottles were unlabeled and unmarked, but Brother Benjamin knew which was which and got the proper wines to their rightful place for whatever occasion. Anyone who attended the Indiana Winegrowers Guild meetings in the 1980s will remember one or another of the St. Meinrad monks delivering grace at the noon meal. Sadly, the vineyard of St. Meinrad was plowed under in 1995 and returned to pasture land. As Brother Benjamin recently explained to the authors, the time and effort required to grow and make their own wine could no longer be justified.

Since the passage of the Indiana small winery law in 1971, individuals within the industry have initiated numerous changes to the state laws in an effort to bring Indiana up to par with other commercial wine-producing states (see the list of laws in Appendix B). One of the more important changes in the state laws concerned Sunday sales. Gerald Huber of Huber Orchard Winery in Borden, Indiana, initiated the change in this law in 1982. It allowed wineries to sell wine by the bottle on Sunday for carryout. The law recognized that Indiana wineries are heavily tourist based and that Sunday is one of the biggest tourist travel days of the week. It has greatly helped the small wineries that often make a large portion of their sales on weekends. In 1985, Bill Oliver, Sr., initiated legislation that allowed a winery to have one off-premise tasting and salesroom location. While less than half the wineries have taken advantage of the second tasting-room permit, in certain situations it has provided wineries with all of their retail sales.

In 1989 Jim Butler, owner of Butler Winery and Vineyards in Bloomington, Indiana, initiated legislation that established the Indiana Wine Grape Council. The council is funded by a penny per bottle of the Indiana state excise tax paid on wine. The council's mission is to enhance the Indiana economy by establishing a successful wine and grape industry. In order to do this, the council is in charge of implementing grape and wine research and market development. The effort is focused on improving the quality of Indiana wines, selecting and matching grape varieties to the Indiana soil and climate, and promoting Indiana wines to consumers. This has been a great stimulus to the industry. In the ten years since its passage, the number of wineries in the state has doubled, the number of gallons produced has increased by 400 percent, and grape acreage has increased by 300 percent. The program is administered by the Purdue University School of Agriculture. It set up a group of wine and grape experts at Purdue, which provides the state with a source of help for its growers and winemakers. The program created faculty positions in enology and viticulture, a marketing specialist position, and one in market promotion. The able personnel hired by Purdue University have ensured the success of the program. Dr. Richard Vine, a former Michigan winemaker, author of several important texts for the wine industry, and wine consultant to American Airlines, was hired as the enologist. He is a highly respected member of the American wine industry and a real asset to the Purdue program. He is now semi-retired but continues to teach a very popular wine appreciation course at Purdue.

Ellen Harkness oversees the wine quality lab at Purdue. She is responsible for the analysis of wines, the improvement of wine quality, and organizing workshops to share this knowledge. She is on the board of directors of the American Wine Society Educational Foundation and was elected chairperson of the eastern section of the American Society for Enology and Viticulture, an international professional wine-growing society.

Dr. Bruce Bordelon is the viticulturalist for the Purdue program. He was hired to help Indiana growers improve grape quality, productivity, and profitability. He has been recognized nationally for his research on small fruits as well as for his viticulture research. One of the most important programs that Professor Bordelon started was the establishment of several research vineyards in the state, which has allowed him to collect climate, pest, and disease information for different regions. Under his tutelage it has been much easier for prospective vineyard owners to make informed decisions, and, as a result, there has been an increase in grape acreage planted.

Several people have served in the marketing position. The first person hired was Theresa Browning, who worked diligently to spread the word about Indiana wines. Cheri Wagner served in the position for a short time after Theresa Browning. Sally Linton, a graduate of Indiana University, now serves as the marketing specialist. She has multiple duties, which include developing and distributing all promotional materials on Indiana wine, leading wine-tasting events, conducting workshops throughout the state, and making public presentations on Indiana wine. Sally is an active member of the Public Relations Society of America and a member of the American Wine Society.

In recent years, there has been a renewed interest in wine-growing in Vevay, Indiana. Paul Ogle, an elderly gentleman of some wealth, wanted to see wine-making return to his hometown. He purchased a large quantity of land in Vevay and made plans for a winery, golf course, and marina complex. He built the Ogle House Inn just below the center of town. Some of the land Ogle purchased included the terraced vineyard site that had once belonged to Jean Daniel Morerod. Ogle cleared the old vineyard site and purchased grapevines for replanting the terraces. When he died at the age of 83 in March of 1989, his vision for Morerod's old hillside vineyard and a new winery complex died with him, but he left behind two foundations that continue to support various community projects in Vevay.

Mr. Ogle also owned the land that had once belonged to Louis Gex-Oboussier, upon which stood an old cabin. Tom and Donna Weaver discovered the significance of the cabin in 1992 and organized Musée de Venoge in 1996, a not-for-profit group whose goal was to purchase and preserve the cabin. The cabin and thirty acres are in the process of being restored to their 1816 appearance, complete with vineyards, fields, and a nature preserve. Eventually, the cabin and grounds will be open for tours by appointment. A living history weekend, during which costumed interpreters explain and demonstrate various aspects of frontier life, is held in October. The timber-frame cottage is typical of French construction in the lower Mississippi Valley but is very rare in the Ohio River Valley, making the Musée de Venoge a special example of early French-Swiss settlement.

In the spring of 1999, the authors had the privilege of touring Vevay in the company of Tom Demaree, co-proprietor of The Ridge Winery. The town remains a small, close-knit river community. The early Swiss wine industry has not been entirely forgotten. While some of the artifacts are hidden or inaccessible, other physical remains are easily found and are celebrated by the townspeople. The Switzerland County Historical Society has displays of early implements used in farming and wine-making. The annual Swiss wine festival, held every year on the third weekend of August, celebrates the region's wine heritage. The street names are another link to the past. Names such as Tell street (named after Swiss hero William Tell) hark back to the traditions of the Old World. Other names, such as Liberty Street and Union Street, reflect the values of the Swiss immigrants' adopted land. And finally, streets with names such as Market Street, Vineyard Street, and Ferry Street recall landmarks of days gone by. Historic documents, including an original copy of Dufour's *The Vine-Dresser's Guide* and Jean Daniel Morerod's account books, are preserved in the vault of one local bank. The Vevay Public Library has a very well-preserved copy of Dufour's rare book, which, amazingly, had been in circulation to the general public until very recently. Many old buildings still stand, and Vevay has a delightful walking tour of the main town area with historical markers denoting significant structures. Some of the original settlers' dwellings are still to be found, including Perret Dufour's home, John Francis Dufour's home, the Roxy house (the home where Twonnet lived in Edward Eggleston's story), and the Morerod home.

The Morerod home is an amazing example of the preservation of Vevay's wine history. The exterior of the home is perfectly preserved, although now approached from the rear, since the road in front of the house was washed away years ago by the Ohio River. As one gazes at the handsome exterior, one would be hard-pressed to believe that the home's greatest treasure was concealed in the cellar. One of Morerod's two great wine casks has been quietly resting in the cellar for nearly 200 years. The back end of the cask has collapsed, but the head facing into the room is still largely intact, as are most of the staves, which is amazing considering the age, changes in ownership, and climate in the cellar. It is also contrary to what had been written about the cask. One of Morerod's descendants, Julie LeClerc Knox, related in an article in 1922 that the casks had been taken apart a few months earlier to remove them from the cellar so that the floor could be repaired. A Hohenberger photograph of 1924 shows two barrels in the cellar still intact. Apparently the existing cask was either reassembled or, more likely, the story was not entirely true. In 1944, she wrote that there was only one barrel in the cellar, which is the case today. This has to be the oldest commercial wine cask in the country and the only one remaining from America's first successful commercial wine industry; it begs for some form of preservation or restoration. Some of Morerod's old vineyard terraces are still visible on the large hill behind the town (these terraces were redone by Paul Ogle) and present a pleasing spectacle that could be improved upon only by the addition of vines.

Morerod casks. This photograph of the 1920s shows Father Morerod's two "great tuns" that were described in the *National Intelligencer* of Washington, D.C., in 1819. When the casks were put in the cellar, one of the casks was full of the vintage of 1818 and was to be kept for eighteen months to two years. The construction of this wine cellar is unique. Wedge-shaped bricks were placed between angled ceiling rafters to increase the thermal mass of the cellar to help maintain constant temperature. (Courtesy of Lilly Library)

Morerod cask, modern photo. This photo was taken in the fall of 1999. There were originally two barrels, but by 1944 only one cask remained. This is the oldest barrel used for commercial wine production in the country. It is one of the great relics of the Vevay wine industry.

After touring the Morerod cellar, the authors and company proceeded to the site of John James Dufour's house and gravesite. We drove several miles east through Markland and down an unpaved farm lane across a field toward the river and parked next to an abandoned tobacco barn, where we were surprised to find that one wall of Dufour's home still stands. A search of the woods to the south of the building turned up the remains of several headstones tumbled on the forest floor, all of them for John James's grandchildren, but there was no visible evidence of John James's crypt or of his final resting place among the overgrowth. Because of a description of the area given in the 1940s by Julie LeClerc Knox, we are convinced that this is the location of Dufour's grave. Perhaps his remains are still there to be found under the tangle of briars and vines.

John James Dufour house, modern photo. The authors were surprised to find that part of Dufour's brick house still stands. The brick walls have spaces for long window openings. These same long windows are noticeable in the 1920s photograph. The old family cemetery where Dufour was buried lies in the woods behind the house. This forgotten relic from the past would make a fine memorial to Dufour.

In many ways the physical remains of Vevay's wine industry have deteriorated, and, without preservation, could be completely lost within a few years. Dufour's crypt disappeared long ago, and his headstone is missing. His house has tumbled in, and the vineyards are gone. One of Morerod's casks is gone and the other is slowly collapsing. There are few people in Switzerland County who know where Dufour's grave and house are located, and the extent and importance of what Dufour accomplished have faded from memory. Vevay is on the cusp of change. A large riverboat casino complex has been built just east of the remains of his house, and there are plans to upgrade the road from Markland Dam to the interstate highway a few miles away in Kentucky. The effect that these projects will have on the community is hard to predict, yet they will undoubtedly bring Vevay closer to our modern world and take the town farther away from its Swiss roots.

On the other hand, historic preservation is going on in Vevay, and the inhabitants seem to have a growing interest in their town's rich heritage. Societies such as the Switzerland County Historical Society and the Musée de Venoge are taking on the task of preserving and educating. Many buildings have been restored or, like Gex's cabin, are in the process of being restored. While the physical relics of America's earliest commercial winemaking may or may not be preserved for the ages, it is the intangible aspect that appears certain to survive. The pioneering spirit of John James Dufour, Father Morerod, and Father Rapp is the true tradition of the Indiana wine industry, and it is this heritage that is happily continued every year with every grape harvested and every bottle of wine produced in Indiana. Such is Indiana's legacy, and what a handsome legacy it is.

The recognition and long-term success of the Indiana wine industry will be dependent upon the extent to which grapes are grown in the state and the degree to which Indiana residents support their native industry. Indiana-grown wines reflect our soil, our climate, and our heritage. The quality of the wines produced in Indiana today has been proven by the awards that wineries have won in competitions from coast to coast. Dufour dealt with a prejudice against "home made" almost 200 years ago. Perhaps that prejudice has begun to turn into a pride in Indiana-made, and, as John James Dufour had hoped, Hoosiers can enjoy wine made "out of the very ground they tread."

11. The Modern Indiana Wineries

THE WORK OF THE SWISS at Vevay, the Germans at New Harmony, and Nicholas Longworth in Cincinnati laid the foundation for the American wine industry. Though their dreams were in many ways unfulfilled, a strange and slow evolution has brought the modern wine industry back to Indiana.

Surely it would warm the heart of John James Dufour to see the rebirth of the Indiana wine industry and its growing and vibrant status. At the time of this writing there are twenty-eight bonded wineries in operation, of which twenty-four are open to the public for retail sales. Wineries have sprung up across the state, and vineyards are planted from Lake Michigan to the Ohio River. (See Appendix C for a list of wineries that have opened since 1971.)

What follows is a snapshot of wineries operating in Indiana today. It is our hope that the reader, armed with knowledge of the past, will travel the state and taste the promise of the future. Please be aware that with a rapidly growing and changing industry, the following list of wineries will very soon be outdated. Up-to-date information can be found at:

www.indianawines.org

NORTHERN INDIANA
Ⓐ Andersons Orchard and Winery
Ⓑ Dune Ridge Winery
Ⓒ Lake Michigan Winery

CENTRAL INDIANA
Ⓓ Chateau Thomas Winery
Ⓔ Easley Winery
Ⓧ Ferrin Fruit Winery
Ⓕ Gaia Wines
Ⓖ Terre Vin Winery

SOUTH CENTRAL
Ⓗ Butler Winery
Ⓘ Butler Vineyard
Ⓙ Brown County Winery
Ⓚ Chateau Thomas Winery
Ⓛ Oliver Winery
Ⓨ Shadey Lake Winery
Ⓜ Simmons Winery

SOUTHERN INDIANA
Ⓝ Chateau Pomije
Ⓞ French Lick Winery
Ⓟ Huber Orchard, Winery
Ⓠ Kauffman Winery
Ⓡ Lanthier Winery
Ⓢ Lanthier Winery Main Street
Ⓣ Madison Vineyards
Ⓤ The Ridge Winery
Ⓥ Thomas Family Winery
Ⓦ Villa Milan Vineyard

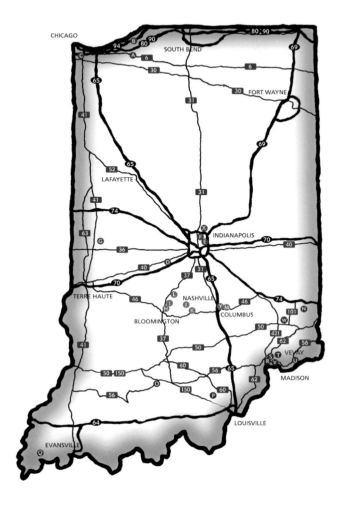

Indiana Wineries

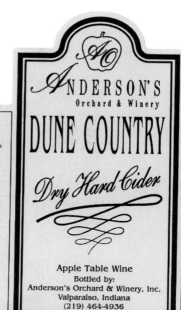

A bit of History:

A family tradition originating in 1927, Anderson's Orchard has grown from a small roadside market to the most beautiful 40 acre family attraction spot in Porter County, Indiana. In 1954, Bill Anderson expanded the family business to its present location with a goal of planting one thousand apple trees each year until the highest ridge in Porter County abounded with apples. Bill exceeded his goal and today the sun shines on over five thousand magnificent fruit-filled trees. "Rosey Bill", one of our own varieties (named after its founder) is just one of over twenty assorted cooking and eating apples you can find in our orchard.

And what better way to complement apples than the introduction of Porter County's first winery established in 1994.

ANDERSON'S
Orchard & Winery

DUNE COUNTRY

Dry Hard Cider

Apple Table Wine
Bottled by:
Anderson's Orchard & Winery, Inc.
Valparaiso, Indiana
(219) 464-4936

GOVERNMENT WARNING: (1) ACCORDING TO THE SURGEON GENERAL, WOMEN SHOULD NOT DRINK ALCOHOLIC BEVERAGES DURING PREGNANCY BECAUSE OF THE RISK OF BIRTH DEFECTS. (2) CONSUMPTION OF ALCOHOLIC BEVERAGES IMPAIRS YOUR ABILITY TO DRIVE A CAR OR OPERATE MACHINERY, AND MAY CAUSE HEALTH PROBLEMS.

CONTAINS SULFITES

7 91130 01004 4

Anderson's Orchard and Winery

Owners: David and Kathy Lundstrom

Address: 430 East U.S. Highway 6, Valparaiso, IN 46383

Phone Number: 219-464-4936

Web site: andersonsvineyard.com

Bonded Winery Number: BW-IN-32 (1994)

Total Acres of Grapes Planted: 10

Varieties of Grapes Planted: Cabernet Sauvignon, Riesling, Traminette, Vignoles, Seyval, Vidal, Chardonel, Foch, N.Y.70.0808.10, N.Y.73.0136.17, Frontenac, Vanessa, Jupiter, and Mars

Types of Wine Made: Very light fruity table wines

DAVE LUNDSTROM first became interested in eastern wineries in 1975. But it wasn't until 1994 that David and his wife Kathy purchased Anderson's Orchard near Valparaiso, Indiana, and started a winery. This 40-acre farm, dating back to 1927, consisted of 5,000 apple trees planted on the highest ridge in Porter County. The winery opened in 1994 and since then has grown to become a family-oriented attraction. It currently offers orchard and winery tours, U-pick apples, a pumpkin patch, a country market and sculpture garden, a bakery, and, of course, a selection of wines. One of their specialties is a dessert-style rhubarb wine. The Lundstroms are renovating the apple orchard and increasing their grape plantings. Dave was elected president of the Indiana Winegrowers Guild in 1999, which should come as little surprise, since he loves the business, and maintains that it has always been a dream of his to open a winery.

CONTAINS SULFITES   FOR SALE IN INDIANA ONLY

Brown County
Winery

Seyval Blanc

Produced and Bottled by Brown County
Wine Company Inc., Nashville, IN BW-IN-19
4520 State Road 46 East, Nashville, IN 47448
Ph. (812) 988-6144   Alcohol 11% by volume

GOVERNMENT WARNING: (1) ACCORDING TO THE SURGEON GEN-
ERAL, WOMEN SHOULD NOT DRINK ALCOHOLIC BEVERAGES DUR-
ING PREGNANCY BECAUSE OF THE RISK OF BIRTH DEFECTS. (2)
CONSUMPTION OF ALCOHOLIC BEVERAGES IMPAIRS YOUR ABIL-
ITY TO DRIVE A CAR OR OPERATE MACHINERY, AND MAY CAUSE
HEALTH PROBLEMS.

Brown County Winery

Owners: Dave and Cynthia Schrodt (majority stockholders)

Address: 4520 State Road 46 E., Nashville, IN 47448

Phone Number: 812-988-6144

Web site: browncountywinery.com

Second Tasting-Room: Old School Way, Nashville, IN 47448; phone
    812-988-8646

Bonded Winery Number: BW-IN-19 (1986)

Total Acres of Grapes Planted: None

Types of Wine Made: Labrusca, fruit wines, and French hybrids

DAVE AND CYNTHIA SCHRODT opened Brown County Winery in 1986. Dave had formerly been the winemaker at Oliver Winery. Cynthia was the executive director of Girls Incorporated of Monroe County. The winery is located in Gnaw Bone, Indiana. A second wine-tasting and salesroom location is behind the Nashville House restaurant in downtown Nashville. The Schrodts have attracted a steady following of loyal customers over the years, who enjoy their light fruity wines and convenient location. They carry a range of grape and fruit wines, which are available for free tasting, and they also have a selection of wine-related gifts in their shop. Open every day.

GOVERNMENT WARNING: (1) ACCORDING TO THE SURGEON GENERAL, WOMEN SHOULD NOT DRINK ALCOHOLIC BEVERAGES DURING PREGNANCY BECAUSE OF THE RISK OF BIRTH DEFECTS. (2) CONSUMPTION OF ALCOHOLIC BEVERAGES IMPAIRS YOUR ABILITY TO DRIVE A CAR OR OPERATE MACHINERY, AND MAY CAUSE HEALTH PROBLEMS.

ALCOHOL 12% BY VOLUME • CONTAINS SULFITES

Butler Vineyards

Indiana
Chambourcin
1999

PRODUCED & BOTTLED BY THE BUTLER WINERY, INC. • 6200 E. ROBINSON RD. • BLOOMINGTON, IN 47408

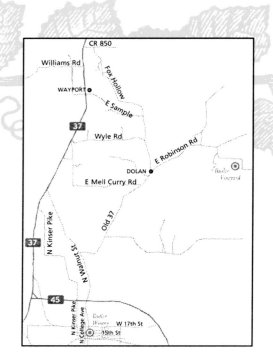

Butler Winery and Vineyards

Owners: Jim and Susan Butler

Address: 6200 E. Robinson Rd., Bloomington, IN 47408

Phone Number: 812-339-7233

Web site: butlerwinery.com

Second Tasting-Room: 1022 N. College Ave., Bloomington, IN 47404

Bonded Winery Number: BW-IN-14 (1983)

Total Acres of Grapes Planted: 4

Varieties of Grapes Planted: Vignoles, Chambourcin, and Chardonel

Types of Wine Made: Chambourcin, Chardonel, Vignoles, Seyval,
Labrusca blends, blueberry, blackberry, black currant, and
hard cider

JIM BUTLER received an undergraduate degree in biology from Indiana University and a master's degree from the University of Minnesota in freshwater biology. He got his start in the Indiana wine industry in 1976 doing lab and cellar work at the Oliver Winery. He was the Olivers' winemaker from 1977 until 1982, when he left to start his own winery. His wife Susan is an office manager for a development company in Bloomington and manages the vineyard tasting-room. Butler Winery opened in December of 1983. From the winery's inception it has focused on producing quality wine from Indiana-grown grapes. Jim also became involved in the Indiana Wine Growers Guild, where he held the position of president from the mid-1980s to the mid-1990s. In 1991, the Butlers purchased land nine miles northeast of Bloomington and began planting a vineyard. In the fall of 1998, they opened a tasting- and salesroom at the vineyard. In the fall of 1999, they moved the entire wine-production process to the vineyard. The in-town location continues to be a wine-tasting and sales location featuring Butler wines as well as a complete line of home wine-making and brewing supplies. The vineyard location offers wine-tasting and sales to the general public as well as to private groups and catered events.

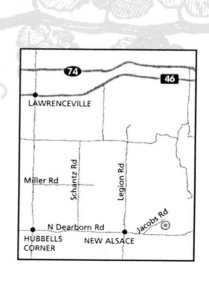

Chateau Pomije

Owner: Terry Shumrick

Address: 25060 Jacob's Road, Guilford, IN 47022

Phone Number: 812-623-4261

Bonded Winery Number: BW-IN-21 (1986)

Total Acres of Grapes Planted: 58

Varieties of Grapes Planted: Vidal Blanc, Concord, Seyval Blanc, Cabernet, Chardonnay, Merlot, and Riesling

Types of Wine Made: Same as varieties planted

CHATEAU POMIJE is located on 100 acres of rolling hills in southeastern Indiana near the town of Guilford. The vineyards were started in 1973, and they have grown from just two acres of French hybrids to eighteen acres of Vinifera and forty acres of hybrids. The winery opened in 1986 and is located in a renovated timbered barn that was originally built in 1891. A restaurant, featuring an enormous 7,000-stone fireplace, is located on the main level and the winery is located below. Grassy lawns lead from the restaurant to a 3-acre lake, which is visible from the dining room through expansive windows. The restaurant features steaks, pork tenderloins, BBQ ribs, and chicken, all served with fresh vegetables, homegrown salads, and bread. The restaurant can accommodate wedding receptions, group tours, and corporate meetings of up to 250 people. A small fee allows the visitor to sample half a dozen of the Schumricks' wines.

North America's premium vineyards in
Rutherford, Napa gave us grapes with rich
extract, spice, and breed. Aged in
American oak, this wine was then blended
with Cabernet Franc for suppleness.
Balanced flavors of cassis, chocolate,
violets, and olives frame the full body.
Serve with red meats, game, yellow cheeses.

International award-winning vinifera wines made
in Indiana from the finest California grapes by
Chateau Thomas Winery, 6291 Cambridge Way,
Plainfield, IN 46168-7904. For more information
call 1-888-761-WINE or check our web site:
www.chateauthomas.com

GOVERNMENT WARNING:
(1) ACCORDING TO THE SURGEON GENERAL,
WOMEN SHOULD NOT DRINK ALCOHOLIC
BEVERAGES DURING PREGNANCY BECAUSE
OF THE RISK OF BIRTH DEFECTS.
(2) CONSUMPTION OF ALCOHOLIC BEVERAGES
IMPAIRS YOUR ABILITY TO DRIVE A CAR OR
OPERATE MACHINERY, AND MAY CAUSE
HEALTH PROBLEMS.

CHATEAU THOMAS WINERY

CABERNET SAUVIGNON
1991 NAPA

PRODUCED AND BOTTLED AT INDIANAPOLIS, IN
BY CHATEAU THOMAS WINERY

TABLE WINE   CONTAINS SULFITES
AVAILABLE ONLY IN INDIANA

Chateau Thomas Winery

Owners: Charles R. and Jill F. Thomas, stockholders
Address: 6291 Cambridge Way, Plainfield, IN 46168
Phone Number: 317-837-9463 or 1-888-761-WINE
Web site: chateauthomas.com
Second Tasting-Room: 225 S. Van Buren St., Suite 3, Nashville, IN 47448
Bonded Winery Number: BW-IN-15 (1984)
Total Acres of Grapes Planted: None
Types of Wine Made: Vinifera wines only

CHARLES R. THOMAS, M.D., is an obstetrician-gynecologist who practiced on the south side of Indianapolis for thirty-two years. In 1970, he became interested in wine-making as a home winemaker. He entered numerous wine competitions and joined several wine groups. He and two other enthusiasts were instrumental in starting the wine competition at the Indiana State Fair in 1974. In 1984, he received his federal winery license and began making Vinifera wines from grapes imported from California, largely because of the unavailability of these grapes locally. The mission of the winery is to produce only Vinifera wines. The first locations of the winery were on the south side of Indianapolis; it moved to a downtown location in 1987, just south of Union Station. That facility was vacated in 1994 and a search began for a new location. In 1994, a retail location was established in Nashville, Indiana, where free tasting, wine sales, and snacks are available. In 1996, Dr. Thomas purchased a site on the south edge of Plainfield for a new winery. The winery purchases grapes from California and Oregon. The grapes are pressed or crushed and then transported to the winery in Plainfield. The winery has a 2,400-square-foot banquet facility area. Current production is 5,000 cases annually.

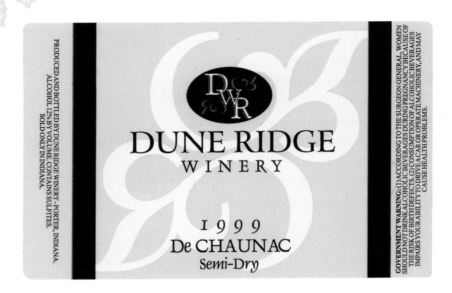

PRODUCED AND BOTTLED BY DUNE RIDGE WINERY - PORTER, INDIANA. ALCOHOL 12% BY VOLUME. CONTAINS SULFITES. SOLD ONLY IN INDIANA.

DUNE RIDGE
W I N E R Y

1 9 9 9
De CHAUNAC
Semi-Dry

GOVERNMENT WARNING: (1) ACCORDING TO THE SURGEON GENERAL, WOMEN SHOULD NOT DRINK ALCOHOLIC BEVERAGES DURING PREGNANCY BECAUSE OF THE RISK OF BIRTH DEFECTS. (2) CONSUMPTION OF ALCOHOLIC BEVERAGES IMPAIRS YOUR ABILITY TO DRIVE A CAR OR OPERATE MACHINERY, AND MAY CAUSE HEALTH PROBLEMS.

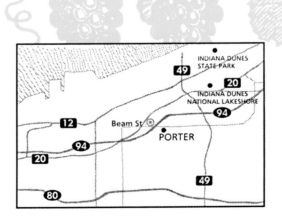

Dune Ridge Winery

Owners: Ken and Kathy Holevinsky

Address: 1240 Beam Street, Porter, IN 46304

Phone Number: 219-926-5532

Web site: duneridgewinery.com

Bonded Winery Number: BW-IN-39 (1996)

Total Acres of Grapes Planted: None

Types of Wine Made: Vidal Blanc, Seyval Blanc, Muscat, cherry, DeChaunac, Chancellor, Blush, Chardonnay, Riesling, and Zinfandel

THIS FAMILY-OWNED winery has been producing wine in small batches since the winery's opening in June of 1998. Owners Ken and Kathy Holevinsky have located their operation in a 1940s-era motor lodge that has been converted into a wine cellar, tasting-room, and blending and bottling facility. They draw on their previous work experience to handcraft their wines. Ken is a mechanical engineer with experience in production management and machinery. Kathy has a degree in microbiology and experience in clinical labs and medical research. Dune Ridge Winery is located only an hour outside of Chicago and minutes from I-80/90 and I-94. The winery grounds consist of a wooded acre at the edge of the Indiana Dunes National Lakeshore, part of the National Park Service. Visitors to the dunes area can add free wine-tasting, a winery tour, and picnicking to the many recreational activities the region has to offer.

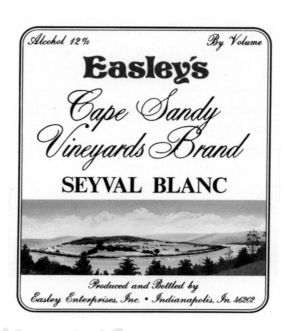

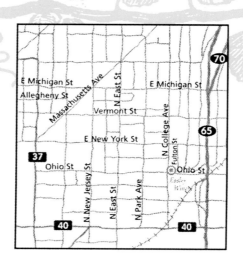

Easley Winery

Owners: Easley Enterprises Inc.

Address: 205 N. College Ave., Indianapolis, IN 46202

Phone Number: 317-636-4516

Web site: easleywine.com

Bonded Winery Number: BW-IN-5 (1974)

Total Acres of Grapes Planted: 18

Varieties of Grapes Planted: French hybrids and Labrusca

Types of Wine Made: Grape wines, champagne, honey mead, cherry
wine, blackberry and raspberry wine, warm mulled wine

IN THE LATE 1960S, Jack Easley was an Indianapolis attorney and
Joan Easley owned Community Market Research Company. The Easleys
helped generate early interest in renewing the Indiana wine industry in
1970 and 1971. They had several meetings in their home in Indianapolis
and helped form a group to change the Indiana prohibition laws. In June
1971, the Easleys secured the land for their vineyard in Crawford County
on the bluffs of the Ohio River. Starting in 1972, a total of 43 acres were
planted with 12 varieties of grapes. In 1974, Jack purchased the former
Fertig Ice Cream plant in downtown Indianapolis, and in June of 1974 he
received a permit to open his winery. The winery has continued to expand
—in 1984 the Easleys purchased a mechanical harvester, in 1986 they
added an automatic bottling line, and in 1997 they added a banquet room.
The original vineyard has since been reduced to eighteen acres, as undesirable varieties have been culled out. Additional grapes are purchased from
other growers in southern Indiana. The winery specializes in sweet, fruity
wines for non-traditional wine-drinkers, which are sold at the winery and
local retail outlets. The winery also sells home beer- and wine-making
supplies, as well as fresh juice in season.

Ferrin's Fruit Winery

Owners: David and Mary Ann Ferrin
Address: 89 First Ave., SW, Carmel, IN 46032
Phone Number: 317-566-9463
Web site: ferrinsfruitwinery.com
Bonded Winery Number: BW-IN-46 (2000)
Total Acres of Grapes Planted: None
Types of Wine Made: Four grape wines and seven fruit wines

SEVERAL YEARS AGO David Ferrin went out to buy a wine rack and returned with a wine-making kit. Since then he has left his 35-year career as a video engineer and become a professional winemaker. He purchased a building in downtown Carmel that previously housed a business office and put in a winery. Visitors can sit at tables or stand at the bar and taste wines that include names such as "Taste of Love," "Crimson Cranberry," "Maiden's Veil," and "Eve's Forbidden Fruit." According to David, "This is not ordinary wine. These are fun, drinkable wines." In the rear of the building is a room called the Speak Easy, a takeoff on the hidden taverns of the 1920s prohibition era. The room can be rented for parties or other events. "I just want people to come here and have a good time," says David.

BEECHWOOD MANSION

French Lick Red

Table Wine

French Lick, Indiana

A Bit of History

Built in 1915, The Beechwood Mansion was home to Ed Ballard, a fabulously wealthy local entrepreneur whose holdings included hotels, casinos, and six circuses including the Buffalo Bill Show. Among the celebrities who mingled at the mansion were composer Irving Berlin, fighter Joe Louis and public enemy number one — Al Capone.

Today, The Beechwood Mansion is home to The French Lick Wine and Coffee Company, where the natural temperature of the mansion's 3000 sq. ft. cellar is ideal for wine production and aging.

Enjoy an educational cellar tour and tasting of fine vinifera, French American, American classic and premium fruit wines, as well as coffees from around the world. Case discounts and in-state shipping available.

GOVERNMENT WARNING: (1) ACCORDING TO THE SURGEON GENERAL, WOMEN SHOULD NOT DRINK ALCOHOLIC BEVERAGES DURING PREGNANCY BECAUSE OF THE RISK OF BIRTH DEFECTS. (2) CONSUMPTION OF ALCOHOLIC BEVERAGES IMPAIRS YOUR ABILITY TO DRIVE A CAR OR OPERATE MACHINERY, AND MAY CAUSE HEALTH PROBLEMS.

CONTAINS SULFITES

Cellared & Bottled by:
French Lick Winery
French Lick, Indiana 47432

For sale in Indiana only.

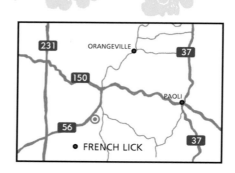

French Lick Wine & Coffee Company

Owners: John & Kim Doty

Address: 8498 W. State Road 56, P.O. Box 169, French Lick, IN 47432

Phone Number: 812-936-2293 or 1-888-494-6380

Bonded Winery Number: BW-IN-34 (1995)

Total Acres of Grapes Planted: 3

Varieties of Grapes Planted: Norton, Vidal, Munson, Vincent, Chambourcin, and Traminette

Types of Wine Made: Native American, French hybrids, fruit, and Vinifera wines

KIM AND JOHN DOTY established the French Lick Winery in 1995. John is a full-time winemaker, and his wife Kim is a postmaster. The winery is located in the historic Beechwood Mansion, a beautiful home that is ideally situated between the area's major tourist attractions, the fashionable French Lick Springs Resort, and the newly restored West Baden Springs Hotel, which boasts a huge dome sometimes referred to as the Eighth Wonder of the World. Wines are produced in the mansion's 3,000-square-foot cellar. John oversees all aspects of the process, from fermentation to the finished product. Kim, an American Wine Society certified judge, works with John to create the blends that go into each wine. The winery has received over 190 gold, silver, and bronze medals since its opening. Currently twenty-five wines are produced under the Beechwood Mansion label. They range from traditional grape wines such as Riesling and Cabernet to the less traditional cherry, blackberry, and rhubarb. All of the wines are available for tasting in the west solarium tasting-room. The tasting-room also offers wine-related gifts, gourmet coffees, teas, and gift baskets. Beechwood Mansion also houses a restaurant and bed and breakfast under different ownership.

Sofa Sisters

Paintings and Serigraphs by
R.J. Hohimer
1-800-876-7450

About the wine

Gaia Wines (guy a: greek
goddess of earth) celebrates
the gifts of earth and the
traditions of wine making.

Our vision is to bring an
enjoyable and educational
experience to an urban
contemporary setting.

LIVE LIFE!
LOVE EARTH!
DRINK GAIA WINES!

Est. 1995
317-634-WINE

Sunset White

GAIA
WINES

AMERICAN WINE
Vidal
Alcohol 10.5% by Volume

Low levels of sulfur dioxide are a natural by-product of wine fermentation. Those with allergies, please note:

CONTAINS SULFITES For those who may not know that wine is meant to enhance food and be consumed moderately, please note:

GOVERNMENT WARNING: (1) ACCORDING TO THE SURGEON GENERAL, WOMEN SHOULD NOT DRINK ALCOHOLIC BEVERAGES DURING PREGNANCY BECAUSE OF THE RISK OF BIRTH DEFECTS. (2) CONSUMPTION OF ALCOHOLIC BEVERAGES IMPAIRS YOUR ABILITY TO DRIVE A CAR OR OPERATE MACHINERY, AND MAY CAUSE HEALTH PROBLEMS.

Produced and bottled by Gaia Wines, Indianapolis, Indiana

Gaia Wines

Owner: Angee D. Walberry

Address: 608 Massachusetts Ave., Indianapolis, IN 46204

Phone Number: 317-634-WINE

Web site: gaiawines.com

Bonded Winery Number: BW-IN-38 (1996)

Total Acres of Grapes Planted: None

Types of Wine Made: Labrusca (Concord, Catawba), fruit, rose petal, mead, sparkling wine, and some Vinifera (Merlot, Chardonnay, and Cabernet Sauvignon)

GAIA WINES opened in May of 1996. Angee Walberry, winemaker and owner of Gaia Wines, is the first woman to own and operate a winery in Indiana. In fact, Gaia Wines is the only solely woman-owned and -operated winery in the country. Gaia (pronounced "guy-a," named after the Greek goddess of the earth) is located in the interesting brick cellars beneath a building in the growing Massachusetts Avenue art district in downtown Indianapolis. The winery offers a contemporary setting in an urban environment. Much of the decor and many of the architectural features come from historic Indianapolis buildings, such as the old downtown L. S. Ayres Building. The winery offers an array of events, including wine appreciation classes, Sunday Jazz, holiday theme parties, and Comedy Improv. The wines range from dry reds to fruit, honey, and rose petal wines. The winery offers wine-tasting and tours to the public and has tasting and banquet areas for private parties. Gourmet catering can be provided by making special arrangements. Gaia features over 300 wine- and grape-related gifts, accessories, gourmet foods, clothing items, decanters, and glassware.

1999
INDIANA

Huber Winery

Vidal Blanc
A dry white table wine.

Alcohol 11% by Volume

PRODUCED
AND BOTTLED BY
HUBER WINERY
19816 HUBER ROAD
BORDEN, INDIANA 47106
1-800-345-WINE

GOVERNMENT WARNING: (1) ACCORDING TO THE
SURGEON GENERAL, WOMEN SHOULD NOT DRINK
ALCOHOLIC BEVERAGES DURING PREGNANCY BECAUSE OF
THE RISK OF BIRTH DEFECTS. (2) CONSUMPTION OF
ALCOHOLIC BEVERAGES
IMPAIRS YOUR ABILITY
TO DRIVE A CAR OR
OPERATE MACHINERY,
AND MAY CAUSE HEALTH
PROBLEMS.

CONTAINS SULFITES

6 43390 21198 6

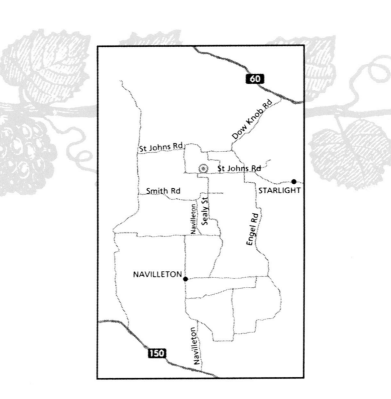

Huber Orchard & Winery

Owners: Ted and Greg Huber

Address: 19816 Huber Road, Borden, IN 47106

Phone Number: 812-923-9813 or 1-800-345-WINE

Web site: huberwinery.com

Bonded Winery Number: BW-IN-11 (1978)

Total Acres of Grapes Planted: 37

Varieties of Grapes Planted: Seyval Blanc, Vidal Blanc, Chancellor, Vignoles, Chambourcin, Villard, Chardonel, Traminette, Cayuga, Concord, Niagara, Catawba, Cabernet, and Cabernet Franc

Types of Wine Made: Wines are made from the varieties grown, as well as peach wine, apple wine, blackberry and raspberry wine, and sparkling wine

SIMON HUBER settled this southern Indiana farm in 1843. He came from Baden, Germany, an area known for its fruit growing and wine-making. From the original 80 acres, the farm has expanded to 600 acres. Seven generations of Hubers have lived on the farm. Ted and Greg Huber own the business and share responsibilities for the daily operations. The farm currently has 100 acres of apples, 125 acres of Christmas trees, 50 acres of peach orchards, 100 acres of seasonal vegetables, and 50 acres of straw-berries. The vineyards cover 37 acres and produce nearly 200 tons of grapes per year, making Huber Winery the largest wine grape–grower in the state. The winery is located underground next to the restored barn (circa 1938) that serves as the wine-tasting and sales area. Approximately twenty styles of grape, fruit wines, and port are produced. The Hubers have won over 600 gold, silver, and bronze medals for their wines. Light lunches are available at the winery. In addition to the winery, the grounds include a cheese and ice cream factory, a bakery, a farm market, U-cut Christmas trees, a petting zoo, a gift shop, and a large banquet facility.

Kauffman Winery

Chancellor

POSEY COUNTY, INDIANA

Fine Dry Table Wine

PRODUCED AND BOTTLED BY
KAUFFMAN WINERY, MT. VERNON, INDIANA

CONTAINS SULFITES

"GOVERNMENT WARNING: (1) According to the Surgeon General, women should not drink alcoholic beverages during pregnancy because of the risk of birth defects. (2) Consumption of alcoholic beverages impairs your ability to drive a car or operate machinery, and may cause health problems."

Kauffman Winery

Owner: Harley Kauffman

Address: 9901 Lower Mt. Vernon Rd., Mt. Vernon, IN 47620

Phone Number: 812-985-3145

Bonded Winery Number: BW-IN-24 (1987)

Total Acres of Grapes Planted: 8

Varieties of Grapes Planted: French hybrid and Labrusca

Types of Wine Made: Dry and sweet grape table wines, fruit wines, apple
and peach wines

HARLEY KAUFFMAN started farming the family farm west of Evansville in 1942. He also worked for twenty-five years as a soil conservation technician for the USDA Soil Conservation Service, retiring in 1980. He and his wife Bettye first planted grapes in 1974 and were part owners of Golden Rain Tree Winery in Wadesville, Indiana. After Golden Rain Tree closed, they supplied grapes to a number of Indiana wineries and opened Kauffman Winery on their farm in 1987. Kauffman Winery is the oldest winery in southwestern Indiana and is one of the nine Indiana wineries located in the Ohio River Valley viticultural area. The Kauffmans produce ten estate-bottled wines that are sold at various locations around Evansville and Mt. Vernon. A tasting-room is under construction that will be open in the fall of 2001.

Lake Michigan Winery

Frostbite Blue Wine

Produced and Bottled by Lake Michigan Winery
U.S. 41 "Calumet Av." At 119th St., Whiting, In. 46394
ALC. 10.5% BY VOL. CONTAINS SULFITES
Ph. 219·659·WINE; 888-TNT-WINE & Fax 219-659-3501
finewine@netnitco.net http://lakemichiganwinery.com
Premium Fruit Wine From Indiana Blueberries.

We are a small boutique winery that uses a family approach to picking, vinting aging & bottling our wine in a careful homespun way. We are carrying on the same natural tradition, improved by modern equipment, as prescribed by our Vevay, Indiana forefathers who originated commercial winemaking in the USA in 1802.

Henry, our cellarmaster and winemaker has studied in France to artfully caress the juice into premium wines, & the fact that we are small allows us to pay more attention to detail.

Call us for fun : we have special events, free tastings, gift baskets, unbelievable ambiance & we are widely known for our "no minimum" personalized label policy. Case discounts available. Enjoy this bottle of wine that we worked hard to produce for you.

Tom Owens, prop.

Lake Michigan Winery

Owner: Tom Owens
Address: 816 119th St., Whiting, IN 46394
Phone Number: 219-659-WINE or 1-888-TNT-WINE
Web site: lakemichiganwinery.com
Bonded Winery Number: BW-IN-27 (1992)
Total Acres of Grapes Planted: None
Types of Wine Made: French hybrid and Vinifera, as well as fruit wines

TOM OWENS was teaching at Hanover College in 1972 when he first learned of wineries in Indiana. He had traveled extensively throughout the world and was familiar with European and California wine regions. Tom's curiosity was piqued by the possibility of growing grapes and making wine in Indiana. After a proposed purchase of Villa Medeo Winery (later known as Scotella) in Madison, Indiana, failed to materialize, Tom purchased 65 acres near the Ohio River in Madison. Ten acres of grapes were planted in 1986. In addition to being a college professor, Tom is a third-generation funeral director in Whiting, Indiana. After rethinking the logistics and marketing possibilities of both the Madison and Chicago areas, Tom decided to relocate the winery to a building he owned near the funeral home in Whiting, Indiana, just a few miles from the Indiana-Illinois border. Lake Michigan Winery opened on July 1, 1992. A grass fire ravaged the vineyard in Madison in 1992, and Tom decided to abandon it and purchase fruit from other growers. Lake Michigan Winery makes thirty different wines, from dry to semi-sweet. Cookouts, hayrides, and grape-stomping festivals that include live entertainment are held in the outdoor wine garden during the summer months.

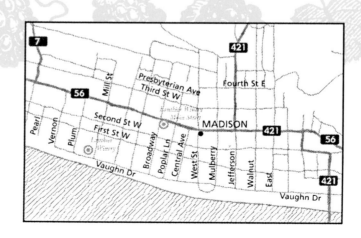

Lanthier Winery

Owners: Chris Lanthier and Tami Hagemier

Address: 123 Mill Street, Madison, IN 47250

Phone Number: 812-273-2409 or 1-800-41-WINES

Second Tasting-Room: 112 East Main Street

Bonded Winery Number: BW-IN-31 (1994)

Total Acres of Grapes Planted: None

Types of Wine Made: Baco, Catawba, Niagara, Concord, and flavored blends. Specialty wines such as dandelion and rose petal are offered throughout the year.

CHRIS LANTHIER AND TAMI HAGEMIER founded Lanthier Winery in September of 1994. Tami was born in Washington, Indiana, and grew up in Columbus, Ind. She attended Purdue University, receiving a nursing degree in 1982. In addition to Lanthier Winery, she owns Always Flowers in Columbus. Chris was born and raised in Wayne, Michigan. He attended Michigan Technological University and received a B.S. in chemical engineering in 1980. He is currently employed at Dow Corning in Carrollton, Kentucky. The winery is located in an eighteenth-century fort built along the river by the early settlers. The walls are 24 inches thick and the windows are narrow "rifle ports." An outpost on the bustling Ohio River waterway, the building underwent major changes during the expansion of Madison. In 1850 the red brick building was added as home to the "Depot Exchange," a rowdy railroad trading post. Over the next 140 years the building had a diverse and colorful life. The old fort became home to such endeavors as a local market, offices for a canning factory, a saloon, a brothel, and between World War II and the 1970s a scrap materials recycling site. Chris and Tami purchased the property in 1990. The state of disrepair required 4 years of intense restoration work. In 1994, Chris released his first commercial wines. The year 1997 added the flood of the Ohio River to the unique history of the site. Eight and a half feet of water and mud flooded the property and closed the winery. With the help of family and friends the winery reopened eight months later. Tours are available on weekends. Homebrewing and wine-making supplies are available in their shop. Call for reservations at their French-Italian restaurant.

MADISON
Vineyards

2000 Estate
Foch Nouveau
Ohio River Valley Table Wine
Produced and Bottled by Madison Vineyards, Inc., Madison, IN 47250

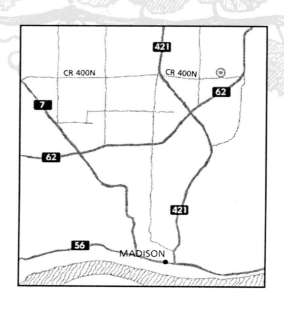

Madison Vineyards

Owners: Steve and Sandy Palmer

Address: 1456 E. 400 North, Madison, IN 47250

Phone Number: 812-273-6500 or 1-888-473-6500

Web site: madisonvineyards.com

Bonded Winery Number: BW-IN-37 (1995)

Total Acres of Grapes Planted: 9

Varieties of Grapes Planted: Seyval Blanc, Cayuga White, Vignoles, Vidal, Niagara, Foch, Rougeon, Cabernet Sauvignon, Merlot, Petit Verdot, and Cabernet Franc

Types of Wine Made: White, red and blush table wine, sparkling wine

In 1994, Steve and Sandy Palmer found a 37-acre site near Madison that fit their grape-growing and wine-making requirements. The site is located between two highways within four miles of the Ohio River and is near a growing tourist area. In 1995, they planted the first four acres of grapes, erected a winery building, and began making wine from purchased juice. Steve works full-time at the winery. Sandy, who continues to work full-time in the insurance field in Indianapolis, joins him on weekends. Their son, Michael, handles advertising and wholesale marketing. Their goal is to "make world-class wines from grapes grown on our property and to successfully market them at reasonable prices."

Oliver Winery

Owners: Bill and Kathleen Oliver

Address: 8024 North State Road 37, Bloomington, IN 47404

Phone Number: 812-876-5800 or 1-800-25-TASTE

Web site: oliverwinery.com

Bonded Winery Number: BW-IN-3 (1972)

Total Acres of Grapes Planted: 21

Varieties of Grapes Planted: Cabernet Sauvignon, Cabernet Franc, Chardonel, Foch, Traminette, Chambourcin, Catawba, and N.Y.70.0809

Types of Wine Made: French hybrid, Vinifera, fruit wines (strawberry, blackberry, cherry, hard cider), Camelot Mead

OLIVER WINERY began during the 1960s in the basement of William W. Oliver, professor of law at Indiana University in Bloomington, Indiana. He planted 5 acres of French hybrid grapes in northern Monroe County. Four years later his production outgrew his cellar. However, Indiana law prevented wineries from selling directly to the public. In 1971, the state legislature passed the Indiana Small Winery Act, which Professor Oliver wrote, allowing wineries in Indiana to produce up to 50,000 gallons for sale either retail or wholesale. Oliver Winery opened in 1973 with 35 acres of grapes and four wines. In the summer of 1983, the professor's son, Bill M. Oliver, took charge of the winery. The demise of the original vineyard due to harsh winters in the late 1970s and early 1980s led to the purchase of Labrusca grape juices from New York. In 1988, Oliver Winery began purchasing Vinifera grapes and juice from the West Coast. They planted 3 acres of grapes in 1994. A large planting in the spring of 2001 brought the total to 21 acres. The winery grounds have been transformed over the years with new production buildings, a pond, a 300-ton limestone environmental sculpture, a post-and-beam tasting-room, and an attractive waterfall at the entrance to the tasting-room.

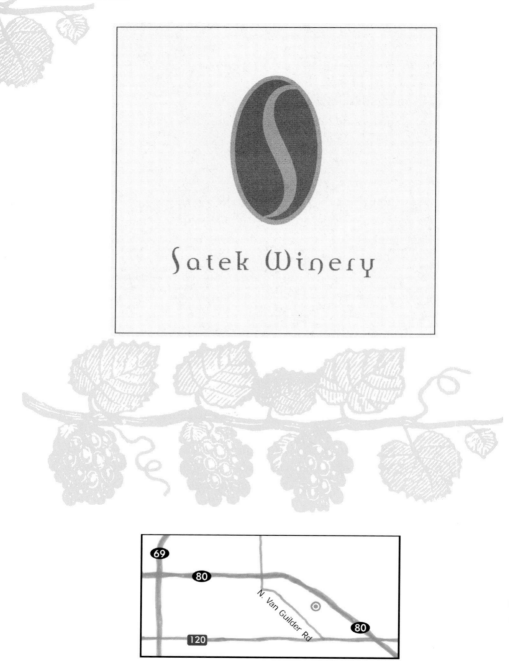

Satek Winery

Owners: Larry and Pam Satek

Address: 6208 N. Van Guilder Road, Fremont, IN 46737

Phone Number: 219-495-9463

Bonded Winery Number: BW-IN-49 (2001)

Total Acres of Grapes Planted: 2

Varieties of Grapes Planted: Seyval blanc, Vidal, Foch, DeChaunac, and Steuben

Types of Wine Made: Red and white, both sweet and dry

IN 1915 PAM SATEK's great-grandfather sold his paint and wallpaper business in Ft. Wayne and retired at the age of 53 to a parcel of land on the hillside above Lake James in northeast Indiana. He planted an orchard that continued producing until his death in 1941. In 1992, the Sateks decided to bring the land back into production and planted 2 acres of grapes.

Larry is also a research chemist. He has made amateur wines since 1976. Pam has served as a school principal for sixteen years. In the summer of 1998, they bought 16 acres bordering the Indiana Toll Road about a mile from the intersection of I-69 and the toll road as a winery site. Construction began in December 2000.

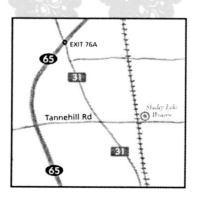

Shadey Lake Winery

Owners: Greg & Pam Schmelz

Address: 1440 Tannehill Rd., Taylorsville, IN 47280

Phone Number: 812-526-0294

Web site: shadeylakewinery.com

Bonded Winery Number: BW-IN-44 (2000)

Total Acres of Grapes Planted: None

Types of Wine Made: Dry fruit wines, blackberry, black raspberry, strawberry, cherry, blueberry, and persimmon. Grape wines include
Chancellor, Niagara, and Concord

GREG SCHMELZ grew up on a small farm near Corydon, Indiana.
Greg's first introduction to wine was the sweet country-style wine that his
father made in the cellar of the farmhouse. Greg left the farm and attended
Purdue University, receiving a B.S. in chemical engineering in 1994. He
now works for Alfa Laval Separation Inc. in Greenwood. Pam Schmelz, a
native of Columbus, Indiana, attended Purdue University and received a
B.S. in electrical engineering in 1992. She followed that up with an M.B.A.
from Indiana Wesleyan University. The Schmelzes made their first wine
after buying a kit in Myrtle Beach, South Carolina, while on vacation in
1995. After five years of amateur wine-making, Greg and Pam decided it
was time to turn the hobby into a business. Shadey Lake Winery takes its
name from a lake surrounded by trees near their home. They obtained their
permits in the spring of 2000 and opened the doors to the public on October
1, 2000. The Schmelzes intend to focus on dry and semi-dry fruit wines.

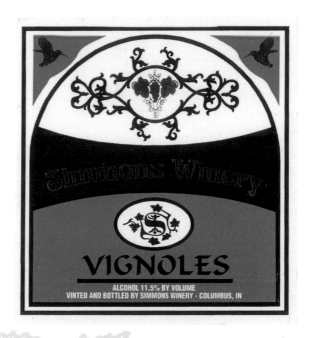

Simmons Winery & Farm Market

Owners: David and Brenda Simmons

Address: 8111 East 450 North, Columbus, IN 47203

Phone Number: 812-546-0091

Bonded Winery Number: BW-IN-45 (2000)

Total Acres of Grapes Planted: $8^1/_2$

Varieties of Grapes Planted: Chardonel, Vignoles, Cayuga White, Chambourcin, Foch, St. Vincent, and Steuben

Types of Wine Made: Chardonel, Vignoles, Cayuga White, Chambourcin, Foch, St. Vincent, Steuben, blackberry, and cherry

DAVID AND BRENDA SIMMONS planted their first grapes on the 115-year-old family farm in 1998. The original plan was to sell grapes to other wineries. However, after visiting several wineries around the state, they decided to open their own. After several years of study and construction, they opened the winery on June 3, 2000. The Simmons also operate a fresh-produce farm market. David farms 800 to 900 acres of corn and beans. Brenda was a high school math teacher who resigned to manage the winery full-time. Together they run the farm, winery, and farm market. The winery is open year-round and fresh produce is available during the summer. Their philosophy for the winery and the produce business is the same: "We want the customer to buy a product that we produce on our farm."

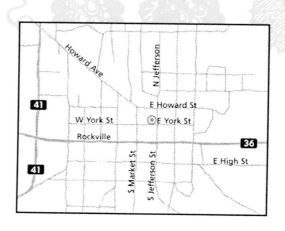

Terre Vin Winery

Owners: Dorothy and Dave Gahimer
Address: 100 W. York St., Rockville, IN 47872
Phone Number: 765-569-5099 or 1-888-965-WINE
Web site: ticz.com/~terrevin/
Bonded Winery Number: BW-IN-33 (1995)
Total Acres of Grapes Planted: 1/10
Varieties of Grapes Planted: Niagara, Catawba
Types of Wine Made: Labrusca, French hybrid, fruit, and some Vinifera

TERRE VIN WINERY is a small family-owned winery. Dorothy Gahimer, winery president, is originally from New York City. She graduated from Hunter College and received a master's degree from Indiana State University. She taught for several years in New York, Virginia, and Indiana. She retired after twenty years as a cataloguer at Indiana State University. Dave is the secretary/treasurer and chief engineer of the winery. He is from Shelby County, Indiana, and is a veteran of the U.S. Navy Submarine Service. He has been head technician in the electrical engineering department of Rose-Hulman Institute of Technology for over twenty-two years. Dave was a home winemaker for many years and decided to change professions for the remainder of his life.

A dozen wines are made from American and French hybrid varieties. Terra Vin wines are named for local places and people. The labels are derived from artwork from family members and friends. The Gahimers have encouraged grape-growers in west central Indiana. Dave served as vice president of the Indiana Winegrowers Guild for three years.

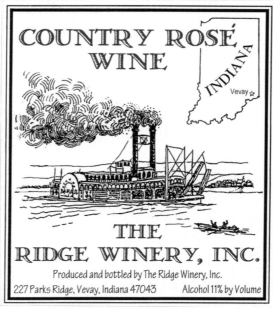

The Ridge Winery

Owners: Mary Jane Demaree, President; Tom Demaree, winemaker
Address: 227 Parks Ridge Road, Vevay, IN 47043
Phone Number: 812-427-2792
Bonded Winery Number: BW-IN-26 (1989)
Total Acres of Grapes Planted: None
Types of Wine Made: Labrusca, fruit wines

TOM AND MARY JANE DEMAREE are co-proprietors of The Ridge Winery, located on their farm on Parks Ridge near Vevay, Indiana, on the Ohio River. Tom is the winemaker. He was previously employed at the Schenley Distillery in Lawrenceburg, Indiana, for twenty-six years and worked in many departments of the distillery. The Ridge Winery originated in 1987 along with an 11-acre vineyard. The hard winter, combined with the deer population, took its toll on the young vines. By spring the vines could not be saved. The Ridge Winery persevered and continued to operate by purchasing fruit and juices from other sources. The Ridge Winery wines are sold through local retail outlets in the Switzerland County area. The winery is not yet open to the public. The Ridge Winery hopes to replant the vineyard once the winery is well established to return a vineyard and winery to the Vevay, Switzerland County, area. The Demarees' daughter and son, Lisa and Eddie, and their families help out at the winery. The Demarees view the winery as an alternative to growing tobacco, and they think that "making wine is a whole lot easier."

This is an old-style Zinfandel, with very ripe fruit of blackberry and raisined cherries, white pepper and chocolate. It has assertive tannins for big foods and the cellar.

Visit our winery at 208 E. Second St. in Historic Downtown Madison, Indiana 47250 or call us at 1-800-948-8466. We would love to hear from you!

Thomas Family Winery

Zinfandel 1999

GOVERNMENT WARNING: (1) ACCORDING TO THE SURGEON GENERAL, WOMEN SHOULD NOT DRINK ALCOHOLIC BEVERAGES DURING PREGNANCY BECAUSE OF THE RISK OF BIRTH DEFECTS. (2) CONSUMPTION OF ALCOHOLIC BEVERAGES IMPAIRS YOUR ABILITY TO DRIVE A CAR OR OPERATE MACHINERY, AND MAY CAUSE HEALTH PROBLEMS.

PRODUCED AND BOTTLED BY THE THOMAS FAMILY WINERY, INC. IN MADISON, IN BW-IN-36 FOR SALE IN INDIANA ONLY 13% ALCOHOL BY VOLUME

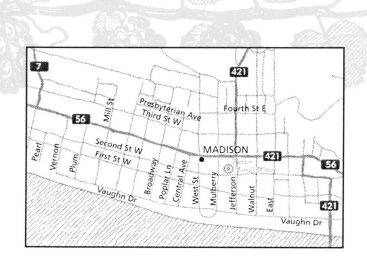

The Thomas Family Winery

Owner: Steven L. Thomas

Address: 208 E. Second Street, Madison, IN 47250

Phone Number: 812-273-3755 or 1-800-948-8466

Web site: thomasfamilywinery.com

Bonded Winery Number: BW-IN-36 (1995)

Total Acres of Grapes Planted: None

Types of Wine Made: Labrusca, French hybrid, some Vinifera, and Gale's
  Hard Cider

STEVE THOMAS is a member of the third generation of a wine-making family. He grew up in central Indiana and lived for a while out west. In 1983, he began making wine at his father's winery, Chateau Thomas. Steve's wife Elizabeth was raised in North Carolina. She worked in the tourism field for fifteen years working with convention and visitors' bureaus and museums. Steve parted ways with Chateau Thomas in 1994. Steve served as president of the Indiana Winegrowers Guild for three years. In the spring of 1995, Steve and Elizabeth moved to Madison, Indiana, to start a winery. They rehabilitated an 1850s stable and carriage house just two blocks from the Ohio River into a winery cellar and tasting-room. The fruit for their wines is purchased from the Midwest and the West Coast. Their wine-making style is very pointedly European, even for the Labrusca wines. Their Gale's Hard Cider is a barrel-conditioned, strong dry cider in the Welsh style. The tasting-room has an old country pub atmosphere and traditional music. Hearth-baked bread, fine cheeses, and salamis are served.

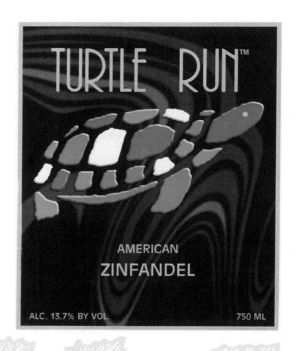

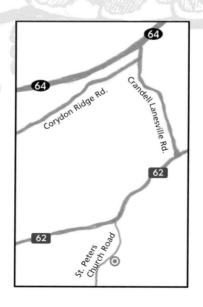

Turtle Run Winery

Owners: Jim & Laura Pfeiffer

Address: 940 St. Peter's Church Road NE, Corydon, IN 47112

Phone Number: 812-952-2650 or 1-866-288-7853 (866-2TURTLE)

Bonded Winery Number: BW-IN-48 (2000)

Total Acres of Grapes Planted: 10

Varieties of Grapes Planted: Chambourcin, Vignoles, Chardonel, Traminette, N.Y.70.0305, and N.Y.74.0308

Types of Wine Made: Red and white, from dry to sweet

Turtle Run Winery, started by Jim and Laura Pfeiffer, is located in the southern part of Indiana near Louisville, Kentucky. Laura majored in interior design at the University of Kentucky and does freelance commercial design work. Jim was bitten by the wine bug after taking a course in the geography of wine at Miami University of Ohio, where he majored in marketing. He thought briefly about going to California to pursue his interest in wine, but he stayed in Louisville where he met his wife Laura. Jim and Laura attended several outdoor concerts at Oliver Winery, and after several visits Jim became curious about midwestern wineries. The first wine they made was from a concentrate. "Luckily it was good enough to drink, so we decided to get more information on starting a winery." Nineteen of their twenty-one wines won awards in the amateur competition at the Indiana State Fair. They looked for land in Kentucky but found that the land was either too expensive or in a dry county. The laws in Kentucky were also more restrictive than in Indiana. In 1997, they purchased land on St. Peter's Church Road in Harrison County near Lanesville, Indiana. Their first vines were planted in 1998, and the first harvest from those vines was in 2000. Their 50-by-50-foot building includes a tasting-room, production area, gift shop, and laboratory. They have plans for a larger building as the vineyard grows.

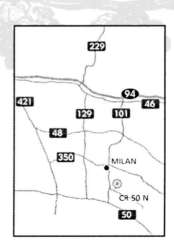

Villa Milan Vineyard

Owners: John and Dorothy Garrett
Address: P.O. Box 248, Milan, IN 47031
Phone Number: 812-654-3419
Web site: seidata.com/villa-milan
Bonded Winery Number: BW-IN-17 (1984)
Total Acres of Grapes Planted: 7½
Varieties of Grapes Planted: DeChaunac, Vidal, Concord, Catawba,
    Maréchal Foch
Types of Wine Made: French hybrids, Labrusca

JOHN GARRETT was a television news reporter in Indianapolis when he and his wife Dorothy decided to move to Milan, Indiana, to plant a vineyard in 1976. The vineyard is located two and a half miles south of Milan atop a scenic hill approached by a steep drive. The Garretts sold their grapes to Indiana wineries and at the City Market in Indianapolis for several years. John was instrumental in establishing the Ohio River Valley viticultural area in 1983. In 1984, John built a cellar into the hillside and started production of his own wines. The winery now has an Italian-style tasting-room where estate-bottled wines are served to the public. John single-handedly built a 32-foot-diameter gazebo for outdoor seating.

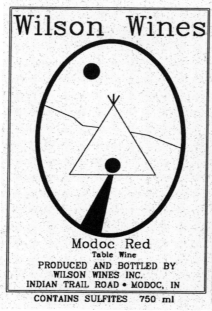

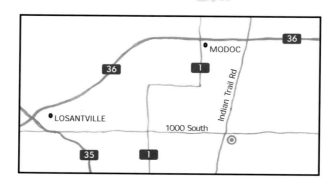

Wilson Wines

Owners: John & Jim Wilson

Address: 10137 Indian Trail Road, Modoc, IN 47358

Phone Number: 765-533-6616

Bonded Winery Number: BW-IN-42 (2000)

Total Acres of Grapes Planted: $^2/_3$

Varieties of Grapes Planted: Foch and Vidal

Types of Wine Made: Apple, raspberry, cranberry, Modoc White, Modoc Red

WILSON WINES is located just south of Modoc, Indiana, on the Wilson family farm. John and Jim Wilson grew up on the farm and eventually found their way back to it. John was working at a factory when his company sent him to Napa Valley, California, for training. He visited a number of wineries and thought what a fun venture making wine would be. His job required him to work in a wet lab, so he had the training for wine-testing. His talents complement those of his brother Jim. Together they began to build the winery by converting the old milk house into a wine cellar. While John worked overtime at the factory, Jim was learning to make wine. The project turned serious after they attended an Indiana Winegrowers Guild symposium. The old blacksmith's building was turned into a winery. John and Jim visited most of the wineries in the state to learn from their successes and avoid their mistakes. They eventually entered their wine in the Indiana State Fair amateur contest and won a few ribbons. Their concept of the winery is that they "always want it to be a place to enjoy wine, food, swap stories, and have a good time."

Winzerwald
Winery

2001
Ohio River Valley

Marechal Foch

ALCOHOL 13.9 % BY VOLUME

Winzerwald
Winery

Produced and bottled by
Winzerwald Winery
26300 N. Indian Lake Rd.
Bristow, IN 47515
1-800-555-5555
www.winzerwaldwinery.com

Marechal Foch

Marechal Foch is estate grown
and is vinted in the old world
tradition of light reds from
southern Germany. Enjoy this
wine with pork, light beef dishes
and lamb. Serve now through 2003.

0 84692 40054 4

GOVERNMENT WARNING : (1) ACCORDING TO THE SURGEON
GENERAL, WOMEN SHOULD NOT DRINK BEVERAGES DURING
PREGNANCY BECAUSE OF THE RISK OF BIRTH DEFECTS. (2)
CONSUMPTION OF ALCOHOLIC BEVERAGES IMPAIRS YOUR
ABILITY TO DRIVE A CAR OR OPERATE MACHINERY, AND MAY
CAUSE HEALTH PROBLEMS.

CONTAINS SULFITES

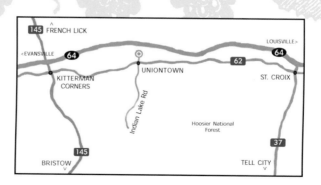

Winzerwald Winery

Owners: Dan and Donna Adams

Address: 26300 North Indian Lake Road, Bristow, IN 47515

Phone Number: 812-357-7000

Web site: winzerwaldwinery.com

Bonded Winery Number: bond applied for but not yet received

Total Acres of Grapes Planted: 2

Varieties of Grapes Planted: Foch, Traminette, and Vignoles

Types of Wine Made: German- and Swiss-style grape wines, fruit table wines, and fortified wine

WINZERWALD WINERY (German for "vintner of the forest") will open in the summer of 2001. The winery is on 85 acres of rolling land in the Hoosier National Forest. The area is likened to the Black Forest area of Germany. Dan previously worked at the largest winery in Wisconsin. The Adamses have been members of the Indiana Winegrowers Guild for six years, and Donna joined the board of directors of the Guild in 2000. They won the Best National Amateur Wine Award at the Indiana State Fair in 1998 with a blush wine made from grapes that family lore says were brought to America from Germany by Dan's ancestors. The Adamses refer to the vine as their "mystery grape."

Appendix A

Location of Firstvineyard, Kentucky

John James Dufour's "Firstvineyard" was located on the big bend in the Kentucky River about four miles above where Hickman Creek joins the river. The Kentucky Vineyard Society purchased 633 acres. No deed has been found which shows the sale of the vineyard land to the Kentucky Vineyard Society or to John James Dufour. However, there is a survey map in the Dufour Family Papers at the Indiana State Library in Indianapolis which covers the area in the big bend of the Kentucky River. The survey map, in conjunction with deed records from Kentucky, allows us to pinpoint the location of Firstvineyard.

In 1816, John James Dufour returned from Europe and had squatters removed from Firstvineyard. What claim he had to the land is hard to determine. In 1828, shortly after the death of John James, his son Daniel Vincent Dufour purchased the land outlined in the survey map from John Hazlerigg, about 938 acres. Daniel Vincent then began selling portions of the land to various people whose names (Wamsley, Rice, and Salter) are written on the survey map. In several instances, the deeds for these properties mention that the land was part of what was "commonly called the vineyard tract." One deed (that of Thomas Wamsley) contains the phrase "as surveyed by John James Dufour." The boundary lines often followed the meanders of the streams. The stream names mentioned on the survey match the stream names in the deeds. When the survey map is laid over a modern topographical map, the fit is amazingly accurate.

There can be no question that the Kentucky Vineyard Society land was at this location. The survey shows a small two-story house near the river. There are also dotted lines that may indicate some sort of fence or enclosure. F. A. Micheau visited Firstvineyard in 1802. His description of the vineyard fits very well in terms of distance from the river, aspect, and slope.

Deeds from Jessamine County, Kentucky, concerning Firstvineyard:

John Hazlerigg to Daniel Vincent Dufour, 9/30/1828, 678 acres, Deed

Book I, pp. 132–133, Jessamine County Deed Books, Kentucky Department for Libraries and Archives, Public Records Division, Frankfort, Kentucky

John Hazlerigg to Daniel Vincent Dufour, 9/30/1828, 260 acres, Deed Book I, pp. 132–133, Jessamine County Deed Books

Daniel Vincent Dufour to Enoch Bruner, 10/2/1828, 35 acres, Deed Book L, pp. 145–146, Jessamine County Deed Books

Daniel Vincent Dufour to Michael Salter, 4/23/1831, 75 acres, Deed Book K, pp. 32–35, Jessamine County Deed Books

Daniel Vincent Dufour to Isaac Rice, 5/10/1832, 51 acres, Deed Book K, pp. 33–35, Jessamine County Deed Books

Daniel Vincent Dufour to Thomas Wamsley, 5/16/1835, 110 acres, Deed Book L, pp. 133–136, Jessamine County Deed Books

Appendix B
Indiana Laws Pertaining to Small Wineries

1971– (P.L. No. 77)
Defined small winery, allowed Indiana small wineries to sell directly to the public. *Laws of the State of Indiana* (Indianapolis: The Burton & Shields Co., Inc., 1971), 391–392.

1973– (P.L. No. 55 and 56)
Reorganized Indiana alcoholic beverage laws, established a wine excise tax of 45 cents per gallon. *Laws of the State of Indiana* (Indianapolis: Central Publishing Co., Inc., 1973), I: 290–450.

1975– (P.L. No. 71 and 73)
Stipulated that the holder of a permit may advertise the name and address of any retailer that sells their wine and that the holder of a small winery permit must pay an excise tax of 25 cents per gallon. *Laws of the State of Indiana* (Indianapolis: Central Publishing Co., Inc., 1975), I: 562–563, 565.

1977– (P.L. No. 93)
Increased small winery production limit from 50,000 to 100,000 gallons per year. *Laws of the State of Indiana* (Indianapolis: Central Publishing Co., Inc., 1977), I: 479.

1978– (P.L. No. 53)
Stipulated that table wine shipped outside of the state does not count toward the production limit of a small winery. *Laws of the State of Indiana* (Indianapolis: Central Publishing Co., Inc., 1978), II: 912.

1981– (P.L. No. 103)
Raised wine and beer taxes 2 cents per gallon and increased liquor taxes 6 cents per gallon, proceeds to go toward an addiction services fund. *Laws of*

the State of Indiana (Indianapolis: Central Publishing Co., Inc., 1981), I: 1085–1091.

1982– (P.L. No. 70)
Allowed small wineries to sell wine on Sunday by the bottle for carryout. *Laws of the State of Indiana* (Indianapolis: Central Publishing Co., Inc., 1982), I: 573–574.

1984– (P.L. No. 58)
Allowed liquor retailers to offer samples of Indiana wines. *Laws of the State of Indiana* (Indianapolis: Central Publishing Co., Inc., 1984), I: 677–678.

1985– (P.L. No. 85)
Allowed small wineries to sell wine from a second location. *Acts 1985: Laws Enacted by the 104th General Assembly* (Indianapolis: Central Publishing Co., Inc., 1985), I: 730–739.

1987– (P.L. No. 104)
Removed the excise tax advantage for small wineries. Increased the excise tax from 27 to 47 cents per gallon. *Acts 1987: Laws Enacted by the 105th General Assembly* (Indianapolis: Central Publishing Co., Inc., 1987), II: 1611–1612.

1989– (P.L. No. 102)
Established the Indiana Wine Grape Council to help develop the Indiana wine industry, funded by 5 cents per gallon of the excise tax on wine. *Acts 1989: Laws Enacted by the 106th General Assembly* (Indianapolis: Central Publishing Co., Inc., 1989), II: 1105–1109.

1996– (P.L. No. 74)
Allowed small wineries to receive temporary permits in order to sell wine by the bottle at festivals, trade shows, and expositions. *Acts 1996: Laws Enacted by the 109th General Assembly* (Indianapolis: Central Publishing Co., Inc., 1989), II: 1645–1646.

1999– (P.L. No. 201)
Allowed small wineries to manufacture ports and sherries. Raised the gallon limit to 500,000 gallons. Renamed "Small Winery" permit as "Farm Win-

ery" permit. *Acts 1999: Laws Enacted by the 111th General Assembly* (India-napolis: Central Publishing Co., Inc., 1999), II: 1302–1306.

1999– (P.L. No. 36)
Reduced residency requirement for opening an Indiana winery from five years to one year. Ibid., I: 219–220.

2001– (P.L. No. 235)
Indiana farm winery brandy distiller's permit.

APPENDIX C
Indiana Bonded Wineries

Bonded Winery Number	Winery Name	City	Year Bond Issued	Year Bond Terminated
BW-IN-1	?	?	?	?
BWC-IN-2	Treaty Line Winery	Liberty	1971	1975
BW-IN-3	Oliver Winery	Bloomington	1972	—
BWC-IN-4	Villa Medeo	Madison	1974	Terminated 1983?
BW-IN-5	Easley Enterprises	Indianapolis	1974	—
BW-IN-6	Swiss Valley Vineyard	Vevay	1974	1988
BW-IN-7	Banholzer Wine Cellars	Hesston	1974	Terminated 1981?
BW-IN-8	?	?	?	?
BW-IN-9	Golden Rain Tree/St. Wendel	Wadesville	1975	1988
BW-IN-10	Rauner & Sons	South Bend	1977	Terminated 1981?
BW-IN-11	Huber Orchard & Winery	Starlight	1978	—
BW-IN-12	Possum Trot Vineyards	Unionville	1978	1991
BWC-IN-13	Schenley Distillers	Lawrenceburg	1982	1991
BW-IN-14	Butler Winery	Bloomington	1983	—
BW-IN-15	Chateau Thomas Winery	Plainfield	1984	—
BW-IN-16	Grazier et Filles	Indianapolis	1984	1989
BW-IN-17	Villa Milan Vineyard	Milan	1984	—
BW-IN-18	Scotella Vineyard and Winery	Madison	1985	1995
BW-IN-19	Brown County Winery	Nashville	1986	—
BW-IN-20	Tall Pines	Terre Haute	1987	1990
BW-IN-21	Chateau Pomije	Guilford	1986	—
BWC-IN-22	PRI-PAC	Lawrenceburg	1987	—
BWC-IN-23	Seagrams Beverage	Lawrenceburg	1987	—

Bonded Winery Number	Winery Name	City	Year Bond Issued	Year Bond Terminated
BW-IN-24	Kauffman Winery	Mt. Vernon	1987	—
BWC-IN-25	American Juice	Gary	1988	1990
BW-IN-26	The Ridge Winery	Vevay	1989	—
BW-IN-27	Lake Michigan Winery	Whiting	1992	—
BWC-IN-28	American Beverage Marketers	New Albany	1992	—
BW-IN-29	Sugar Grove Winery	Mooresville	1994	1998
BW-IN-30	?	?	?	?
BW-IN-31	Lanthier Winery	Madison	1994	—
BW-IN-32	Anderson's Orchard & Winery	Valparaiso	1994	—
BW-IN-33	Terre Vin Winery	Rockville	1995	—
BW-IN-34	French Lick Wine & Coffee Company	French Lick	1995	—
BW-IN-35	Borns Winery	Madison	1995	1996
BW-IN-36	The Thomas Family Winery	Madison	1995	—
BW-IN-37	Madison Vineyards	Madison	1995	—
BW-IN-38	Gaia Wines	Indianapolis	1996	—
BW-IN-39	Dune Ridge Winery	Porter	1996	—
BW-IN-40	?	?	?	?
BW-IN-41	St. Joe Valley Winery	Mishawaka	1997	1999
BW-IN-42	Wilson Wines	Modoc	2000	—
BW-IN-43	Private Label Vintage	Laconia	1999	—

Bonded Winery Number	Winery Name	City	Year Bond Issued	Year Bond Terminated
BW-IN-44	Shadey Lake Winery	Taylorsville	2000	—
BW-IN-45	Simmons Winery & Farm Market	Hope	2000	—
BW-IN-46	Ferrin's Fruit Winery	Indianapolis	2000	—
BW-IN-47	Leser Winery and Vineyard	Vincennes	2000	—
BW-IN-48	Turtle Run Winery	Lanesville	2000	—
BW-IN-49	Satek Winery	Fremont	2001	—

Notes

page | 1. IN THE BEGINNING

1   "Colonists at Paris Island plant a vineyard" in Thomas Pinney, *A History of Wine in America* (Berkeley, Los Angeles, London: University of California Press, 1989), 11.

1   Climate in the New World in Pinney, *A History of Wine in America*, 12–13.

1–2   Grape-growing in colonial Virginia in Pinney, *A History of Wine in America*, 15–22.

2   Decline in tobacco markets in David Joel Mishkin, *The American Colonial Wine Industry: An Economic Interpretation*, vol. 1 (New York: Arno Press, 1975), 224.

2–3   Other attempts to grow grapes on eastern seaboard in Pinney, *A History of Wine in America*, 29–46.

4   George Washington and grape-growing in Donald Jackson and Dorothy Twohig, eds., *The Diaries of George Washington*, vol. 2 (Charlottesville: University of Virginia Press, 1976–1979), 52; and John C. Fitzpatrick, ed., *The Writings of George Washington from the Original Manuscript Sources, 1745–1799*, vol. 27 (Washington, D.C.: United States Government Printing Office, 1938), 55.

4   Philip Mazzei and Jefferson in R. de Treville Lawrence, Sr., ed., *Jefferson and Wine*, vol. 1 (The Plains, Va.: Vinifera Wine Growers Association, 1976), 133.

4   Jefferson's opinion of adulterated wine in Lawrence, *Jefferson and Wine*, vol. 1, 128, 3.

4–5   Wine imported from the Netherlands and England in Mishkin, *The American Colonial Wine Industry*, vol. 1, 116–121.

5   French plant grapes on the Wabash River in H. C. Bradsby, *History of Vigo County, Indiana* (Chicago: S. B. Nelson & Co., 1891), 109.

5   King of the Ball in Ronald L. Baker, *French Folklife in Old Vincennes* (Terre Haute, Ind.: Hoosier Folklore Society, 1989), 24–25.

5–6   Lieutenant Fraser's opinions about Wabash River wine in Lt. Alexander Fraser, "Report of Lieutenant Fraser," in *Indiana Historical Society Publications*, comp. J. Dunn, vol. 2 (Indianapolis: Bowen Merril Co., 1895), 410–411.

6	Thomas Hutchins's opinions about Wabash River wine in Thomas Hutchins, "A Topographical Description of Virginia, Pennsylvania, Maryland and North Carolina," in *Indiana as Seen by Early Travelers*, comp. Harlow Lindley (Indianapolis: Indiana Historical Commission, 1916), 8.
6	"They go into the woods" in Eugene F. Bliss, "Dr. Saugrain's Note-Books, 1788," *Proceedings of the American Antiquarian Society* XIX (Worcester, Mass.: The Society, 1908), 229.
6	"One finds both on the hills and on the plain a great quantity of grapes" in The Scioto Company, "Description of the soils, etc., of that Portion of the United States Situated between Pennsylvania and the Rivers Ohio, Scioto, and Lake Erie," in *The Centennial Anniversary of the City of Gallipolis, Ohio*, trans. John H. James. 2nd ed. Vol. 3 (Columbus: Ohio State Archaeological and Historical Society, 1895), 88.

2. WANDERING IN THE WILDERNESS

8	Dufour's maimed arm in John James Dufour, *The American Vine-Dresser's Guide* (Cincinnati: S. J. Browne, 1826), 8.
8	Dufour's birth in Julie LeClerc Knox, *The Dufour Saga, 1796–1942* (Crawfordsville, Ind.: Howell-Goodwin Printing Co., 1942), 30.
8	Fête des Vignerons in Richard Vine, *Wine Appreciation* (West Lafayette, Ind.: Learning Systems, 1988), 530–531.
8	Dufour family as grape-growers in Perret Dufour, *The Swiss Settlement of Switzerland County Indiana*, vol. XIII (Indianapolis: Indiana Historical Commission, 1925), 7–8.
9	"When I took the resolution to come to America" in Dufour, *The American Vine-Dresser's Guide*, 7–8.
9	Benjamin Franklin's advice to Dufour's father in Knox, *The Dufour Saga*, 16.
10	"The revolution has allowed the wines of France and Savon into the Canton of Bern" in John James Dufour to Albert Gallatin, Feb. 1, 1801, trans. Thomas Harris, Albert Gallatin Papers, Library of Congress, Washington, D.C., 2.
10	"The convulsions and wars that are now raging in Europe" in Contract between Swiss Settlers, April 30, 1800, enclosed in J. J. Dufour to Cincinnati Land Office, February 11, 1801, Cincinnati Historical Society Research Library.
10	Dufour's expenses for his 1796 journey across the Atlantic in Perret Dufour, trans., "Daybook of John James Dufour," in *The Swiss Settlement of Switzerland County*, vol. XIII, 247.
10–11	Dufour's tour of eastern vineyards in Dufour, *The American Vine-Dresser's Guide*, 23–24.
11	Legeaux and the Pennsylvania Vine Company in Pinney, *A History of Wine in America*, 109–110.
11	Legaux's letter to Thomas Jefferson in Pinney, *A History of Wine in America*, 111.

11	"But none of the different and numerous trials" in Dufour, *The American Vine-Dresser's Guide*, 18.
11–12	"As I had seen but discouraging plantations" in Dufour, *The American Vine-Dresser's Guide*, 18.
12	Dufour's trip to Pittsburgh in "Daybook of John James Dufour," 257–263.
12	Gallatin's support of opening of Northwest Territory in Raymond Walters, Jr., *Albert Gallatin: Jeffersonian Financier and Diplomat* (New York: Macmillan, 1957), 94–96.
12–13	Washington's acreage in Eugene E. Prussing, *The Estate of George Washington, Deceased* (Boston: Little, Brown, and Co., 1927), 322, 342–343, 345.
13	Dufour's letter to Washington in John James Dufour to George Washington, Dec. 19, 1796, trans. Eric Jourdain, The Papers of George Washington, Item 223, Alderman Library, University of Virginia, Charlottesville, Virginia.
13	"I do not intend to swell the masses of land speculators" in John James Dufour to George Washington, Dec. 19, 1796.
13	"I resolved therefore on a visit to see if any remains of the Jesuits' vines were still in being" in Dufour, *The American Vine-Dresser's Guide*, 18–19.
14	"I found the same kind of grapes up the Kentucky, and Mississippi rivers" in Dufour, *The American Vine-Dresser's Guide*, 21.
14	"But I found only the spot where that vineyard had been planted" in Dufour, *The American Vine-Dresser's Guide*, 19.
14	Dufour's preparations for trip up the Ohio River in "Daybook of John James Dufour," 273–275.
14	"'The barge sunk and he had a great deal of trouble'" in Dufour, *The Swiss Settlement of Switzerland County Indiana*, vol. XIII, 8.
14	Dufour replaces damaged biscuits in "Daybook of John James Dufour," 275.
15	Business transactions in Cincinnati in "Daybook of John James Dufour," 277.
15	"'We turned up the main street'" in Fortescue Cuming, *Sketches of a Tour to the Western Country*, vol. 4 (Cleveland, Ohio: The Arthur H. Clark Co., 1904), 182.
15	Dufour encouraged to start a vineyard in Dufour, *The American Vine-Dresser's Guide*, 8.
15	Dufour proposes a vineyard in Kentucky in John James Dufour, "Letter to the Citizens of Kentucky," *Kentucky Gazette*, Jan. 17, 1798.
16	"One hundred acres of third rate land at two dollars" in Dufour, "Letter to the Citizens of Kentucky."
16	"Now, ye citizens of Kentucky" in Dufour, "Letter to the Citizens of Kentucky."
16	"I with a number of well disposed citizens" in Dufour, "Letter to the Citizens of Kentucky."
16	Dufour offers to take payment in shares of stock in Dufour, "Letter to the Citizens of Kentucky."
16–17	Dufour's search for a site in Kentucky in "Daybook of John James Dufour," 277–279.

17   Dufour buys a horse in "Daybook of John James Dufour," 279–281.
17   Gallatin's proposal to sell Northwest Territory in small lots in Walters, *Albert Gallatin*, 133–135.
17   Description of New Geneva in William Bining, "The Glass Industry of Western Pennsylvania, 1797–1857," *Western Pennsylvania Historical Magazine* 19 (Dec. 1936): 255–257.
17   Glassworks in New Geneva in Bining, "The Glass Industry of Western Pennsylvania," 256–257.
18   Dufour's trip along Zane's Trace in "Daybook of John James Dufour," 283–289.
18   Public notice by Kentucky Association for the Establishment of a Vineyard in J. Russel, "Public Notice," *Kentucky Gazette,* Sept. 19, 1798.
18–19   Trip to Hickman Creek in "Daybook of John James Dufour," 289–291.
19   "I reported to the Vineyard Company" in "Daybook of John James Dufour," 291.
20   "Prepared to go and begin the work on the company's land" in "Daybook of John James Dufour," 293.
21   "Furnish at his own charge" in Michael L. Cook and Bettie A. Cook, *Kentucky Court of Appeals Deed Books A–G,* vol. I (Evansville, Ind.: Cook Publications, 1985), 219–221.
21   "Monticello . . . had been abandoned" in Dufour, *The American Vine-Dresser's Guide,* 22–23.
21   Too dangerous to go to Europe in John James Dufour, "Letter to the Directors of the Vineyard Society in Kentucky," *The Kentucky Gazette,* July 3, 1800.
21–22   Dufour purchases vines and tools in Dufour, *The American Vine-Dresser's Guide,* 24; "Daybook of John James Dufour," 293.
21   "Left Philadelphia again for Kentucky" in "Daybook of John James Dufour," 295.
22   Dufour sells the last of his lead in "Daybook of John James Dufour," 295–299.
22   Kentucky Vineyard Society incorporated in William Littell, *The Statute Law of Kentucky,* vol. 2 (Frankfort, Ky.: Johnston and Pleasants, 1810), 268–270.

3. THE SWISS COLONY

23   Covenant with friends and relatives in Switzerland in Contract between Swiss Settlers, April 30, 1800, enclosed in J. J. Dufour to Cincinnati Land Office, February 11, 1801, Cincinnati Historical Society Research Library.
23   "The immense and fertile continent of the new world" in Contract between Swiss Settlers.
23   "Those who have the wisdom and courage to quit the frivolous and dangerous resources" in Contract between Swiss Settlers.
24   "Our friend J. J. Dufour" in Contract between Swiss Settlers.
24   "I shall only observe that when I procured the vines" in John James

Dufour, "Letter to the Kentucky Vineyard Society," *Kentucky Gazette,* July 3, 1800.

25   "Although extremely painful, yet I conceive it to be my duty to inform you" in "Letter to the Kentucky Vineyard Society."

25   "I have now witnessed the effect of every season of the year" in "Letter to the Kentucky Vineyard Society."

25   Kentucky Vineyard Society collects funds from shareholders in Kentucky Vineyard Society, "Reply to Dufour Letter," *Kentucky Gazette,* July 3, 1800.

25   Dufour's contract with Kentucky Vineyard Society shareholders in Michael L. Cook and Bettie A. Cook, *Kentucky Court of Appeals Deed Books, A–G,* vol. I (Evansville, Ind.: Cook Publications, 1985), 221.

26   Sale of land in Northwest Territory in *U.S. Statutes at Large, 6th Congress, 1st Session,* vol. 2 (Washington, D.C.: Government Printing Office, 1937), entry for May 10, 1800.

26   Sale of land in Ohio begins in *U.S. Statutes at Large,* May 10, 1800.

26–27   1800 presidential election in Henry Adams, *The Life of Albert Gallatin* (London: J. B. Lippincott and Co., 1880), 240–262.

27   "May the virtuous and independent sons of Switzerland" in "Grand Festival," *Kentucky Gazette,* Jan. 26, 1801.

27–28   "They refused, not because they cannot attest to the progress and success that I've had" in John James Dufour to Albert Gallatin, Feb. 1, 1801, trans. Chris Momenee, The Papers of Albert Gallatin, Library of Congress, Washington, D.C., 2.

28   Dufour's preference for land along the Ohio River in John James Dufour to Albert Gallatin, Feb. 1, 1801, 1.

28   "That is why I believed that Congress" in John James Dufour to Thomas Jefferson, Feb. 1, 1801, trans. Thomas Harris, The Thomas Jefferson Papers, Series 1, Library of Congress, Washington, D.C., 2.

30   "To settle upon the land the families above mentioned" in Dufour, "Petition to Congress," 2.

30   Dufour corresponds with Cincinnati Land Office in John James Dufour, "Letter to Cincinnati Land Office," Feb. 11, 1801, The Cincinnati Historical Society Research Library, Cincinnati, Ohio, 1.

30   Dufour records his land purchase in Perret Dufour, trans., "Daybook of John James Dufour," in *Swiss Settlement of Switzerland County,* by Perret Dufour. Vol. XII (Indianapolis: Indiana Historical Commission, 1925), 302–303.

4. THE SWISS SETTLE IN INDIANA

31   "All poor people who have . . . only the means to make the trip" in John James Dufour to Thomas Jefferson, Jan. 1, 1802, trans. Thomas Harris, The Thomas Jefferson Papers, Series 1, Library of Congress, Washington, D.C., 1.

31   Friends and relatives leave Switzerland in Perret Dufour, trans. "Daybook of John James Dufour," in *Swiss Settlement of Switzerland County,*

by Perret Dufour. Vol. XIII (Indianapolis: Indiana Historical Commission, 1925), 219.

31   Families in Swiss group in Dufour, *Swiss Settlement of Switzerland County,* 11.

31   Golay family in Ruby Golay Stoner, comp., *David Golay, His Ancestors and Descendants* (Des Moines, Iowa: Ruby Golay Stoner, 1984), 20–22.

31   John James responsible for siblings in "Daybook of John James Dufour," 219.

32   Jean Daniel Morerod in Julie LeClerc Knox, *The Dufour Saga, 1796–1942* (Crawfordsville, Ind.: Howell-Goodwin Printing Co., 1942), 70.

32   Ninetieth Psalm read as families depart Switzerland in Harlow Lindley, "Introduction," in *The Swiss Settlement of Switzerland County Indiana,* by Perret Dufour, xv.

32   Ninetieth Psalm read at funerals in Vevay High School, *Brief History of Switzerland County Indiana* (Vevay, Ind.: Vevay High School, 1913), 6.

32–33   Families depart for the United States in "Daniel Dufour's Account of His Voyage From Switzerland to Virginia in 1801," trans. D. C. Brown, Dufour Papers, Indiana State Library, Indianapolis, Indiana, 1–12.

33   Journey to Pittsburgh in Dufour, *Swiss Settlement of Switzerland County,* 12.

33   Swiss group borrows money to continue journey in Dufour, *Swiss Settlement of Switzerland County,* 229; and Lewis Sanders, "J. J. Dufour—First Vineyard Society of Kentucky—Settlement of Vevay, Indiana," in *Transactions of Indiana Horticultural Society, 1872* (Indianapolis: R. J. Bright, State Printer, 1872), 128.

33–34   Dufour's proposal for a vineyard in Tennessee in John James Dufour, "Letter to the Tennessee Gazette," *Tennessee Gazette,* July 29, 1801.

34   Dufour travels to meet family and friends in "Daybook of John James Dufour," 302–303.

34   Newspaper announcement of arrival of Swiss group in the *Cincinnati Western Spy,* July 29, 1801.

34   Fourth of July celebration described in *Kentucky Gazette,* July 6, 1801.

34–35   "My brothers and all their company," in "Daybook of John James Dufour," 302–303.

35   "[The Swiss Colony desires] about three sections of land on the banks of the Ohio" in John James Dufour to Thomas Jefferson, January 15, 1802, trans. Thomas Harris, The Thomas Jefferson Papers, Series 1, Library of Congress, Washington, D.C., 1–2.

35   "I foresee the time when the Ohio will compete with the Rhine" in John James Dufour to Thomas Jefferson, January 15, 1802, 2.

36   "This petition is more or less the same" in Daniel Dufour to Albert Gallatin, January 12, 1802, trans. Chris Momenee, The Papers of Albert Gallatin, Library of Congress, 1–2.

36   "Be it enacted" in *U.S. Statutes at Large* (Washington, D.C.: Government Printing Office, 1937), entry for May 1, 1802, 47–48.

36   "They thought the steep hillsides unfavorable" in Sanders, "J. J. Dufour," 129.

37   Thomas Hopkins's land purchase in Dufour, *Swiss Settlement of Switzerland County*, 36–37. The lands chosen by the colony and entered on June 11, 1802, were the partial sections 13, 14, 22, 23 and 27, as well as the complete sections 12 and 15 in Township 2 N, Range 3 W.

37   "I will cut down the first tree on our lands" in Dufour, *Swiss Settlement of Switzerland County*, 12.

37   Covenant drawn at Firstvineyard in Dufour, *Swiss Settlement of Switzerland County*, 19.

37   Boralley family in Dufour, *Swiss Settlement of Switzerland County*, 362.

38   "However the success did not answer the expectation" in F. A. Michaux, "Travels to the Westward of the Allegheny Mountains," in *Early Western Travels, 1748–1846*, ed. Reuben Gold Thwaites. Vol. 3 (Cleveland, Ohio: The Arthur H. Clark Co., 1904), 208–209.

38   "Three years . . . we were in full expectation" in John James Dufour, *The American Vine-Dresser's Guide* (Cincinnati: S. J. Browne, 1826), 9.

39   "Very much surprised" in "Cultivation of the Vine, by an American Navy Officer," *American Farmer* 7 (Dec. 1825): 301.

39   Hybrid grapes in Bernard McMahon, *The American Gardner's Calendar, 1806* (Philadelphia: published by William Fry, 1806).

40   In the mid-1990s the USDA Plant Genetics Unit in Geneva, New York, received several grape cuttings from a gentleman in Terryville, Conn., that were said to be the "Alexander" grape. However, inquiries by the authors to Mr. Warren Lamboy in Geneva confirmed that the variety cannot be verified as the true "Alexander" or "Cape" of the early 1800s.

40   Clay finances journey of John Francis DuFour to Washington in James F. Hopkins, ed., *The Papers of Henry Clay*, vol. 1 (Lexington: University of Kentucky Press, 1959), 162.

40   "Started off through the then almost trackless wilderness" in Knox, *The Dufour Saga*, 44–45.

41   "The Bearier J. F. Dufour" in John Brown to Thomas Jefferson, Feb. 20, 1805, The Thomas Jefferson Papers, Series 1, Library of Congress, Washington, D.C.

42   "They appear to possess a body capable of becoming good" in Thomas Jefferson to John Brown, Feb. 23, 1805, The Thomas Jefferson Papers, Series 1, Library of Congress, Washington, D.C. A small tribute to this journey was paid at the Indiana Building in the Chicago Fair of 1932. Julie Leclerc Knox stated that "there was a curiously interesting relief map of the state, with characteristic little figures, marking distinctive features. A miniature rider, leading a pack horse, laden with casks, identified Vevay, typifying this incident." Julie LeClerc Knox, *The Dufour Saga*, 57.

41–42 Land purchases of Swiss colonists in Dufour, *Swiss Settlement of Switzerland County*, 306–307.

42–43 Golays in New York in Stoner, *David Golay, His Ancestors and Descendants*, 20–22.

43   "The family has ceased being in partnership" and "In consequence of our

dissolution of partnership" in Dufour, *Swiss Settlement of Switzerland County*, 307.

43   "By the above division each of my brothers and sisters" in Dufour, *Swiss Settlement of Switzerland County*, 308–309.

43–44   "*Ora et labora*" in Jean Jacques Dufour, "Letter from a Father in Switzerland to his Children in America," *Panoplist and Missionary Magazine* XIII (June 1817), 248–249.

44   Looking for saltpeter in Dufour, "Daybook of John James Dufour," 309, 311; and Samuel Brown to James Brown, Nov. 10, 1804, in *The Register of the Kentucky State Historical Society* 35 (1937): 123–124.

44   "Have placed the vineyard in the care of Jean Francois" in Dufour, *Swiss Settlement of Switzerland County*, 309, 311; and John J. Dufour to John Francis Dufour, Jan. 15, 1806, Jessamine County Deed Book B, County Deed Books, Jessamine County, Kentucky, 163.

44   Henry Clay finances Dufour's trip east in Dufour, *Swiss Settlement of Switzerland County*, 318–319. Dufour looks for investors in Washington in Dufour, *Swiss Settlement of Switzerland County*, 318–319; see advertisements for Dufour's steam engine in the *National Intelligencer and Advertiser*, Feb. 19, 21, and 24, 1806.

45   "The Bearer is one of the Swiss Emigrants" in John Brown to James Madison, Feb. 22, 1806, The James Madison Papers, Library of Congress, Washington, D.C., 1.

45   Dufour visits vineyard of Legaux in Peter Legaux, "Journal of the Pennsylvania Vine Company," March 23, 1806, American Philosophical Society Library, Philadelphia, Pennsylvania.

45   "I briefly answered" in Dufour, *The American Vine-Dresser's Guide*, 34.

45   George Morgan in Max Savelle, *George Morgan: Colony Builder* (New York: Columbia University Press, 1932), 233. Historian U. P. Hedrick wrote that Morgan started a vineyard in 1796 in *History of Horticulture in America to 1860* (New York: Oxford University Press, 1950), 83–84.

46   Dufour arrives in Switzerland in Perret Dufour, *Swiss Settlement of Switzerland County*, 320–343.

5. OUT OF THE VERY GROUND THEY TREAD

47   John David and John Francis Dufour fulfill contractual obligations of John James at Firstvineyard in Michael Cook and Bettie Cook, *Kentucky Court of Appeals Deed Books A–G*, vol. 1 (Evansville, Ind.: Cook Publications, 1985), 219–221.

47   Increase in grape production in Perret Dufour, *Swiss Settlement of Switzerland County*, vol. XIII (Indianapolis: Indiana Historical Commission, 1925), 25.

47–48   Yields from first vineyard at New Switzerland in John James Dufour, *The American Vine-Dresser's Guide* (Cincinnati: S. J. Browne, 1826), 10–11; and Dufour, *Swiss Settlement of Switzerland County*, 25.

48   "The plan was well laid" in Dufour, *The American Vine-Dresser's Guide*, 9–10.

49   John Stuart on the Kentucky River in John G. Stuart, "A Journal Re-
      marks; or, Observations in a Voyage Down the Kentucky, Ohio, Missis-
      sippi Rivers &c.," *Register of the Kentucky Historical Society* 50, no. 170
      (1952): 13.

49   Swiss settlers' dislike of slavery in L. H. Bailey, *Sketch of the Evolution
      of Our Native Fruits*, 3rd ed. (New York, London: Macmillan, 1911), 34.

49   Cheaper land in slave territory in John James Dufour to Albert Gallatin,
      February 1, 1801, trans. Chris Momenee, The Papers of Albert Gallatin,
      Library of Congress, Washington, D.C., 1.

49   John Francis and John David Dufour leave Firstvineyard in Dufour,
      Swiss Settlement of Switzerland County, 15, 25–26.

50   Swiss at Crozier Mill in Bennet H. Young, *A History of Jessamine County,
      Kentucky* (Louisville: Courier-Journal Job Printing Co., 1898), 59.

50   "Some vineyard workers are leaving on the same ship as we are" in Ruby
      Golay Stoner, comp., *David Golay, His Ancestors and Descendants* (Des
      Moines, Iowa: Ruby Golay Stoner, 1984), 14.

50–51 "New Swisserland is situated on the right bank of the Ohio river" in John
      Francis Dufour, "New Swisserland," *Niles' Weekly Register*, Nov. 2, 1811,
      140.

51   "Hail, Bettens and Morerod!" in Dufour, *Swiss Settlement of Switzerland
      County*, 71.

52   "Last night our boats were anchored under a very high bank" in Lydia
      Bacon, "Ohio River To Vincennes," in *Travel Accounts of Indiana*, comp.
      Shirley McCord (Indianapolis: Indiana Historical Bureau, 1970), 61.

52   "The culture of the vine has been successfully introduced" in David
      Baille Warden, "A Statistical, Political and Historical Account of North
      America," in *Indiana as Seen by Early Travelers*, comp. Harlow Lindley
      (Indianapolis: Indiana Historical Commission, 1916), 230.

53   "We were now in sight of a Swiss settlement" in John Mellish, *Travels
      through the United States of America* (Philadelphia: John Mellish, 1818),
      371.

53–54 Native Americans, earthquake at New Switzerland in Dufour, *Swiss
      Settlement of Switzerland County*, 31–32.

54–55 Petition for special extension to pay for land in "Petition to Congress by
      John James Dufour and Associates," in *The Territorial Papers of the
      United States*, comp. and trans. Clarence Edwin Carter, vol. VIII (Wash-
      ington, D.C.: United States Printing Office, 1939), 224–225; Jonathan
      Jennings to Samuel McKee, June 10, 1813, in *The Territorial Papers of
      the United States*, 260.

55   Congress grants petition in August 2, 1813, "An Act Giving Further
      Time to the Purchasers of Public Land, Northwest of the River Ohio, to
      Complete Their Payments," in *U.S. Statutes at Large*, vol. 6 (Washing-
      ton, D.C.: Government Printing Office, 1813), 126.

55–56 Kentucky Vineyard Society in John Bradford et al., "The Shareholders
      of the Vineyard Association," *Kentucky Gazette*, Oct. 5, 1813.

56   "This town just laid out on a liberal plan" in John Francis Dufour,
      "Vevay," *Kentucky Gazette*, Oct. 5, 1813.

57	"Daniel Debeltaz . . . advises tavern keepers and others" in Daniel Debeltaz, "Forward," *Niles' Weekly Register,* July 24, 1813.
57	Congress passes license law in *U.S. Statutes at Large,* vol. 6, August 2, 1813, 72.
57	Gex license in "License to a Retailer of Merchandise, Including Wine," Oct. 31, 1814, Gex Family Papers, SC 620, Indiana Historical Society, Indianapolis. Our efforts to find records of other licenses were unsuccessful.
57–58	Petition for exemption from licensing in "Petition to Congress by Vinedressers of Switzerland County," *The Territorial Papers of the United States,* vol. VIII, 311–312.
58	"They have now greatly augmented the quantity of their vineyard grounds" in Samuel R. Brown, "The Western Gazetteer," in *Indiana as Seen by Early Travelers,* 154–155.
58–59	"This is the commencement of the vintage" in William Tell Harris, "Vevay to Harmony," in *Travel Accounts of Indiana,* comp. and ed. Shirley McCord (Indianapolis: Indiana Historical Bureau, 1970), 92–93.
60	"Vevay . . . is a pleasant flourishing town" in Edmund Dana, "Geographical Sketches on the Western Country Designed for Emigrants and Settlers, 1819," in *Indiana as Seen by Early Travelers,* 205.
60–61	Governor Jennings samples Vevay wine in Dufour, *Swiss Settlement of Switzerland County,* 149.
61	Lottery for the canal in J. Bigelow to John Francis Dufour, April 15, 1818, Dufour Family Papers, B-106, Indiana State Library, Indianapolis, Indiana.
61	Canal begun in C. G. Harraman, *History of Switzerland County Indiana* (Owensboro, Ky.: Cook-McDowell Publications, 1980), 1032–1033.
62	"The people of this vast continent" in Dufour, *The American Vine-Dresser's Guide,* 7.

6. THE VEVAY WINEMAKERS

63	Initial entries in John James Dufour's account book in Perret Dufour, trans., "Daybook of John James Dufour," in *Swiss Settlement of Switzerland County,* by Perret Dufour. Vol. XIII (Indianapolis: Indiana Historical Commission, 1925), 341–347.
63	"We continued to descend the Rhone with great rapidity" in John James Dufour, *The American Vine-Dresser's Guide* (Cincinnati: S. J. Browne, 1826), 101–102.
64	"They abandoned the place to an American tenant" in Dufour, *The American Vine-Dresser's Guide,* 10.
64	Vincent Dufour purchases land in John Hazlerigg to Daniel V. Dufour, Sept. 30, 1828, Jessamine County Deed Book I, County Deed Books, Jessamine County, Ky., 132–133.
64	"Dufouria" in Lewis Sanders, "J. J. Dufour—First Vineyard Society of Kentucky.—Settlement of Vevay, Indiana," in *Transactions of Indiana*

<table>
<tr><td></td><td>Horticultural Society, 1872, ed. W. H. Ragan (Indianapolis: R. J. Bright, State Printer, 1872), 129.</td></tr>
<tr><td>64</td><td>Peach brandy in C. G. Harraman, History of Switzerland County Indiana (Owensboro, Ky.: Cook-McDowell Publications, 1980), 1004.</td></tr>
<tr><td>67</td><td>"I did a little better yet" in Dufour, The American Vine-Dresser's Guide, 131–132.</td></tr>
<tr><td>67</td><td>Jean Daniel Morerod's wedding in Julie LeClerc Knox, The Dufour Saga, 1796–1942 (Crawfordsville, Ind.: Howell-Godwin Printing Co., 1942), 72.</td></tr>
<tr><td>68–69</td><td>Morerod and Bettens families plant vineyards in Dufour, Swiss Settlement of Switzerland County, 12, 22; and Harlow Lindley, "Introduction," in Swiss Settlement of Switzerland County, by Perret Dufour, xviii.</td></tr>
<tr><td>69</td><td>Morerod's homestead in Knox, The Dufour Saga, 72.</td></tr>
<tr><td>69–70</td><td>Morerod's wine sales in Account Book of Jean D. Morerod, microfilm F.139, Indiana Historical Society, Indianapolis, Indiana.</td></tr>
<tr><td>70</td><td>"We stopped at Vevay" in William Hall, "Journal of William Hall," in Journal of Illinois State Historical Society, ed. Jay Monaghan. Vol. 39 (Springfield: Illinois State Historical Society, 1946), 47–48.</td></tr>
<tr><td>70–71</td><td>Morerod in the national press in "A Friend to the Industry," "On the Grape Vine, with Its Wines, Brandies, Salt and Dried Fruits, No. II," American Farmer 1, no. XXXV (Nov. 26, 1819): 281.</td></tr>
<tr><td>72</td><td>"A measure of manifest importance" in "A Friend to the Industry," "On the Grape Vine, with Its Wines, Brandies, Salt and Dried Fruits, No. IV," American Farmer 1, no. XXXVII (Dec. 10, 1819): 294.</td></tr>
<tr><td>72</td><td>John Adlum in R. de Treville Lawrence, Sr., ed., Jefferson and Wine, vol. 1 (The Plains, Va.: Vinifera Wine Growers Association, 1976), 123.</td></tr>
<tr><td>72</td><td>Morerod in the international press in Leo Schelbert, "Vevay, Indiana, and Chabag, Bessarabia: The Making of Two Winegrower Settlements," Yearbook of German-American Studies 25 (1990): 118–119.</td></tr>
<tr><td>73</td><td>Gex recommends the Ohio Valley in Gex-Oboussier to Jean I. Mennet, September 28, 1803, Gex-Oboussier Papers, SC 620, Indiana Historical Society, Indianapolis, Indiana.</td></tr>
<tr><td>73</td><td>"If [one] wishes to come, and live leisurely" in Gex-Oboussier to Jean I. Mennet, September 10, 1804.</td></tr>
<tr><td>73</td><td>Gex loses wife and brother-in-law in Gex-Oboussier to Jean I. Mennet, March 24, 1808.</td></tr>
<tr><td>73</td><td>"I made for Perdonnet early in 1808" in Gex-Oboussier to Jean I. Mennet, January 10, 1809.</td></tr>
<tr><td>73</td><td>Gex marries Marriane Golay in Ruby Golay Stoner, comp., David Golay, His Ancestors and Descendants (Des Moines, Iowa: Ruby Golay Stoner, 1984), 91.</td></tr>
<tr><td>73</td><td>"Caused by the needs of my establishment" in Gex-Oboussier to Jean I. Mennet, December 27, 1819, Indiana Historical Society, Indianapolis, Indiana.</td></tr>
<tr><td>74</td><td>"Upon entering the home of Mrs. Oboussier" in Stoner, David Golay, His Ancestors and Descendants, 41.</td></tr>
</table>

74	Invoice for shipment of two chests in Gex-Oboussier to Joseph C. Breckinridge, May 19, 1815, Breckinridge Family Papers, Library of Congress, Washington, D.C.
74	"Mr. Morerod sell[s] his wine at two Dollars" in Gex-Oboussier to Joseph C. Breckinridge, May 19, 1815, Breckinridge Family Papers, Library of Congress, Washington, D.C.
74	Tarrascon brothers in Boster, "Tarrascon Brothers, James Berthoud and Co. to Gex," October 17, 1816, trans. Thomas Harris, Gex Papers, SC 620/F3, Indiana Historical Society, Indianapolis, Indiana.
75	James B. Clay drinks his father's wine in Dufour, *Swiss Settlement of Switzerland County*, 128–129.
75	Louis Golay manages a vineyard in Stoner, *David Golay, His Ancestors and Descendants*, 43.
75	Francis Louis Siebenthal as a blacksmith in Dufour, *Swiss Settlement of Switzerland County*, 187.
75–76	Jacob Weaver biographical information in Jacob Weaver to His Father and Brothers, March 28, 1815 and September 5, 1814, Jacob Weaver Papers, Indiana Historical Society, Indianapolis, Indiana.
76	"On the 15th of May we had a very sevear frost" in Jacob Weaver to His Father and Brothers, May 5, 1816 and Oct. 13, 1816.
76	Jacob Weaver describes his farm in Jacob Weaver to His Father and Brothers, Dec. 12, 1817.
76	John Daniel Dufour and politics in Knox, *The Dufour Saga*, 35.
76	John Daniel Dufour and Massachusetts Missionary Society in Samuel Mills and Daniel Smith, *Report of a Missionary Tour* (Andover: Flagg and Gould, 1815), 56.
77	John Francis Dufour and politics in Knox, *The Dufour Saga*, 42–47.
77–78	"*Vevay* was laid out in the fall of 1813" in "Vevay, Indiana," *Niles' Weekly Register*, July 13, 1816, 347.
78	"The Vineyards in the vicinity of that place" in "American Wine," *Niles' Weekly Register*, August 23, 1817, 416.
78	Crop of 1817 in Jacob Weaver to His Father and Brothers, July 6, 1817 and Dec. 12, 1817.

7. TROUBLE IN PARADISE

80	Population of Vevay in Perret Dufour, *Swiss Settlement of Switzerland County*, vol. XIII (Indianapolis: Indiana Historical Commission, 1925), 33.
80	Buildings in Vevay in "Vevay, Indiana," *Niles' Weekly Register*, July 13, 1816, 347.
80	Wine production in Vevay in Dufour, *Swiss Settlement of Switzerland County*, 25, 29, 33–34.
81	Banks in the Midwest in Richard C. Wade, *The Urban Frontier* (Cambridge, Mass.: Harvard University Press, 1959), 164–165.
81	Land prices in St. Louis in *The Urban Frontier*, 164.
81	Loans recalled in *The Urban Frontier*, 166.

82   "He had emigrated last summer" in "Nuttall's Travels into the Arkansas Territory, 1819," in *Early Western Travels 1748–1846*, ed. Reuben Gold Thwaites. Vol. 13 (Cleveland, Ohio: The Arthur H. Clark Co., 1905), 63.

82–83   "Wine is got to be very cheap" in Jacob Weaver, Vevay, Switzerland Co. to His Father and Brothers in Bloomingdall, Ulster Co., New York, March 28, 1815 and September 6, 1818, Jacob Weaver Letters, 1814–1824, SC 1548, Indiana Historical Society, Indianapolis, Indiana.

83   Economic recession and "our country is very extensive" in Jacob Weaver to His Father and Brothers, Jan. 25, 1819 and July 30, 1920.

83   "No money" and falling prices in Jacob Weaver to His Father and Brothers, Nov. 11, 1821 and Jan. 11, 1824.

83   Shortage of bottles in Tarrascon Brothers to L. Gex, Oct. 17, 1816, trans. Thomas Harris, SC 620/F3, Indiana Historical Society, Indianapolis, Indiana.

83   "Farmers can only raise own food and clothing" in Gex-Oboussier to Jean I. Mennet, September 1, 1823, Gex-Oboussier Papers, SC 620, Indiana Historical Society, Indianapolis.

83   Price of Morerod's wine in Account Book of Jean D. Morerod, Microfilm F. 139, Indiana Historical Society, Indianapolis, Indiana.

84   Dufour leads delegation from Vevay to meet Lafayette in Dufour, *Swiss Settlement of Switzerland County*, 84.

84–85   "As we crossed the public square," "We had hardly returned to Mr. Febiger's," and "The general arrived" in A. Levasseur, *Lafayette in America*, trans. John D. Godman. Vol. 2 (Philadelphia: Corey and Lea, 1829), 177, 175, 176. Interestingly, Godman, the translator of the volume, disagreed savagely with Levasseur's opinion of the wine and stated so in a footnote.

85–86   Dufour's promise to Congress in John James Dufour, "Petition to Congress," Feb. 1, 1801, The Thomas Jefferson Papers, Library of Congress, Washington, D.C., 2.

87   Circular soliciting information about vine culture, Jan. 13, 1825, in Broadside Collection, Indiana Historical Society, Indianapolis, Indiana.

87   "It will be found something like presumption in me" and "the grand book of nature" in John James Dufour, *The American Vine-Dresser's Guide* (Cincinnati: S. J. Browne, 1826), 1, 11.

89   "The Kentucky Vineyard Society, may be . . . considered as the beginner" in Dufour, *The American Vine-Dresser's Guide*, 8.

89   "I will also try to save the character of our Cape grapes" in Dufour, *The American Vine-Dresser's Guide*, 5.

89–90   "To that may be added another obstacle" and "The time will come" in Dufour, *The American Vine-Dresser's Guide*, 32–33, 39.

90   "The first explicit account of the vine diseases" in L. H. Bailey, *Sketch of the Evolution of Our Native Fruits* (New York: Macmillan, 1898), 93.

91   "The different diseases" and "The Mildew or *Charbon*," in Dufour, *The American Vine-Dresser's Guide*, 205–206.

91   "It is very likely that two diseases are confounded" in Bailey, *Sketch of the Evolution of Our Native Fruits*, 93–94.

91	Girdling in Dufour, *The American Vine-Dresser's Guide*, 199–201; and A. J. Winkler, James A. Cook, W. M. Kliewer, and Lloyd A. Lider, *General Viticulture*, 2nd ed. (Berkeley: University of California Press, 1974), 346.
91–92	Dufour's advice about grape-growing in Dufour, *The American Vine-Dresser's Guide*, 230, 161, 112–113, 173, 124.
92–93	Dufour's efforts to fight phylloxera and mildew in Dufour, *The American Vine-Dresser's Guide*, 74–75, 222.
93	Silkworms in Dufour, *The American Vine-Dresser's Guide*, 99, 108.
93	Dufour's advice about wine production in Dufour, *The American Vine-Dresser's Guide*, 241, 270–271, 265–266, 254–255, 291–293, 265, 298.
94	"A Vine-Dresser's Guide . . . may fairly claim" in Thomas Pinney, *A History of Wine in America* (Berkeley: University of California Press, 1989), 123–125.
94	"And the day must come" in "American Wines," *Putnam's Magazine* IV (Nov. 1854): 505.
94	Death of Dufour's wife in Bailey, *Sketch of the Evolution of Our Native Fruits*, 41.
94	Conflict between John James and John David in John David Dufour v. John James Dufour, Circuit Court Records Book, 1825–1829, Switzerland County Court Records, Switzerland County Courthouse, Vevay, Indiana, April Term 1825, 287, and Oct. 31, 1826, 193.
94	Death of John James Dufour in Bailey, *Sketch of the Evolution of Our Native Fruits*, 41.
95	Dufour's estate in "Estate of John James Dufour," March 1, 1827, Circuit Court Records Book, 1825–1829, Switzerland County Court Records, Vevay, Indiana, 255; "Estate of John James Dufour," April 12, 1828, 378, 369; and "Estate of John James Dufour," August Term 1832, 79.
95–96	Dufour's grave in Julie LeClerc Knox, *The Dufour Saga, 1796–1942* (Crawfordsville, Ind.: Howell-Goodwin Printing Co., 1942), 28–30; Bailey, *Sketch of the Evolution of Our Native Fruits*, 41; and Anonymous, "Burial Place of Jean Jacques Dufour," Paper on Burial Site, Switzerland County File, Switzerland County Public Library, Vevay, Indiana. Knox gives the following inscription, which is slightly different: "Jean Jaques Dufour, loyal and courageous leader of the Swiss family who founded Vevay. Friend of Jefferson. Buried on his old land entry."
96	Deaths of original settlers in Dufour, *Swiss Settlement of Switzerland County*, 362; Ruby Golay Stoner, comp., *David Golay, His Ancestors and Descendants* (Des Moines, Iowa: Ruby Golay Stoner, 1984), 35, 12, 94; Dufour, *Swiss Settlement of Switzerland County*, 362; and Knox, *The Dufour Saga*, 165–166.
97	"In his will was expressed a desire" in Julie LeClerc Knox Scrapbook, Miscellaneous Newspaper Articles, 1894, Switzerland County File, Switzerland County Public Library, Vevay, Indiana.
97	Morerod's descendants and WCTU in Julie LeClerc Knox, "Some Reminiscences of Vevay," *Indiana Magazine of History* 25 (1929): 305; and Knox, *The Dufour Saga*, 15.

97	"Long after the vineyards were abandoned" in Knox, *The Dufour Saga,* 73.
97–98	"The vines however have degenerated" in Karl Postel, "The Americans as They Are; Described in Tour through the Valley of the Mississippi," in *Indiana as Seen by Early Travelers,* comp. Harlow Lindley (Indianapolis: Indiana Historical Commission, 1916), 522.
98	Prince's dedication and mention of Gex in William Prince, "Dedication," in *A Treatise on the Vine,* by William Robert Prince (New York: T. J. Swords, Carville, Bliss and Collins, 1830), iii, 383.
98–99	Rafinesque and descriptions of wine in Constantine Rafinesque, *American Manual of Grape Vines and the Method of Making Wine* (Philadelphia: Printed for the Author, 1830), 35, 43.
99	Dufour's ideas linked with "grape-variety racism" in Lucie T. Morton, *Winegrowing in Eastern America* (Ithaca and London: Cornell University Press, 1985), 25.
99	"They turned attention to our native vine" in Alden Spooner, *The Cultivation of American Grape Vines, and Making of Wine* (Brooklyn: A. Spooner and Co., 1846), 12.
100	"He came hobbling out of his room into the sunlight" in Edward Eggleston, *Roxy,* 2nd ed. (Ridgeway, N.J.: Gregg Press, 1968), 141.
100–101	"The traveler who visits this spot to-day" and "Grape-growing, as a business, has long since perished at Vevay" in Bailey, *Sketch of the Evolution of Our Native Fruits,* 31–32, 40.

8. NEW HARMONY

103	Birth of Rapp and his success as a winemaker in William E. Wilson, *The Angel and the Serpent,* 2nd ed. (Bloomington: Indiana University Press, 1967), 7; and Karl J. R. Arndt, *George Rapp's Harmony Society, 1785–1847* (Philadelphia: University of Pennsylvania Press, 1965), 48.
103	Rapp's religious conflict in Germany and arrival in Pennsylvania in Karl J. R. Arndt, ed., *A Documentary History of the Indiana Decade of the Harmony Society, 1814–1824,* vol. 1 (Indianapolis: Indiana Historical Society, 1975), ix–x.
104	Rapp's letter of introduction to Jefferson in Clarence Edwin Carter, ed., *The Territorial Papers of the United States,* vol. 7 (Washington, D.C.: U.S. Government Printing Office, 1939), 209.
104	Jefferson's advice to Rapp in Arndt, *George Rapp's Harmony Society,* 65–66.
104–105	"The cause of the great emigration from Württemburg" in Arndt, *George Rapp's Harmony Society,* 67.
105–106	Beginning of Rapp's group in the United States in Arndt, *George Rapp's Harmony Society,* 70–75.
106	"The land where they live presently is too small" in Arndt, *George Rapp's Harmony Society,* 86.
106	Harmonists unsuccessfully petition Congress in Arndt, *A Documentary History of the Indiana Decade of the Harmony Society,* vol. 1, x; Arndt, *George Rapp's Harmony Society,* 84–90.

106–107	Improvements to property in Pennsylvania and growth of Harmonists in Arndt, *George Rapp's Harmony Society,* 105–106, 121.
107	Harmonists fined for refusing to serve in the Napoleonic Wars in Arndt, *George Rapp's Harmony Society,* 128–131.
107	Connoquenessing Creek was not a suitable avenue for shipping in Wilson, *The Angel and the Serpent,* 33.
107	"There we built a city named Harmonie" in Frederick Rapp to Joseph Leobold, July 10, 1816, in Arndt, *A Documentary History of the Indiana Decade of the Harmony Society,* vol. 1, 235.
108	Rapp quotes scripture in Arndt, *George Rapp's Harmony Society,* 121.
108	"By the way, my spirit will not be at rest until I have been to the Wabash" in George Rapp to Frederick Rapp, April 20, 1814, in Arndt, *George Rapp's Harmony Society,* 128–131.
108–109	Rapp purchases land along the Wabash, "So we set our course for the Wabash," and "The Wabash is a large stream of water" in George Rapp to Frederick Rapp, May 10, 1814, in Arndt, *A Documentary History of the Indiana Decade of the Harmony Society,* vol. 1, 7–8.
109	"The first people of the Harmonie left for the Indian territory" in Frederick Rapp, "Memorandum on Departure of First Harmonists for Indiana Territory," June 20, 1814, in Arndt, *A Documentary History of the Indiana Decade of the Harmony Society,* vol. 1, 11.
109–110	"Having heard through many channels of your vineyards" in John Francis Buchetti to Harmony Society, June 25, 1814, in Arndt, *A Documentary History of the Indiana Decade of the Harmony Society,* vol. 1, 11–12.
110	Harmonists advertise and sell their Pennsylvania land in Arndt, *George Rapp's Harmony Society,* 135–140.
110–111	Moving to New Harmony in Arndt, *George Rapp's Harmony Society,* 63; Arndt, *A Documentary History of the Indiana Decade of the Harmony Society,* vol. 1, 11, 41, 65, 72, 93, 113, 116, 124–127.
111	"I sent Fleckhammer and Gerber to the Swiss with compliments" in George Rapp to Frederick Rapp, Sept. 27, 1814, in Arndt, *A Documentary History of the Indiana Decade of the Harmony Society,* vol. 1, 48.
111	"The vines have been delivered to the Swiss," in Arndt, *A Documentary History of the Indiana Decade of the Harmony Society,* vol. 1, 77.
111–112	"Today at Judge Park's" and "I expect to make enough wine after a while" in John L. Baker to George Rapp, July 20, 1814, and George Rapp to Frederick Rapp, Nov. 8, 1814, both in Arndt, *A Documentary History of the Indiana Decade of the Harmony Society,* vol. 1, 20, 71.
112	"Forschner is sick and his boy" in George Rapp to Frederick Rapp, Nov. 8, 1814, in Arndt, *A Documentary History of the Indiana Decade of the Harmony Society,* vol. 1, 20, 68–70.
112–113	Planting at New Harmony in [George Rapp] to Frederick Rapp et al., December 10[-18?], 1814, and George Rapp to Frederick Rapp, March 10, 1815, both in Arndt, *A Documentary History of the Indiana Decade of the Harmony Society,* vol. 1, 83, 107.
113	"Our town lyeth on a handsome plain" in Frederick Rapp to George

Sutton, March 28, 1816, in Arndt, *A Documentary History of the Indiana Decade of the Harmony Society,* vol. 1, 203–204.

113   "Last year we built a vineyard here" in [Frederick Rapp] to Joseph Leobold, July 20, 1816, in Arndt, *A Documentary History of the Indiana Decade of the Harmony Society,* vol. 1, 236–237.

114   Harmonists had twelve acres in David Thomas, "Travels through the Western Country in the Summer of 1816," in *Indiana as Seen by Early Travelers,* comp. Harlow Lindley (Indianapolis: Indiana Historical Commission, 1916), 133.

114   "The Vines able to bear are full of great Clusters of grapes" in Frederick Rapp to David Shields, July 25, 1818, in Arndt, *A Documentary History of the Indiana Decade of the Harmony Society,* vol. 1, 557.

114   "They have cleared, fenced and cultivated" in "Harmony as Seen by an English Traveler," in Arndt, *A Documentary History of the Indiana Decade of the Harmony Society,* vol. 1, 799.

114   "They have a fine vineyard in the vale" in Arndt, *George Rapp's Harmony Society,* 277.

114   Imported grapevines from Germany in John Reichert and Romelius L. Baker to Beloved Fathers and Friends, Oct. 20, 1822, in Arndt, *A Documentary History of the Indiana Decade of the Harmony Society,* vol. 2, 479–480.

114   "Our Orchards well sat with the best kind" in [Frederick Rapp] to Samuel Worcester, Dec. 19, 1822, in Arndt, *A Documentary History of the Indiana Decade of the Harmony Society,* vol. 2, 511–512.

114   "Their little town" in William Herbert, "A Visit to the Colony of Harmony in Indiana," in *Indiana as Seen by Early Travelers,* 329.

114   "I went to the orchard on the Mount Vernon road" in Karl Bernhard, "Travels through North America, during the Year 1825 and 1826," in *Indiana as Seen by Early Travelers,* 429.

114–115 Wine and brandy at New Harmony in George Rapp to Frederick Rapp, June 22, 1816; Elisha Harrison to [John L.] Baker, Oct. 1, 1816; Elisha Harrison to Frederick Rapp, Dec. 24, 1816; and Frederick Rapp to George Rapp, June 27, 1817, all in Arndt, *A Documentary History of the Indiana Decade of the Harmony Society,* vol. 1, 227, 399, 254, 276, 346.

115   Selling New Harmony wine in [Frederick Rapp] to William Burtch, Oct. 7, 1820; Frederick Graeter to Frederick Rapp, Aug. 20, 1822; Sophia Hobson to John L. Baker, April 17, 1823; John L. Baker to Frederick Rapp, Nov. 22, 1823; and [Frederick Rapp] to Samuel Patterson, Nov. 29, 1823, all in Arndt, *A Documentary History of the Indiana Decade of the Harmony Society,* vol. 2, 116–117, 444–445, 562, 628, 726, 738.

116   Mixing wine and whiskey in [George Rapp] to Frederick Rapp et al., Dec. 10[-18?], 1814; [John L. Baker] to Abishai Way & Co., March 27, 1819; and Ferdinand Ernst, "Visit to Harmonie on the Wabash, Starting July 18, 1819," all in Arndt, *A Documentary History of the Indiana Decade of the Harmony Society,* vol. 1, 81, 679, 745.

116 Customer response to New Harmony wine in Henry R. Schoolcraft, "Scientific Observer Visits Harmony, Reports on Footprints in Stone," July 1821; and William Newnham Blane, "Young English Gentleman Reports on His Travels to Harmony," Dec. 1822, both in Arndt, *A Documentary History of the Indiana Decade of the Harmony Society,* vol. 2, 258, 523.

116 "They brew beer and make wine" and "The doctor on the Wabash advised him when he lay sick with fever" in Elias Pym Fordham, "At Harmonie," May 6, 1818; and Godfrey Haga to Frederick Rapp, Dec. 16, 1814, both in Arndt, *A Documentary History of the Indiana Decade of the Harmony Society,* vol. 1, 515, 88.

116–117 "At noon we ate dinner with our entire family" in George Rapp to Frederick Rapp and William Smith, April 18, 1823, in Arndt, *A Documentary History of the Indiana Decade of the Harmony Society,* vol. 2, 564.

117 "At Rapps we tasted some excellent wine made at Harmony" in Karl J. R. Arndt, ed., *Harmony on the Wabash in Transition* (Worchester, Mass.: Harmony Society Press, 1982), 749.

117 "There are about 2000 acres of land in a high state of cultivation" in Arndt, *George Rapp's Harmony Society,* 295.

117 Harmonists leave New Harmony in Wilson, *The Angel and the Serpent,* 81.

117 "Incidentally, with the good German dinner we drank excellent wine" in Arndt, *George Rapp's Harmony Society,* 341.

117 "We came, finally, to say farewell to old Rapp" in Arndt, *George Rapp's Harmony Society,* 458.

118 Gex moves to New Harmony in Arndt, *Harmony on the Wabash in Transition,* 764.

118 "From the mills we went to the vineyard" and Gex family at New Harmony in Bernhard, "Travels through North America," 425; and George B. Lockwood, *The New Harmony Movement* (New York: Appleton and Co., 190), 177.

118 Owen stops wine production at New Harmony in Lockwood, *The New Harmony Movement,* 5; and Maximillian, Prince of Wied, "Travels in the Interior of North America," in *Thwaite's Early Western Travels,* ed. Reuben Gold Thwaites. Vol. 22 (Cleveland, Ohio: The Arthur H. Clark Co., 1906), 183.

9. INDIANA WINE, 1827–1919

120–121 Nicholas Longworth in John F. von Daacke, "Sparkling Catawba, Grape Growing and Wine Making in Cincinnati, 1800–1870" (Ph.D. diss., University of Cincinnati, 1964), 12–13; and C. W. Elliot and Nicholas Longworth, "Wine Making in the West," *Horticulturalist,* June 1848, 315–316.

121 "On Wednesday the 16th ult. rode down with a small party" in T. A., "The Vintage in Our Neighborhood," *Western Farmer,* Oct. 1840, 17.

121	"He is an enterprising man of Swiss descent" in J. Kirtland, "For the Western Farmer and Gardener: Cultivation of the Grape," *Western Farmer*, March 1842, 135.
122	"Mr. Mottier, who has a flourishing vineyard near town" in "American Wine," *Western Farmer*, April 1844, 201.
122	"It seems that there is a great interest beginning to be excited in this neighborhood" in John E. Mottier, "Cultivation of the Vine," *Western Farmer*, June 1844, 250.
122	Sparkling Catawba in Nicholas Longworth, "American Wine," *American Agriculturalist*, April 1850, 119.
122–123	Cincinnati Horticultural Society competition in D. B. Lawler, S. P. Foote, M. Flagg, Jacob Resor, and Elisha Brigham, "Report of the Committee on Wine," *Western Farmer*, 1845, 255.
123	Wine production along the Ohio River in Paul C. Morrison, "Viticulture in Ohio," *Economic Geography* 12 (1936): 119, 74.
123	Quotes from Buchanan's wine text in Robert Buchanan, *Culture of the Grape and Wine-Making* (Cincinnati: Moore, Wilstach, Keys and Co., 1852), 18–19.
124–125	"Dufour, with that loyalty and love for his favorite grape" and "The poor old vigneron" in Editor, "The Last Words of John James Dufour," *Cozzen's Wine Press*, Feb. 20, 1858, 172.
125	Longworth obtained cuttings from Adlum in S. I. Mosher, "Further History of the Catawba Grape," *Western Horticultural Review*, 2 (Jan. 1852): 194.
125	"Still, the vine-growers owe to Mr. Dufour and his associates" in Buchanan, *Culture of the Grape and Wine-Making*, 67.
126	"I will name a circumstance at the vintage of 1846" in Elliot and Longworth, "Wine Making in the West," 319.
126	Mottier and the Delaware grape in von Daacke, "Sparkling Catawba," 73.
126	"None of it . . . has yet made for itself a respectable market" in Meltzer Flagg, "Wine in America and American Wine," *Harper's New Monthly*, June 1870, 112.
127	Decline of Cincinnati winegrowing in Lucie T. Morton, *Winegrowing in Eastern America* (Ithaca, N.Y.: Cornell University Press, 1985), 28–29.
127	Popularity of Concord grape in Morton, *Winegrowing in Eastern America*, 33.
127	Indiana wine production in United States Census Office, 8th Census, *Agriculture of the United States in 1860* (Washington, D.C.: Government Printing Office, 1864), 40; and "The Vineyard of Mr. Chase" in "Native Wine," *Border Star* (Westport, Mo.), March 7, 1860.
128	"Below Cincinnati are the vineyards" in William Cullen Bryant, ed., *Picturesque America; or, The Land We Live In*, vol. 2 (New York: D. Appleton and Co., 1872), 165.
128–129	Census reports on grape production in Indiana in United States Department of Agriculture, *Report upon Statistics of Grape Culture and Wine*

Production in the United States for 1880 (Washington, D.C.: Government Printing Office, 1881), 5; United States Department of Agriculture, *Viticulture Statistics of Grape Growing and Wine Production in the United States* (Washington, D.C.: Government Printing Office, 1891), 601–606; and United States Census Office, 8th Census, *Agriculture of the United States in 1860* (Washington D.C.: Government Printing Office, 1864), 40; United States Department of Agriculture, *Report upon Statistics of Grape Culture and Wine Production in the United States for 1880,* 5, 15–18.

129　　　Hermann Jaeger and black-rot fungus in Morton, *Winegrowing in Eastern America,* 31; and Pierre Galet, *A Practical Ampelography,* trans. Lucie T. Morton. 2nd ed. (Ithaca, N.Y.: Cornell University Press, 1980), 220–222.

129–130　"Planting only the few varieties that resist Rot sufficiently" in Hermann Jaeger to J. Lacksteder, Jan. 3, 1890, SC-2038, Indiana Historical Society, Indianapolis, Indiana.

130　　　Pre–World War I wineries in Indiana in James L. Butler interview with Dr. Donald MacDaniel, July 1999.

131–132　Dry laws in the nineteenth century in David L. Colvin, *Prohibition in the United States* (New York: George H. Doran Co., 1926), 33, 140, 334–335.

132　　　Temperance Republicans defeated in Colvin, *Prohibition in the United States,* 345.

132　　　Growth of numbers of saloons, decline in dry counties in Indiana prior to prohibition in Colvin, *Prohibition in the United States,* 366, 374.

132　　　"God loves to see us happy" in Thomas Pinney, *A History of Wine in America* (Berkeley: University of California Press, 1989), 86.

10. THE MODERN INDIANA WINE INDUSTRY

134　　　Cost of enforcing prohibition in Edward Behr, *Prohibition: Thirteen Years That Changed America* (New York: Arcade Publishing Co., 1996), 233.

135　　　Eastern wine industry begins to revive in U.S. Office of the Commissioner of Internal Revenue, *Annual Report of the Commissioner of Internal Revenue* (Washington, D.C.: Government Printing Office, 1938), 155.

135　　　National Grape Growers Association sends members to Vevay in Julie LeClerc Knox Scrapbook, Miscellaneous Newspaper Articles, Post-Prohibition, Switzerland County File, Switzerland County Public Library, Vevay, Indiana.

135　　　Liquor Control Act in August G. Mueller, Secretary of State, *Acts of Indiana General Assembly* (Indianapolis: Wm. B. Burford Printing Co., 1935), 1056, 1135–1136.

137　　　Leon Adams and trend toward consumption of drier wines in Lucie T. Morton, *Winegrowing in Eastern America* (Ithaca, N.Y.: Cornell University Press, 1985), 47–49.

138   Hybrid vines in France in Hudson Catell and H. Lee Staufer, *The Hybrids* (Lancaster, Penn.: L & H Photojournalism, 1978), 8.

138   "The Wise Creator has endowed the seeds of every sort of fruit" in John James Dufour, *The American Vine-Dresser's Guide* (Cincinnati: S. J. Browne, 1826), 39.

139   Growing interest in locally produced wines in Morton, *Winegrowing in Eastern America,* 49.

141   Restrictions on selling wine to the public lifted in Indiana in Larry A. Conrad, Secretary of State, *Acts of Indiana General Assembly* (Indianapolis: The Burton Shields Co., 1971), 391.

143   Birth of Indiana Winegrowers Guild in Ben Sparks, "Articles of Incorporation of the Indiana Winegrowers Guild Inc.," Article II, in possession of authors.

144   Criteria for AVAs in *Code of Federal Regulations, Title 27, Part 9* (Washington, D.C.: Government Printing Office, 1979).

144–145 Wine at St. Meinrad in Russ Bridenbaugh, "Monks at St. Meinrad Archabbey Cultivate Vineyards for Religious Use," *Herald Times* [Bloomington, Indiana], July 3, 1991.

148   Morerod casks taken apart in Julie LeClerc Knox, "Pioneer Homesteads," *Indiana Magazine of History* XVIII (1922): 375.

Index

JAMES L. BUTLER

and his wife, Susan, own Butler Winery and Vineyards in Bloomington, Indiana. Before becoming involved in the wine-making business, Jim attended Indiana University, where he majored in biology. He later received a Master's degree from the University of Minnesota Department of Ecology and Behavioral Biology. In 1976 the Butlers returned to Bloomington, where they opened their winery in 1983. Jim served as president of the Indiana Winegrowers Guild for ten years and has been a member of the Indiana Wine Grape Council since 1990.

JOHN J. BUTLER

received an undergraduate degree in history at Purdue University. He is currently studying twentieth-century U.S. history in the doctoral program at Indiana University. He and his brothers literally grew up in the wine-making business, living above their family's winery in downtown Bloomington.

Book and Jacket Designer: Sharon L. Sklar
Copy Editor: Kate Babbitt
Compositor: Sharon L. Sklar
Typefaces: Adobe Caslon and Castellar
Book and Jacket Printer: Thomson-Shore